THE
GREAT
CHRISTIAN
REVOLUTION

Other books by Otto Scott:

THE
GREAT
CHRISTIAN
REVOLUTION

HOW CHRISTIANITY TRANSFORMED THE WORLD

OTTO SCOTT

The Reformer Library
Windsor, New York

First Printing 1994 by Uncommon Books, Federal Way, WA 98003
Second Printing 1995 by The Reformer, Windsor, N.Y. 13865

Chapters 1 through 19 of the present work originally appeared with slight differences
as "The Great Christian Revolution," Part III of *The Great Christian Revolution,* a
symposium, © 1991 by Ross House Books, Vallecito, California. ISBN 1-879998-02-
5. Part III of this symposium has been reprinted by special permission from Ross House
Books.

ISBN 1-887690-04-2 pbk. (previously ISBN 0-968381-1-3)

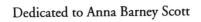

Dedicated to Anna Barney Scott

Contents

Foreword

Henry Adams was a famous nineteenth century American personage, noted for his scholarship, political acumen, and high position, who left behind one of the most unusual autobiographies in history. It left unmentioned most of the details of his private life, and described only those experiences that he believed advanced his education. He wrote about these in the third person, as though viewing himself in retrospective from the outside. The results dazzled the nation for a time, but have since been expertly smothered by the schoolteachers. A few brief excerpts at what the very perspective Mr. Adams recalled might be helpful today for those concerned about that combination of teaching and learning known as education.

"One day in June 1854, young Adams walked for the last time down the steps of Mr. Dixwell's school in Boylston Place and felt no sensation but one of unqualified joy that this experience was ended. Never before or afterwards in his life did he close a period so long as four years without some sensation of loss—some sentiment of habit—but school was what in life he commonly heard his friends denounce as an intolerable bore. He was born too old for it. The same thing could be said of most New England boys. Mentally they never were boys. They were fully five years more mature than the English or European boy for whom schools were made. For the purpose of future advancement, as afterwards appeared, these first six years of a possible education were wasted in doing imperfectly what might have been done in one, and in any case would have had small value. The next regular step was Harvard College."[1] He was 16.

Later, he wrote, "The four years passed at college were, for his purposes, wasted. Harvard College was a good school, but at bottom what the boy disliked most was any school at all. He did not want to be

---

1. Adams' autobiography, first privately printed when he was 66 in 1904, was titled *The Education of Henry Adams*, and limited to 100 copies.

one in a hundred[2] —one percent of an education. He regarded himself as the only person for whom his education had value, and he wanted the whole of it."

Before he left Harvard, while still fretting about waste and boredom, Adams was invited to privately read with James Russell Lowell in his study. That practise, previously unknown in the college, was one that Lowell had brought back from Germany. This led, of course, to conversations, and were more enjoyable for Adams than a classroom. Adams was encouraged by Lowell to continue his schooling, after Harvard, in Germany.

After his Harvard graduation, Adams attended the University of Berlin. There, he said he "found the lecture system in its deadliest form as it flourished in the thirteenth century. The professor mumbled his comments; the students made, or seemed to make, notes; they could have learned from books or discussion in a day more than they could learn from him in a month, but they must pay his fees, follow his course, and be his scholars, if they wanted a degree. To an American the result was worthless."

Adams decided that if one wanted to grasp Civil Law, "the student had only to read the Pandects or the commentators at his ease in America, and be his own professor." Berlin ended Adams' formal schooling—but not his education. He had learned, at 21 and at considerable expense to his parents, that teachers cannot pour knowledge into anyone's head, that students have to do their own learning, and that schools as areas of higher learning are greatly overrated.

In that event, Adams left Germany with a shaky grasp of the language and spent some time soaking in the culture of Rome. It was, for him, a city whose history "dwarfed teachers." He called it a bewildering complex of ideas, experiments, ambitions, energies; without her the Western world was pointless and fragmentary; she gave heart and unity to it all." He was later to conclude that Gibbon never understood its value in Christian history. That Rome was still guillotining criminals in the public street in 1859 upset Browning, who blundered upon such a scene. But Adams thought that the indignant English poet "a middle-aged gentlemanly figure" seemed slightly ridiculous against "the back-

---

2. His Class of 1858 numbered a hundred.

drop of the Circus Maximus [and] the Christian martyrs flaming as torches. . . ." That, however, was written years later in thoughtful retrospect, as one of the stages in his education.

By the time he reached that assessment, he was elderly. He had by then seen the world from the special vantage of his father's office who was an American ambassador to Britain during our Civil War. He had grown to know—and despair—of Washington D.C.; had taught history in Harvard, and had become a very famous—still famous—American scholar. His twin masterpieces in maturity were *Mont Saint-Michel and Chartres: A Study of Thirteenth-Century Unity,* and *The Education of Henry Adams: A Study of Twentieth-Century Multiplicity."*

"The *Chartres* was finished and privately printed in 1904. The *Education* was more difficult. [H]e used to say, half in jest, that his great ambition was to complete St. Augustine's *Confessions,* but that St. Augustine, like a great artist, had worked from multiplicity to unity, while he, like a small one, had to reverse the method and work back from unity to multiplicity."[3]

In the end, illness intervened. In Adams' view, his educational Odyssey remained incomplete, but its fame spread. A printed version appeared in 1907, and another in 1918,[4] issued by the Massachusetts Historical Society. My copy was printed in 1924, and was the 25th edition to appear. I cite him because he was not only one of the few nineteenth-century American intellectuals, but one who was wise enough to know, and to say, that education is largely self-taught.

༄

Teachers, after all, can only teach. It is the student's task to learn. This was made clear to me by a young man from Cambridge University who was hired to be my tutor when I was thirteen years old. My parents and I were living in the Copacobana Hotel in Rio. I was daily enjoying the ocean surf, available across the tiled Avenida Rio Branco, and spending happy afternoons amid mounds of books of action fiction. I recall Peter B. Kyne and *Subjugation of Cappy Ricks, Scaramouche* and piles of Rafael Sabatini, Jeffrey Farnol, and other now unhappily forgotten authors of

---

3. Editor's *Preface* by Henry Cabot Lodge, September 1918.
4. The year that Adams died.

historical and action fiction. A tutor was, in my eyes, unnecessary. I was educated enough. My father thought otherwise.

So did the young Englishman. To my astonishment, he came to that conclusion within ten minutes after our first session. That began when he asked me to tell him the history of the United States. I gaped at him. Nobody had ever expected me to do that before. I stumbled through the effort. There was a long silence while the tutor stared at me. Finally he said, "You stupid little boy. You don't even know the history of your own country."

He leaned forward, "The fact is, the United States grew up behind the shield of the British Navy. It was that Navy that enabled your clipper ships to travel the oceans of the world, carrying goods in and out of your country. It was British money that enabled you to build your transcontinental railroad, and British capital that supported your mining and cattle industries in the West. Were you never taught that?"

I had not. The next step came when he handed me a book to read. "Finish it by the next session," he said, and left leaving me somewhat shaken.

On the next occasion he said, "Did you read the book?" I nodded. "Did you like it?" I said, "Yes." He said "Why?"

It had not, until then, occurred to me that I could dislike a book. A nonfiction book was to be obeyed, not disputed. The tutor disabused me.

"You stupid little boy," he said. "It is a foolish book. A boring book. A worthless book." He then proceeded to demolish the book. It had, obviously, been a test—and one that I had failed. He handed me another book and said, "Read it and report on it the next time."

He left, and I realized that I was supposed to evaluate what I read. My next book report was much more careful. I read and I *thought* or tried to think. My comments were more deliberate, but still favorable. The tutor then said, "Have you thought of this? Or that?" I had not, but I was not willing to be humiliated again, and I argued, somewhat ineptly. For the first time, he smiled at me. "That's better," he sad, and we began to discuss the book in more reasonable terms. He agreed that what I liked had merit. I listened to his criticisms with a sense of being taught what was interesting to learn. My tutoring had begun.

What I experienced, in other words, was both the blunt candor of

English boarding schools and the famous tutorial method of Oxford and Cambridge. In this the pupil is stretched and not stifled. The purpose is to force him to react, to think, and to apply himself. It is a method reserved through the centuries to crowned heads and to the wealthy. It is the best of all methods, and is one being used to great advantage by those parents who teach their children themselves. It is one in which the pupil, and not the teacher, does most the work. The sessions are (or should be) short: a very few hours a week for the teacher; longer hours for the pupil.

The home-school parent who assumes the role of tutor is providing the best known, longest-tested approach known to educational history. That is the reason that home-school children are now welcomed at every university in the land. Home schooling produces young men and women who are literate in the best sense, well-mannered, normal and self-confident. The myth is that they miss the benefits of "socialization" and "democracy" in unsafe schools, with prejudiced teachers, unruly crowds, and biased lessons. In contemporary America, *nobody,* can escape rubbing elbows with every race, every ethnic background, and every level of citizen. It is best to have this experience when one is equipped to discern the difference between ability and pretence, morality and stupidity, propinquity and friendship. And, when one can defend what one knows and believes. It is, after all, crucial to understand and respect differences, but one must first establish one's own identity. Education is slow; socialization is quick.

≈

One of the lessons of education is that history is heavy with both successes and failures. Science relies on history in order to pursue what has worked, and to avoid repeating what has failed. Business abandons losing experiments in the pursuit of profits. History tells us what has worked and what has not. We have to develop the ability to recognize these lessons in whatever sector we choose, if we hope to enjoy full and rewarding lives.

The ability to do this is called education. To assist the sincere student to achieve skill, I have reintroduced the influence of Christianity into this history of the civilization we enjoy. I am well aware that there are many Christian histories. There are also too many histories of this civilization which mention Christianity only briefly and negatively. That is more than a flaw: it is to *falsify* history.

If Christianity had not appeared, Rome would have continued its fall and been succeeded by the warlike tribes of pagan Europe. The culture of the ancients, with their wars, human sacrifices, injustices and barbarities would have continued repetitively until today, like the incoherent histories of Asia and Africa.

It was Christianity alone that brought intellectual and spiritual hope, an end to human sacrifices, and the recognition of individual rights to the world. No other religion ever created a church that limited governments. That limitation enabled the free Christians of Europe to clear the land of great forests, to tame the wild beasts and wild tribes, to develop better methods of agriculture and manufacture, to build cities, to create cultures that were diverse but united in a single faith, to erect the largest, richest, and most polyglot civilization the world has ever known.

This book tells you the significance of Christianity to our civilization. It also tells you, if you have eyes to see, that no civilization has ever risen without a faith, and that none have ever outlasted the loss of its faith. It reminds you of the sacrifices, setbacks, and triumphs of Christians through roughly 1,600 years. It points—like a tutor in print—toward your own evaluation of what you have inherited (no matter who you are), what it means to keep this civilization—and what it could mean to lose it.

No matter what the unfortunate students in our anti-Christian schools are told, this *is* a Christian civilization. Its marvels, spread throughout the world, could not have been conceived, let alone created, by any other civilization. Christianity, in other words, revolutionized the world.

Chapter One

PAGANISM'S PRICE

———— ?❧ ————

To be governed not by the past,
but by knowledge of the past —
different things.

— Lord Acton

We live at a time of pagan revival but are naïve about the realities of paganism. We are deceived in part because modern paganism uses new terms, and partly because pagan history has been misrepresented by the majority of modern scholars.

Many scholars admire what J. C. Stobart called *The Grandeur that was Rome and the Glory that was Greece*. That "grandeur" was based on slavery, used torture as an instrument of the courts, and human sacrifice as part of religion and politics. Such sacrifices, said Acton, "were the turning-point at which paganism passed from morality to wickedness."[1]

Such abominations were labeled diabolic by the Israelites and the early Christians. The Hebrew word for pagan deities in the Bible is translated three ways: as demons, idols or vanities. This is underscored by the diabolic nature of certain pagan rites, which grew progressively more degraded.

Virtually all "classical" scholars shrink from describing the lack of individual rights under paganism, and are remarkably silent about paganism's human sacrifices. When the eminent English historian Macaulay, an ardent admirer of ancient Greece and Rome, denied that human sacrifices were conducted throughout the span of both these societies, Lord Acton wrote a memorable, irrefutable essay to disabuse him.[2]

---

1. Lord Acton, *Selected Writing,* vol. 3 (Indianapolis, IN: Liberty Classics, "Human Sacrifice," 1985), pp. 395–442.

2. Ibid.

Euripides described the Greek sacrifice of Iphigenia; Herodotus described human sacrifices in Egypt, Plato spoke of human sacrifices as "a common custom." In Rome sacrifices "for magical purposes" were outlawed from 95 B.C., but human sacrifices for religious and political reasons were conducted in public for as long as Rome was pagan.

In 63 B.C. Cataline and his accomplices sacrificed a boy and ate his bloody flesh to ratify their oath of conspiracy. Julius Caesar sacrificed mutineers in the name of Mars; Augustus, Nero, Caligula, Commodus, Marcus Aurelius—indeed, all the Roman emperors until Constantine—ordered human sacrifices.

Julian the Apostate, who tried to restore paganism and persecuted Christians, "filled his palace at Antioch with the corpses of human victims. . . . After his death the body of a woman was found hanging by her hair in a temple at Carrae. He had inspected her entrails to divine the issue of his campaign. . . ."

That was the "glory that was Greece" and the "grandeur that was Rome." But ending human sacrifices in the civilizations erected by the elegant barbarians of Greece and Rome was only one of the tasks that confronted Christians.

Church leaders confronted and converted the Saxons, who customarily decimated their prisoners. Rhadagaisus, a Saxon leader, sacrificed a Roman Christian every day—and continued to do this at the time of Charlemagne, who died in A.D. 842. The Franks practiced human sacrifice long after Clovis, who died in A.D. 511. The Germans abandoned the worship of Odin slowly and reluctantly over a long period. The Scandinavians sacrificed humans to the God of battle, to avert drought, and as a religious rite till the middle of the eleventh century.

Nor was Europe the only arena of human sacrifice. Even as Calvin wrote, Christians from Spain were suppressing the hideous, widespread and incessant human sacrifices of the Aztecs and Toltecs of Central America.

ع

That is not to say that the Europe of Calvin's day was a peaceful place. It was, in fact, more brutal and turbulent than modern Christians seem able to credit. In the sixteenth century a long-gathering rebellion against the excesses of the Papacy, the State and its Princes, the clergy and its

Cardinals, Bishops and Popes broke into flames. These flames were fed on all levels—top, middle and bottom—for the elite was often as frustrated by the Vatican and its clergy as were ordinary people.

It's not possible, however, to understand the Reformation without understanding what it was that needed reform. The late Middle Ages, from the plague-riddled fourteenth century onward, had been a time of declining faith amid rising prosperity. The Renaissance, a term covering a time of material advance and spiritual decline that lasted nearly 300 years, led to the rise of absolutism and a loss of individual political rights in nearly all western Europe.

> ⁊◆

Such a tangled period cannot be described in detail. Its prototype was the Emperor Frederick II of Germany,[3] whom Burckhardt defined as the first ruler "of the modern type."[4]

Frederick destroyed the feudal state with its common faith, interlocking allegiances, individual rights and Biblically-based limits on government. He forced the people into becoming "a multitude destitute of will and the means of resistance, but profitable to the utmost degree to the exchequer. He centralized, in a manner hitherto unknown in the West, the whole judicial and political administrations." Elections were forbidden. "Taxes, based on a comprehensive assessment and distributed in accordance with Mohammedan usage, were collected by . . . cruel and vexatious methods."[5]

"This was in marked contrast to the thousand years we now call the Middle Ages," wrote Lord Acton, "when representative government, unknown to the ancient pagans, was almost universal. The methods of election were crude, but the principle that no tax was lawful that was not granted by the class that paid it was recognized, not as the privilege of certain countries, but as the right of all. . . . [S]lavery was everywhere (in Christendom) extinct, and absolute power was deemed more intolerable and more criminal than slavery. The right of insurrection was not

---

3. 1194–1250.
4. Jacob Burckhardt, *The Civilization of the Renaissance in Italy* (Phaideon Publishers, 1965), p. 2.
5. Ibid., p. 2, 3.

only admitted but defined as a duty sanctioned by religion. Even the principles of the Habeas Corpus and the methods of the Income Tax were already known. The issue of ancient politics was an absolute state planted on slavery. The political order of the Middle Ages was a system of states, in which authority was restricted by the representation of powerful classes, by privileged associations and by the acknowledgments of duties superior to those imposed by man.

"In the days when every State made unity of belief its first care," he continued, "it came to be thought that the rights of men, and the duties of neighbors and of rulers toward them, varied according to their religion; and society did not acknowledge the same obligations to a Turk or a Jew, a pagan or a heretic, or a devil worshipper, as to an orthodox Christian. As the ascendancy of religion grew weaker, this privilege of treating enemies on exceptional grounds was claimed by the State for its own benefit; and the idea that the ends of government justify the means employed was worked into a system by Machiavelli . . . ."[6]

Machiavelli rationalized despotism, but he also advised rulers to be careful to maintain what we today would call public relations: the patronage of the arts and artists together with conspicuous charities, in order to create popularity, and to mask their hold on power. This double-edged advice provided, in Acton's words, a sop to the consciences of even "very religious kings. [Because] he made the bad and the good very much alike." Rulers came to believe that their tenure depended upon lack of scruples.

This moral decline seemed rewarded by a widespread increase in luxury attendant upon commerce, inventions, explorations and innovation. Christian certainties began to fade in the discovery of seemingly successful non-Christian cultures and civilizations.

Meanwhile the Papacy kept losing spiritual stature and prestige. In the fourteenth century there were two pseudo-popes, two sets of cardinals and two papal courts. Then a third claimant appeared. Finally a church Council deposed all three and elected Martin V. But the shock lingered: the awareness that worldly ambitions absorbed the Vatican's attention spread far and sank deep.

Although ancient Rome had persecuted Christians, fed martyrs to

---

6. Acton, *op. cit.,* vol. 1, pp. 36, 37.

wild beasts, sacrificed humans as though they were animals, approved the crucifixion of our Lord Jesus and collapsed through continued corruption, Italian scholars began to hail the pagans as wiser, and their times as superior to the Christian.

Few observed, when this trend began, that to turn toward the graves of Rome and Greece was to revert to an evil past—and to turn away from the Christian faith. Some later said the Italians were attracted by pride in their ancestors and Italy's once-great role in the world. But that rings hollow: flights to the past usually betray discontent with the present.

Whatever the reasons, Italians began to extol the pagans, revive their writings and customs and unearth their statuary, paintings and plays. Inherent in these physical and intellectual exhumations, however, were ancient intellectual diseases that had led both Greece and Rome into the abyss: arguments that led to the despairing conclusion that life is pointless and chaotic.

Enormous sums were spent for translations, copyists, old manuscripts. Ancient names were restored: Plutarch and Polybius, Cicero, Quintilian and a long parade reappeared. Nor did the Church remain aloof. Restraints that had, through the centuries, gathered, protected and translated antique manuscripts but had restricted the circulation of the diabolic were swept away by the flood.

Popes subsidized vast pagan collections. Latin moved out of the Church and beyond the clergy into new Latin Schools which separated the children of the well-to-do from the poor, who were taught in local languages.

ૐ

This led to the rise of a new group: the Humanists, scholars once destined for the clergy who chose secular careers. The Humanists imitated the ancient poets, essayists, authors, lecturer-teachers, satirists and romancers.

At first they appeared singly, like stars. Dante, in the early Renaissance, led the transition. His *Divine Comedy* treated the ancient and Christian worlds as parallel, much as an earlier period mingled figures from the Old and New Testaments. He placed pagans and Christians together in Heaven, Purgatory and Hell—where all, improbably, reflected the politics of Florence.

Since the Christian version of history was then well-known, Dante's pagan personages appeared fresh and interesting. In effect, he limned a universal society in the next life; a supernatural world state; a celestial Church.

Renaissance Humanists followed Dante's lead. Eventually they abandoned the Christian viewpoint almost entirely, and began to write secular histories patterned on Livy and Tacitus, and biographies a la Plutarch.

The rise of new writers, the recovery of perspective in painting, the appearance of new/old techniques in sculpture and the recovery of ancient theater and culture seemed dazzling and fresh.

But the unearthed past withered contemporary innovation. In Florence in 1300 laborers could cite Dante in Italian; by 1400 learning had deteriorated into Latin tags and citations. Men looked to antiquity for answers to all problems; literature became imitative. Medicine rediscovered Galen and his absurd theories about "humors" at the expense of medical research. Hard-won municipal and individual rights faded as Humanists extolled tyrannical Roman laws, which despots were quick to adopt. And the impact of a licentious past upon morals and behavior was disastrous.

Swayed by Humanists, Italians came to accept the pagan theory of free will. Law, in any real sense, collapsed. "Their belief in God began to waver," wrote Burckhardt, "and their view of the government of the world became fatalistic." They embraced the paradoxical theory that Man is philosophically free, while unable to exercise free choice in the real world.

People sought escape from this intellectual cul-de-sac by plunges into astrology and magic. Blind fortune, they came to believe, rules the world. Like the immature everywhere, they retained a vague sense of good and evil, but lost their belief in sin.

The idea of eternal life was rejected in favor of earthly fame. Paganism deepened as the Renaissance extended. Cities appointed official astrologers. From the fourteenth to the sixteenth centuries, universities had official "stargazers." Even the Popes relied on horoscopes.

By the beginning of the sixteenth century Italy was in a deep moral crisis. But the Renaissance was not, by then, limited to Italy. It had spread throughout all Europe, rotting morals everywhere.

European rulers, centralizing their power, found the way smoothed by this spiritual decline. France, Spain, the Holy Roman Empire (a partly fictional claim fostered by the Emperor of Germany) competed to simultaneously influence the Vatican while contending for control of the Papal States—for success in either could deliver Christendom into new hands.

Ferdinand, crafty king of Spain, seized control of Naples, Sicily and Sardinia; France controlled Milan. Such inroads into rich, splintered Italy reflected big power rivalries.

Meanwhile at Oxford, John Wyclif denounced the Pope as Antichrist and questioned church doctrines. So did Jan Hus, a Czech. Dissident religious movements increased. The Vatican, engrossed in secular power struggles, argued that it was heretical to question its doctrines and issued spiritual threats backed by very real temporal force.

ॐ

Luther, a penniless monk with a master's degree, visited Rome on behalf of his monastery in 1510. There he saw "gorgeous churches and more gorgeous rituals, the pagan splendor of the paintings, the heathen gods still almost worshipped in the adoration of the art which had formed them. . . ."[7]

He was shocked. "Everything is permitted in Rome," he said later, "except to be an honest man."

Later, as a 35 year old professor of philosophy at Wittenberg, he was preaching on Sundays when the Dominican monk John Tetzel arrived in Saxony. Tetzel was raising money for the new, splendid St. Peter's Cathedral, designed by Michelangelo, being constructed under Pope Leo X. Tetzel was selling "Dispensations" that allowed purchasers to break church rules: to eat meat on Fast Days, to marry a close relative, to commit adultery without penalty and so on.

Indulgences were similar, but could only be cashed in Heaven, to which the Church alone had the keys. There heavenly credits could be balanced against sins committed on earth. If the Indulgences amounted

---

7. James Anthony Froude, *Short Studies of Great Subjects* (London, England: Longman, Green and Co., 1888), p. 92.

to a greater total than the sum of one's sins on earth, the gates of Heaven opened automatically.

Tetzel, in other words, sold earthly and spiritual pardons. The Vatican was his manufacturer; Saxony his sales territory. The Archbishop of Mayence, a friend of Erasmus the Humanist, would receive half of all the money Tetzel collected.

The monk's progress was triumphant. To doubt the value of his wares was to risk excommunication—a penalty that meant ostracism and ruin; death in life.

An earlier generation would have meekly bought the Indulgences, Tetzel and the Archbishop would have divided the proceeds, and the Papal caravan would have moved on. In a month the campaign would have run its course.

But Wyclif had risen. Jan Hus had risen (and been burned alive). Printed satires had appeared against the Church and circulated in the tens of thousands. Anticlerical polemics had appeared. A younger generation was restless; the air was heavy with dissent in Germany, the Netherlands, France, Switzerland, and Scandia.

Luther wrote a protest against Tetzel's campaign to the Archbishop of Mayence. When it was ignored he nailed another to the church door at Wittenberg, arguing that God, and not a Pope, forgave sins; that it was better to give alms than buy Indulgences, that the repentant do not seek to escape punishment: they seek it. That he who helps his neighbor buys his own pardon—and 91 other propositions he offered to debate.

His challenge was in Latin, the educated language. But a new class of men had appeared who were neither scholars, nobles nor clergy, but printers, workingmen who, somehow, learned Latin and Greek and the other languages of Europe as well. They translated whatever seemed to them commercially viable, printed and distributed books and pamphlets for sale at fairs and stalls. They were men earning a living by using new techniques invented and developed by unknowns from their own ranks; men unaware (as are most men) that they were instruments of God.

One of these, known only to Heaven, paused to read Luther's challenge. He translated it into German, printed it and began to sell copies. Another (or perhaps the same printer) translated the German into French and began to print and sell copies in France and parts of

Switzerland; still others translated and sold copies in Spanish, in Flemish, in Dutch, and in Italian. In due course a copy was handed to Pope Leo X.

He read it, smiled, and said, "A drunken German wrote this. When he had slept off his wine he will be of another mind."

But the Reformation had dawned.

જ

Between 1517 and 1520, 300,000 copies of Luther's writings were sold throughout Europe. That was a tremendous number at a time when print had uncanny power. "For the first time in history a great reading public judged the validity of revolutionary ideas through a mass medium which used the vernacular languages together with the arts of the journalist. . . ."[8]

Luther was invited to the Vatican but wisely declined. He debated Eck, a famous theologian, who cited various Papal Bulls and Edicts while Luther cited the Bible. That ended with both men furious.

In 1519 Charles V, Hapsburg ruler of the Netherlands, inherited the Spanish Crown and was elected Emperor of Germany. That did not bode well for Luther, for Charles V was unusually devout, and Luther's relations with the Vatican had grown tense. By then, Luther had moved irrevocably into Reform, questioned Papal infallibility, and even the General Council of the Church.

જ

But even an age steeped in theology had other, more immediate concerns. Syphilis carried people off in days at first, weeks later and— still later—in months. It appeared first in Naples and was later blamed by each nation upon its nearest rival. Theologians discerned God's judgment on an evil period. In 1519, meanwhile, Cortez entered Mexico and met, for the first time, Montezuma, ruler of the bloodthirsty Aztecs. The Portuguese expanded their commercial empire to Burma; Magellan left Europe to try to circle the world by water.

---

8. E. I. Eisenstein, *The Advent of Printing and* the *Protestant Revolt,* cf. *Renaissance and Reformation History* (Minnesota Burgess Printing Co., 1974), p. 235.

In 1520 the Pope issued a Bull against Luther: an ultimatum to obey or be excommunicated. In response Luther issued three brief books criticizing the distinctions between the clergy and the laity, the sole right of the Pope to interpret Scripture and to call a General Council of the Church. All three, he said, had to be overturned.

He also rejected the right of the Vatican to interfere with Princes (an argument that attracted powerful support), said the Scriptures were the final authority for doctrine or practice, and urged Germany to reject the Papacy. He recommended a national church and the expulsion of all Papal delegates. This struck a popular chord.

Luther's *Open Letter* created a sensation. Presses ran around the clock, turning out new editions. His national appeal fell on fertile ground throughout the North.

When he received the Papal Bull, Luther burned it in public. When the Writ of Excommunication reached him, he burned that as well. He criticized all Sacraments except Baptism and the Lord's Supper (the only ones mentioned in the New Testament). Then he issued a third manifesto on *Christian Liberty* in which he stated that faith alone, and not good works, makes a man good; his good works follow from faith. "The tree bears fruit; the fruit does not bear the tree."

His remarks on liberty were equally incisive. "A man firm in his faith in the divinity and redeeming sacrifice of Christ enjoys not freedom of will, but the profoundest freedom of all: freedom from his own carnal nature, from all evil powers, from damnation, even from law; for the man whose virtue flows spontaneously from his faith needs no commands to righteousness."

These arguments flowed across Europe like molten lava, igniting the Reformation. Reformers began to meet secretly at Cambridge while Luther's works were being burned at Charing Cross. Entire areas of northern Germany appeared openly against the Vatican. Toward the end of 1520, Luther proclaimed that no man could be saved unless he renounced the Vatican. In effect, Luther excommunicated the Pope.

೭♦

This confrontation between an indomitable individual and a vast international organization is stirring and mysterious to contemplate, even across the gulf of centuries. Europe was menaced by Turks who controlled the eastern Mediterranean and North Africa and were at the gates of Hungary. Yet European ships moved around the globe expanding European influence, power and Christian principles. Simultaneously, Europe was in the throes of a great religious upheaval.

In 1521 Charles V summoned Luther to a personal meeting at the Imperial Diet at Worms. All that stood between Luther and death at the hands of the Emperor at that point was the protection of the Elector of Saxony, who said, "There is much in the Bible about Christ, but not much about Rome."

The Elector extracted a safe-conduct from the Emperor for Luther's trip to and from Worms. But the temptation to seize and punish Luther must have been extreme. Charles V was, after all, only 21 years old. At that age he held title to more lands, people and riches than any man in history. He was emperor of Germany, King of Spain, Sardinia, Sicily and the Netherlands, ruler of Milan and lesser regions. His titles would overflow a page; his soldiers were masters of vast areas.

Charles V could have ignored the Elector, but Germany was still largely feudal and the Emperor's power not absolute. Germans still enjoyed many of the rights and powers the Renaissance had, elsewhere, swept away. Charles didn't want to make a difficult situation worse.

That Luther entered Worms in triumph was no surprise to the Papal observers. They had reported anti-Vatican sentiment in northern Germany three years before. At Wittenberg, Luther's stronghold, the university faculty, students and citizens were all for him. One former Humanist and theologian, professor of Greek at 21, was Philipp Schwartzert (Black Earth), whose guardian Hellenized his name to Melancthon. Small, homely and seemingly timid, his eloquence entranced classes of four and five hundred, including Luther.

Another zealous Wittenberg professor was Andreas Bodenstein, generally called Carlstadt (his birthplace). At 30 Carlstadt held the chair of Thomistic philosophy and theology, and had anticipated Luther in 1517 by publishing 152 theses against Indulgences.

Luther, in other words, spoke not only for himself. He met the Emperor on April 17–18, 1521. The youthful Charles sat on a raised dais surrounded by men in gleaming armor, mitered Archbishops and richly dressed nobles. Luther seemed overawed. Asked to recant the heresies in his books, he asked for time to consider. Charles gave him a day.

That night men came to Luther's lodgings to encourage him. By the next day he had recovered. Asked again if he would recant "heretical" passages, Luther replied that passages about ecclesiastical abuses were "by common consent just." The Emperor leaned forward and said explosively, "No!"

Asked again, in Latin, if he would recant, Luther answered in German, "My conscience is bound to the word of God, and it is neither safe nor honest to act against one's conscience. God help me! Amen!"

When the questioning ended, he walked out holding one hand high, like a victorious German knight who had unhorsed his opponent. It was a significant gesture. He had, in fact, come through a great ordeal. The Emperor frowned after him.

Charles thought it was "self-evident that the right of each individual to interpret Scripture, and to accept or reject civil or ecclesiastical authority according to private judgment or conscience, would soon erode the very foundation of social order."[9]

In a private conference the next day, the Emperor showed a statement citing his august Catholic lineage that ended by saying that Luther's safe-conduct would be honored, but that proceedings against him would be undertaken later. He asked the Electors to approve.

Four Electors agreed and signed but Luther's protector, the Elector of Saxony, abstained. So did the Elector of the Palatinate. News of the statement and the Emperor's intention leaked from the chambers (probably by servants) within hours. That night anonymous hands posted "on the door of the Town Hall and elsewhere in Worms, placards being the German symbol of social revolution, the peasant's shoe."[10]

૨७

Luther hid till 1522. Early that year Carlstadt issued an iconoclastic call against images. That was a call against a past in which images had proliferated all across western Europe. Crosses and statues, shrines and paintings were an integral part of pilgrimages. Statues were the focus of devotions; relics abounded.

---

9. Will Durant, *The Story of Civilization*, vol. 6 (New York, N.Y.: Simon and Shuster, 1957), p. 357.

10. Ibid., p. 362.

The Vatican, following the defeat of iconoclasts at the Second Council of Nicaea in 787, had long encouraged imagery in the Church. The reasoning too convoluted to describe fully in this section, argued that the Incarnation of the second person of the Trinity in Jesus meant that God Himself had reinterpreted the meaning of the Second Commandment, because there had appeared a living image of whom it was possible and legitimate to make an icon or image.

Through the centuries since that decision, "the sheer numbers of religious images that still survive (let alone what once existed) argue eloquently for the importance that seeing had for believers. The image was not peripheral to medieval Christianity. It was a central means. . . . Participation in the Sacraments was relatively rare; communion with the saints through their representations was a common if not daily experience. In the later Middle Ages it was accepted by the church that Christians should not only learn their faith through visual representations, but should also express their faith through reverencing these."[11]

In a manner we today can understand, "images begot images." They ranged from huts to palaces, from roads to buildings, from churches to shrines. The Vatican produced arguments in defense of images. Those who did not choose (or were unable) to go on pilgrimages could serve a penance before an image; a devotional system was created.

Meanwhile, there were profits in imagery. Carvers, painters, gold and silversmiths and other artisans found employment; worshippers bedecked images with jewelry and laid gifts before the saints. As time passed, the figures and displays of churches and cathedrals became increasingly ornate and provided poignant contrasts to the humble situation of the congregations. Yet many accepted these splendors as signs of the glories of Heaven.

Carlstadt considered images tangible evidence of the idolatries—both physical and intellectual—that had carried the faith to near-paganism. While Luther hid from the agents of the Emperor, Carlstadt led demonstrators in Wittenberg to strip the churches of statues, paintings and hangings. Nor did he stop there: he had his followers break into a church library, where they pulled crucifixes from the wall,

---

11. Margaret Aston, *England's Iconoclasts: Laws Against Images*, vol. 1 (Oxford: Clarendon Press, 1988), pp. 21, 22.

and defaced book illustrations.

In effect, Carlstadt transformed an intellectual rebellion into a religious revolution. His actions in Wittenberg served as a catalyst to what would become an inextricable element in the Reformation: the destruction of physical images, shrines and all religious artifacts.

The Reformers came to believe that "widespread destruction was necessary for the renewal of an entire religious system . . . we must . . . give them the credit of consciously believing that they were shaping a complete new order. They saw, as none of their predecessors had seen so clearly, the possibilities of controlling minds through imagery or the destruction of imagery, loading or unloading mental processes with visual effects. These are methods that have been taken to new limits in our day."[12]

Luther was shocked. He saw in the breakers of images a destructive impulse released in the name of religion; "a spirit hidden in them which is death-dealing, not life-giving, and which at the first opportunity will also kill men, just as some of them have begun to preach."[13]

Luther also wondered if it was necessary to destroy every image, and if people should take the law into their own hands. Finally, he argued that eliminating idolatry in the heart came before eradicating imagery in the churches.

Nevertheless, Carlstadt had catalyzed the Reform, which began to move among the people more rapidly than authorities—or even Reform leaders could trace. Augustinian friars at Wittenberg abandoned their monastery and began to preach Lutheranism. While Melancthon prepared an exposition of Biblically based theology, Carlstadt demanded that Mass be said in the vernacular, that the Eucharist be given in bread and wine without fasting or confessions, that monks as well as secular priests should marry and have children. Luther agreed with these arguments.

In hiding Luther completed the first new translation of the New Testament since Jerome's *Vulgate,* which had appeared in the fourth century. At a time when no Greek or Latin dictionary into German existed, this was remarkable. Even more remarkable was the fact that its

12. Ibid., p. 5.
13. Ibid., p. 9.

language was superior to any previous German work. It (and Luther's later translation of the Old Testament) set a standard of German prose unsurpassed to this day.

Then Luther learned, to his anger and disgust, that his New Testament was being widely suppressed. This led him, in a book titled *Civil Power,* to say that "Princes are not to be obeyed when they command subservience to superstitious errors."

That rationale for resistance had immediate consequences. Outbursts against priests and demolition of altars increased to such an extent that Luther, alarmed on a new front, issued *Warning Against Insurrection and Rebellion.* He realized that the people had suffered, but stressed that disorder would worsen their situation.

But arguments once raised do not simply vanish. Some wanted to burn religious paintings as well as destroy altars; others appeared to claim divine inspiration and special skills to interpret the Bible. Some said that baptism should be deferred till maturity; others said that the Kingdom of God was at hand and that the ungodly would soon be destroyed.

Such echoes alarmed Luther. He shaved the thick beard he had grown in hiding and reappeared to preach in Wittenberg. He urged an end to destructive behavior, using a variety of arguments. But the wind had been raised, and it continued to rise.

※

In the 1520s Luther was the most popular author in Europe. His books sold not only at stalls and fairs, but (by wandering peddlers and students) house to house. In Paris his works outsold all others. He was popular in Spain, France, Italy, the Netherlands, Switzerland, and England. He alone unconsciously moved the center of publishing from Italy to northern Europe where it has remained ever since.

Meanwhile the storm he had summoned rose to hurricane levels. Starving knights besieged the city of Trier and were counterattacked by the archbishop. Luther began to disassociate himself from rebellion.

Priests and nuns poured from the Church and rushed toward marriage. Great princes began to convert to the Reform. The new Pope, Adrian VI, elected in 1521, demanded Luther's arrest from the Elector of Saxony. The Elector refused: he and other German rulers had decided to support Luther. In 1524 another new Pope, Clement VII, a Médici, sent a Cardinal to Germany but he succeeded only in spurring the anti-Vatican movement. When the Cardinal warned the German Diet against unchecked religious schism, the peasantry erupted.

≈

Peasants had rebelled before, but never on so sweeping a scale. That they should have been excited by Luther's successful defiance of Popes and the Emperor, his teaching that every man is a priest before God and that all Christians can become free through faith was understandable. It was also understandable that many confused Luther's definition of spiritual freedom with their earthbound situation.

Speakers arose to say that Luther's New Testament proved the clergy had deceived the people; that it promised that the poor would inherit the earth immediately. Some called for an end to all taxes and passports, fines and duties, licenses and permits; for the election of all officials by universal suffrage, and at the same time, a return to the medieval system of fixed bread prices.

Popular historian Will Durant, academically underrated but often insightful, said, "In the Germany of that age the Church and state were so closely meshed—clergymen played so large a role in social order and civil administration—that the collapse of ecclesiastical prestige and power removed a major barrier to revolution."

Violence flared. Thomas Munzer called for the death of all the Godless, gathered an army and even cannon. By the end of 1524, 30,000 armed peasants in South Germany demanded an end to all taxes, tithes and feudal dues.

Under leaders too numerous to mention and arguments tedious to recall, peasant armies captured and sacked cities, indulged in orgies, murder and pillage. Bands ran riot in nearly all of Germany, demanded ransoms, pillaged churches, committed arsons, looted castles and mon-asteries.

In May an alarmed Luther issued a pamphlet *Against the Robbing and Murdering Hordes of Peasants.* It was vehement enough to shock all factions.

His cold water appeared just as the rulers began to regain the upper hand. Munzer and his cannon were met and conquered, and 5,000 of his followers were slaughtered. In Alsace 20,000 peasants were killed in the same month that Luther's pamphlet against rebellion had appeared. Hideous deaths for rebels were ordered by the Markgraf Casimir, and killings continued until the Diet of Augsburg urged moderation in August, 1525.

In Austria, which Charles V had ceded to his younger brother Ferdinand, the rebellion lasted another year. By the time it ended 130,000 peasants had been killed in battle or by execution. The Swabian League alone executed 10,000. Hundreds of castles and monasteries had been ruined; more hundreds of towns depopulated and impoverished. Over 50,000 homeless roamed the roads or hid in the woods. Widows and orphans were numerous. Not till the Thirty Year's War a century later was Germany to suffer so much.

Peace did not restore the old order. Because many rebel groups had destroyed the charters that recorded their feudal dues, new ones— sometimes more rigorous, sometimes less—were drawn. Concessions were made in some areas, such as Austria, Hesse, and Baden. But in other areas—especially east of the Elbe—serfdom was made more rigorous.

One important result was that the authorities came to a shocked realization of the power of the press. Peasants echoing phrases of Luther out of context and with eccentric interpretations made it clear that books and pamphlets are not innocuous. Censorship appeared everywhere. All Europe drew similar conclusions. Charles V characterized the Peasant's War as a Lutheran movement; rulers in Southern Germany repledged their allegiance to the Vatican and ordered men executed for having, even briefly, accepted Luther's position.

❧

Luther himself ruefully accepted the fact that his theory of private judgment and dissent had opened unexpected gates. He was shocked at the appearance of the Anabaptists (Again-Baptizers), a sect that contained lesser sects that exalted the individual conscience above the State, the Church and even the Bible.

Although some Anabaptists adopted severe manners and dress and recommended moral austerities, they stretched Luther's argument of spiritual freedom from sin into a concept of political freedom. They denounced all governments, and all obedience to governments. They refused to swear oaths of allegiance, to accept military service, and preached religious toleration for all.

Religious toleration was, however, a position that neither the sixteenth century nor any of its predecessors had ever accepted as valid. Neither the Vatican nor its forebears believed that error should have equal rights with truth.

To allow the practice of Satanism, which is what the Church fathers considered paganism, to enjoy equal status with Christianity, was obviously impossible.

If the early Church had accepted toleration (which was proposed to it by the Roman authorities from the start), Rome would have remained three-quarters pagan. Infanticide and human sacrifice would have existed alongside Christianity. The depravity of the Roman elite would have been allowed to mock and subvert the austerity of Christian congregations. Such a state of affairs was clearly impossible; it was never seriously regarded by the Church fathers, let alone accepted as a moral and permanent solution.

૨➋

Luther had come to regard the Pope as Antichrist and the leader of a revived paganism. The Reform was an effort to revitalize Christianity, and to recall Christians to their principles. Rebellion against the Reform was a threat to the faith. He said with some reason, "The devil, having failed to put me down with the help of the Pope, was seeking my destruction through the preachers of destruction and blood."

To avert that ruin, Luther called upon the Princes of Germany to protect his church. He provided them with the spiritual position they needed to defy the Vatican while retaining a stable social order; to get rid of the Papal bureaucracy within their realms and to assume control of both Church and State.

That this placed the Lutheran church under the State was, to Luther, no more than the normal traditional situation. All Christendom in the sixteenth century agreed that society is held together by a common religion. The idea of diverse religions in a single State was, by philosophers, historians, theologians, laymen and clergy alike, held to be anarchic. The rise of a competitive religion within a single State was, by all rulers, held to be treasonous.

Luther, looking into the Bible, held that rulers are divinely appointed. The Princes, in turn, provided Lutheranism a shelter from the Vatican. The price Lutheranism paid for that protection later was what Acton termed "that character of political dependence and that habit of passive obedience which it has ever since retained."[14]

---

14. Acton, *op. cit.*, vol. 2, p. 101.

Chapter Two

THE RENAISSANCE

———— ❧ ————

But his heart was swollen,
And turned aside
By deep, interminable pride.
— Byron

The Renaissance did not end with Luther or stop in Italy. Luther had released pent-up German protests and arguments again the Vatican, but by the 1520s Europe had seen many such rebellions and defections. Lutheranism did not, to the Pope, seem too threatening. The struggle of European princes against the Vatican States seemed immediate and important.

The aristocracy of Europe had adopted the attitudes of the Italian despots and lived in unexampled luxury, but this pride was irritated by the inescapable influence of the Vatican. Its taxes and bureaucracy, property and prelates, its paralleling and sometimes dominating authority within the realm, ruled from afar by a personage who claimed sovereignty over all temporal as well as the spiritual kingdoms—earth and heaven together—was a constant irritant.

An example that rulers and aristocrats considered more favorable was provided by the Sicilian Monarchy. There was a model of how a state, its rulers and aristocrats, could be free of Rome without upsetting or altering the faith of the people.

The Norman conquerors of Sicily had defied the Vatican and controlled both church and state on the island to a degree unparalleled outside Byzantium. The Kings of Aragon, who succeeded the Normans, maintained the same bad relations despite Bulls of Excommunication and an interdict that lasted nearly seventy years. The wily Ferdinand of Aragon, maternal grandfather of Charles V, finally ended that unpleasantness by having the Kings of Sicily appointed hereditary papal

Legatees (ecclesiastics invested with the power of the Holy See).

That inspired Henry VIII to ask for the same authority to be given to Cardinal Wolsey, his principal minister *a latere* (in secret). This was granted, and the Cardinal had hopes of becoming Pope. Charles V, warring with France, encouraged Wolsey's ambition. In turn, Wolsey encouraged Henry VIII to believe that by helping Charles V fight France, England might regain French territories; perhaps even the French Crown.

By 1523 the Cardinal's hopes began to fade. Two successive enclaves failed to bring him the triple tiara. The elevation of the younger Clement VII, a Médici, finally convinced the English Cardinal he had been tricked. He began to talk his master away from Charles V and toward an alliance with France.

In January 1525, before Wolsey's new goal surfaced, England learned that Francis I not only lost a great battle at Pavia, Italy, but had also been taken prisoner. The King of France was held for ransom in Madrid for a year, while Charles V plotted the conquest of Italy.

On learning of Charles V's victory, Henry VIII sent in his bill. He wanted to be made King of France, and wanted the money Charles owed him to be repaid.

Charles V refused everything. He would not help England obtain any part of France. He would not marry Henry's daughter. Instead of paying his debts, he asked for more money.

Cardinal Wolsey then made a new deal. The Regent of France agreed to pay England as much money to drop Charles, as Charles would receive for the French king's ransom. Henry VIII, who had followed the advice of the universally detested Wolsey, was in that fashion privately paid but publicly humiliated.

Ordinarily such an unpalatable result would have led Wolsey to the scaffold, for Henry VIII was a tyrant of unusual qualities. He had all the presence, wit and learning expected of a Renaissance prince—and was as unscrupulous as any Médici, Colonna or Sforza. Yet, when the goal of rivalling the Plantagenets appeared within reach, Henry VIII dropped the whole matter—and continued to listen to Wolsey.[1]

The English king's reasons were deeply personal. He had tired of his

---

1. Acton, *op. cit.*, vol. 2, p. 265.

wife. Wolsey, through his strong connections at the Vatican, promised to have the royal marriage annulled or divorced despite its long duration.[2] Officially Henry stated that he feared he had violated the injunctions in Leviticus by marrying his brother's widow. This was, he feared, the reason the three sons he had by Catherine had died almost upon birth. The King had sinned involuntarily, he said, and the Lord had punished.

The Queen was older than Henry. Her looks were prematurely faded; her eldest children dead. She watched in dismay as the long alliance between her country, Spain, and England was severed and new ties drawn with France.

This situation made the English uneasy. "It called to mind the havoc of the civil war, and the murders in the Royal House, which in the seven preceding reigns had seven times determined the succession."[3] It was feared that Henry would have a series of mistresses and that his inheritance would be contested by bastards. The King's soul, the monarchy and Wolsey's own position, wrote Acton later, were all in jeopardy.

Meanwhile the Vatican trembled before Charles V. In captivity, Francis I proposed that he join the Emperor in an assault on Rome, and together place the Pope under control, once and for all. That proposition, tempting though it was, was rejected—but provides an insight into the temper of the times. In March 1526 Francis I was released, and the Pope put himself at the head of a Sacred League joined by France and helped by England. Italians sought to rally one another against the Spanish threat.

In April 1527 Henry VIII, infuriated over Charles V's failure to acknowledge England's claims, signed a treaty with France, agreed that his daughter Mary would marry into the French royal house, and simultaneously shipped another large sum of money to the Vatican to promote his divorce.

But in July 1527, the Duke of Bourbon, who had broken with the King of France, and had allied himself with Charles V, led a force of Spanish, German and Italian mercenaries to the successful conquest of

---

2. They were married in 1509.
3. Acton, *op. cit.*, vol. 2, p. 266.

Milan. After that triumph, he looked south, toward the Vatican—and the Pope had more immediate concerns than approving a divorce for the King of England.

ạ❦

The Duke of Bourbon's army consisted of 14,000 German Lutheran *landsknechts,* 5,000 Spaniards and 3,000 Italian mercenaries. The Spaniards, less numerous than the Germans under Bourbon, were universally feared. Their centuries-long struggles against the Moors had taught them patterns of cavalry and torture. In addition to their cruelty—unparalleled in Europe—the Spaniards were inured to campaigning amid gruelling conditions. They could march and fight long after soldiers from softer nations would collapse. They were notorious for being physically filthy and unwashed. Chamberlin says they were "one of the most odoriferous armies in history."

The Italians who made up the rest of Bourbon's army were mercenaries: men without allegiance or conscience, capable of everything for money; nothing for honor.

That army moved toward Rome and the Pope in early 1527; only its Germans claimed a religious motive. All the soldiers were unpaid and unfed, and lived by robberies from the peasantry. Quarrelsome and hungry, anxious for booty, women, drink and food in that order, they were as vicious a group of men as any ever assembled.

ạ❦

They arrived at the gates of Rome on May 5, 1527. It was, at that moment, the richest city in Europe. Within its walls 50 great families maintained as many miniature states, each independent. Their wars, once savage, had gradually relaxed to occasional poisonings, secret assassinations, endless agreements and disagreements. Each enclave had great pride of family, but none of race. They did not regard themselves as Italians, but as family members.

That some were cardinals had no religious significance whatever; the office had become political. Though a pope might make a meritorious selection, most appointments were openly purchased, after tortuous negotiations. Popes, chosen by the cardinals, represented these Roman families, who regarded the Papacy as their joint possession; the source of their wealth and power.

Beneath this rich crust, the people native to Rome comprised only 16 percent of the population. The Venetian ambassador noted that virtually all the native Romans were without a trade and lived in abject poverty. Prostitution was a major Roman industry. The artists who transformed the city into a showplace came from Florence, Sienna, Venice, Mantua and other parts. The banks were dominated by Florentines. The service trades were dependent upon residents from other cities.

Calls to volunteer for military duty fell upon indolent and indifferent ears: it seemed impossible that anyone would seriously damage the beautiful Holy City. Even the weather cooperated with the attackers: a heavy, unprecedented mist appeared at dawn to keep them invisible to the defenders along Aurelian's wall.

Although Bourbon was among the first to fall, mortally wounded, from one of the ladders placed along that wall, the invaders eventually found unprotected openings, and poured into the city. The leader of the defense, discovering this, ran down the street shrieking that all was lost.

Hadrian had built a great circular mausoleum on the west bank of the Tiber. In the late fifteenth century the first Borgia Pope, Alexander, and his successor Julius II "carved out dungeons and storerooms in the solid heart of the drum, and on its surface erected halls and residential buildings . . . a little city high above the dusty streets of Rome." All this was called the Castle Sant' Angelo. It was to this that the Pope, eleven cardinals, 3,000 noncombatants including ambassadors, priests, diplomats, scholars, servants, citizens, 500 soldiers and 90 survivors of the Swiss Guard retreated. Their main protection was artillery, which kept the bulk of the invaders at bay across the river.[4]

From this refuge, which lacked enough supplies to be tenable for very long, Clement VII could hear the shrieks of women and see men fleeing from murderers. The mixed soldiery of Bourbon, lacking controls, plunged into depravities unequalled even by the barbarian invaders of centuries before. The Germans, said one survivor later, were terrible but still human (and even, on occasion, spared some nuns), the Italian

---

4. Chamberlin, *The Sack of Rome* (Dorset Press, 1985), pp. 185–186.

mercenaries were depraved, but the Spaniards were fiends.

Only a sadist can regard the descriptions of the sufferings of Rome without a shudder. They included public perversities to which its most aristocratic and tenderly reared women were subjected, and the hideous sufferings of those men unfortunate enough to miss a quick death. Those who refused to tell where they hid their money, silver or other treasures lost their lives. The Germans were the most methodical: they weighed each coin on scales and recorded the totals.

Famous names were caught in the maelstrom: Benvenuto Cellini served as a bombardier at Sant' Angelo and later claimed to have brought down Bourbon; Machiavelli, the admirer of power politics, careworn at 57, was there in the last month of his life; the painter Peruzzi was first tortured, then forced to paint a portrait of the dead Bourbon, released and then recaptured, re-tortured and re-robbed. Giovanni da Udine was tortured and robbed and allowed to flee; Caravaggio the brawler and painter fled for his life, Parmigiano painted portraits of *landsknechts* and was allowed to live as a reward. Writers fared worse, being poorer. Cananova the poet was last seen begging for food, the humanist Angelo Colocci was twice taken, paid two ransoms and then had to watch as his manuscripts were burned; Angelo Cresi the lawyer was dragged from a sickbed to his death, Julianus Camers committed suicide, Francesco Cherea the comedian fled to later establish the *Commedia del'Arte*. He was one of the few fortunate. Meanwhile Aretino, the famous pornographer-poet-blackmailer, sent Clement VII a note saying, "It is the will of God that you find yourself at the mercy of the Emperor, and therefore in a position to experience both divine mercy and imperial clemency."

One can almost hear his laughter as he wrote that pitiless pun.

❧

Inside the Castle of Sant' Angelo the Pope agreed to pay an immense ransom. Similar conditions were imposed on the ambassadors and the rich who had taken refuge with him; that was a normal part of the war at the time.

In Madrid the Emperor publicly denied his private pleasure by ordering prayers and processions for the Pontiff's release: a release he could order at any time. His advisors talked about Spanish rule over Rome in the future, and some thought "that the Sacred Chair in Rome be . . . utterly and completely abolished."[5]

Charles V withstood that temptation. To have his foot on the Pope now and in the future was sweet enough. From the moment of that decision for generations to come, Madrid would decide the course and policy of the Vatican—and Henry VIII's chances of Papal approval of his divorce from the aunt of Charles V silently disappeared.

❧

The moment is worth a stare. During the previous autumn, in 1526, Suleiman the Magnificent had led 300,000 Turks against Hungary, defeated a tiny Hungarian army of 30,000, killed Louis II, the King of Hungary, and captured Buda. The Turks then carried off 200,000 Hungarians into slavery. That left the throne of Hungary vacant. It was claimed by the archduke Ferdinand of Germany, the younger brother of Charles V. He had hereditary claims to offer, but his connection to the most powerful prince in Christendom undoubtedly helped him to obtain the crown. The House of Hapsburg, therefore, ruled Austria, Hungary, Spain, the Netherlands, Sicily, Burgundy—and the Papacy.

These events, tumbling as they did upon one another, are almost too much to assess. As always, the full significance of the Sack of Rome (as it became known) took time to grasp.

It later became clear that what had happened to Rome, to the Papacy, to the Catholic Church, was that the Judgment of God had descended. The ambitions of the priests and their immense, fabled organization had been greatly reduced as far as temporal power was concerned. But the punishment spread far beyond the Vatican.

The people of Italy fell from their pinnacle as the leaders of Europe to people who were to live under conquerors. A series of occupiers would break them into fragments of a people: remnants. The Italian Humanists would see their literary prestige destroyed; their witticisms turned acrid, their vaunted historicism mocked. The nation that introduced the Renaissance was the first to find its fruits hollow; its splendors reduced to theatrics, its people regarded with easy contempt for generations to come.

---

5. Ibid., p. 196.

Beyond that stretched the lesson taught by the invading army. The Lutherans from Mindelheim, the torturing Spaniards, the mercenary Italians of Bourbon's army all claimed to be Christians. Once tempted by helpless women, quaking civilians and an absence of controls, they had turned into monsters.

Nothing could more definitely fix, into the horrified mind of all watching Europe, the innate depravity of Man. That phrase, and even that observation, was yet to be reformulated, but Europe's mental and psychological landscape had been altered to make it receptive when it did appear—and that time was not too far off, for Calvin in 1527 was eighteen and beginning his university studies.

Chapter Three

THE REFORMATION

─────── ?◍ ───────

And ye were as a firebrand
Plucked out of the burning.

— Amos

When Henry VIII received a Papal Bull threatening him with anathema[1] if he divorced Queen Catherine, Wolsey was banished. He gave his palace at Whitehall to the King in a transparent effort to avert vengeance. His enemies moved to charge him with various offenses, but Henry, with ostentatious mercy, refused. In true Renaissance fashion, he preferred to let Wolsey suffer in anticipation.

Meanwhile most English Catholics and all but one Bishop sided with the King against the Pope. That was no surprise, for Pelagius, the father of the free-will doctrine, was English.

From this time onward, the English were steadfast in defiance of Roman authority. They were, historically, the first colony to successfully throw off Roman rule. During succeeding centuries their religion fused with their national spirit, and they regarded Europe with suspicion and disdain.

Throughout the Middle Ages they "manufactured world chronicles in which the English played a prominent role. In the fourteenth and fifteenth centuries, armed with ancient claims and grudges, they inflicted their historic visions and myths on the hapless French. Quite when they first took note of the fact that they were the successor-race to the Jews is impossible to determine. It must have occurred early in the sixteenth century. . . .

"Henry VIII's controversy with Rome gave an enormous impulse to

─────────────

1. A curse usually accompanied by excommunication.

these probings into the past. Suddenly, history became politics; records and libraries were scrutinized for immediate public objects. King Arthur made his formidable appearance in the debate with Pope Clement. . . . [T]hey read Gildas and Nennius, Geoffrey of Monmouth and . . . historians who built on fantasies. Some believed Christianity had been brought to Britain by Joseph of Arimathea on the express instructions of the Apostles; some thought the agent was St. Paul. . . . But all the versions had one thing in common: Britain had gotten the faith directly from the apostolic succession—hot as it were, from the Holy Land— without the intermediary of Rome. The Popes had nothing to do with it."[2]

Belief in these myths was not restricted to any group; it was racial more than theological. By the sixteenth century, the English had no hesitation in choosing their King over a Pope.

≷❧

The Swiss states also resisted empire builders. They repelled Charles the Bold (Duke of Burgundy) in the west and the German Emperor Maximilian and absorption into the Holy Roman Empire in the east.

Mutual protection kept the Cantons against suicidal wars with each other, but not toward pacifism. During 1500–12 they took advantage of troubled Italy to seize control of Bellinzona, Locarno, Lugano and other areas south of the Alps. But after 1515 the Federation, which consisted of German, French and Italian speaking Cantons[3] abandoned ambitions for neutrality, peace, trade and prosperity.

Until Luther the Cantons were technically Catholic, but really Humanist. Nearly all Swiss priests had concubines. Zurich and some other Cantons established civic control of clergymen and taxed church properties. In 1510 Geneva received Papal permission (in return for the use of Swiss soldiers) to regulate the "monasteries, convents and public morals within its domain." In other words, before Luther's theses, local authority triumphed over the Vatican in Zurich and Geneva.

≷❧

---

2. Paul Johnson, *A History of the English People* (New York, N.Y.: Harper and Row, 1985), p. 175.

3. Some spoke several languages.

Zwingli was born in the present Swiss Canton of Saint-Gall in 1484, and schooled in the College at Bern and the University of Vienna. He studied theology under Wyttenbach, who attacked indulgences, clerical celibacy and the Mass. At 22 he earned his master's degree and became a priest. He continued to study, learned Greek, read pagan writers, and corresponded with Pico della Mirandola and Erasmus, by whom he was deeply influenced.

Despite his priesthood he had liaisons with several women, and became a pastor in Schwyz. A Protestant before Luther, his sermons were similar. In 1518 he became a vicar or "people's priest" in Zurich. When a Milanese friar appeared to sell indulgences in Zurich, Zwingli protested and the Vatican—reacting to events in Germany—recalled the ecclesiastical salesman.

In 1519 the plague struck Zurich; a third of the people died in six months. Zwingli stayed, toiled with the sick, fell victim himself. His popularity soared after he recovered; in 1521 he became head priest of the Grossmunster (Great Minister), and led the Reformation in Zurich.

Zwingli made the sermon the center of the service. Before that, the sermon had counted for little; Mass and Communion for nearly everything. He thought that Christianity should return to its original simplicity. When the Vatican protested, Zwingli cited the New Testament and was held innocent of heresy. After that all Zurich clergymen were ordered to preach only from the Scripture.

The Zurich Council, pressed by Reformers, also issued orders to remove all religious images, relics and ornaments from the churches. Catholics retained some civic rights but were forbidden public office. Monasteries and nunneries were closed or turned into hospitals or schools; large numbers of monks, nuns and priests married. Saint's days vanished as did pilgrimages, holy water and Masses held for the dead. By the end of 1524, Zurich created a Privy Council with authority to regulate religious as well as civic matters, with Zwingli as its unofficial leader. The Bible became the basis for all law.

ॐ

The Reformation split the Swiss Confederation, as it split all Europe. Bern, Basel, Schaffhausen, Appensill and Grison favored Zurich; the other Cantons were hostile. Five Cantons—Lucerne, Uri, Schwyz,

Unterwalden and Zig—formed a Catholic League to suppress all Hussite, Lutheran and Zwinglian movements. Archduke Ferdinand of Austria pledged his assistance to the Catholics and incidents erupted between the two groups.

The Protestant leader in Basel was Johannes Hausschein, who had Hellenized his name, which meant house lamp, into Oecolampadius. A prodigy who wrote Latin poetry at twelve, he also mastered Greek and became a Hebraist. "He made a name for himself in the pulpit of St. Martin's Church and in the chair of theology at the university, as a reformer and moralist. . . ."[4] Luther acclaimed him after he attacked Vatican abuses, and in 1525 Oecolampadius adopted Zwingli's positions on all but predestination, which he denied.

When the Council at Basel proclaimed freedom of worship, Oecolampadius protested and demanded suppression of the Mass. When the Council delayed, a crowd moved into the churches with hammers and axes and destroyed all "discoverable" religious images.

The Council then abolished the Mass. Erasmus, Beautus Rhenanus and most of the professors of the university left. Their attitudes were epitomized by Erasmus, who politely deplored the excesses of the church—until men took action. That alarmed him. "As for me," he wrote to Archbishop Warham, "I have no inclination to risk my life for truth. We have not all strength for martyrdom; and if trouble come, I shall imitate St. Peter. Popes and emperors must settle the creeds. If they settle them well, so much the better; if ill, I shall keep on the safe side."

వ

Events, however, overtook Erasmus and those Humanists who snuggled so long inside the church while deprecating its excesses. When Protestantism first appeared in The Netherlands said Froude, the great English historian, "before one single Catholic had been ill-treated there, before a symptom of a mutinous disposition had shown itself, an edict was issued by the authorities for the suppression of the new opinions."

All the people in the United Provinces were told to "hold and believe" the doctrines of the Holy Roman Catholic Church. "Men and women,"

---

4. Durant, *op. cit.,* p. 410.

said the edict, "who disobey this command shall be punished as disturbers of public order. Women who have fallen into heresy shall be buried alive. Men, if they recant, shall lose their heads. If they continue obstinate, they shall be burnt at the stake."

"The Inquisition shall inquire into the private opinions of every person, of whatever degree; and all officers of all kinds shall assist the Inquisition at their peril. Those who know where heretics are concealed, shall denounce them, or they shall suffer as heretics themselves. Heretics who give up other heretics to justice, shall themselves be pardoned if they will promise to conform for the future."[5]

Under this edict, in the Netherlands alone, more than fifty thousand human beings were coldly murdered.

⁊❧

In 1529 a Protestant missionary from Zurich tried to preach in the Catholic Canton of Schwyz and was burned at the stake. Zurich declared war, but then the two Cantons agreed that neither was to attack the other over religious differences, and in lands common to the two Cantons: a majority vote would determine religious regulations. Zwingli, unable to obtain freedom for Protestantism in Catholic areas, predicted that such a peace could not last long. (It lasted twenty-eight months.)

Protestantism had grown, in little more than a decade, into a formidable force. Half of Germany was Lutheran. Many important German cities: Ulm, Augsburg, Wurttemberg, Mainz, Frankfurt-am-Main and Strasbourg leaned toward Zwingli.[6]

Philip, the Landgrave of Hesse, invited Luther, Melancthon and other German protestants to meet Zwingli, Oecolampadius and other Swiss Protestants in his castle at Marburg in September, 1529. Luther and Zwingli agreed on many points, but disagreed over the Eucharist. Zwingli considered it only a symbol, but Luther chalked the words *This Is My Body* on a table.

The German leader stalked away, refusing Zwingli's hand. Later he drew up seventeen articles including transubstantiation, signed by the

5. Froude, *op. cit.*, vol. 1, pp. 49, 50.
6. Protestantism was first launched in cities and spread to the countryside later.

Lutheran Princes who declared they would reject alliance with any group that would not do the same.

Zwingli returned to a Zurich where trade dropped due to religious differences; his popularity sank. In 1531 he sent a letter explaining his views to Francis I, reflecting his lifelong admiration of Erasmus, saying that Christians, on reaching Paradise, would find there "Hercules, Theseus, Socrates, Aristides, Numa, Camillus, the Catos, the Scipios. . . . What could be imagined more joyful, pleasing, and noble, than this sight?"

This shocked Luther, who decided that Zwingli must be a heathen.

In May, Zurich and its allies voted to compel Catholic Cantons to allow freedom of preaching. When they refused, the Protestant Cantons launched an economic blockade. The Catholic Cantons declared war. The armies met at Kappel in October, 1531, with the Protestants badly outnumbered, 1,500 to 8,000. Zwingli was slain, together with 500 others. The Catholics quartered his body and burned it on a dunghill.

૨ઐ

Two years earlier, in 1529, England held its "Reformation Parliament," reflecting Henry VIII's anger at the Vatican. Commons passed an "Act of Accusation" charging the clergy with making laws without the consent of Parliament or the King, levying fines against laymen, distributing benefices "to certain young folks, calling them their nephews," (meaning priest's children), and asking the King for the "reformation of these ills."

The Bishops said abuses were individual errors,[7] claimed their Courts were just and asked for help in "reducing heresy." They also reminded the King that they served God rather than the Throne—which was not especially politic.

The King delayed while he pressed Commons to excuse him from repaying loans made to him by his subjects.[8] Meanwhile Commons reduced clerical authority in several sectors.

In late 1530 Henry and his Prime Minister, the Duke of Norfolk,

---

7. An inveterate bureaucratic rationale.
8. Durant notes that "depreciation of the currency now exempts governments from such honest burglary."

launched proceedings against Cardinal Wolsey, who was acting as Archbishop of York. Wolsey's physician was questioned under torture and provided evidence. An arrest warrant was served at the Archbishop's castle, where Wolsey had transferred enough personal goods to burden 160 horses and 72 carts. In cold November, Wolsey said good-bye to his household and left for London.

At Sheffield he came down with dysentery and stopped. Soldiers arrived and he resumed his journey, but two days later was so weak he was allowed to stop in Leicester Abbey. There, on his deathbed, he said what Cavendish reported and Shakespeare adapted, "If I had served my God as diligently as I have my King, he would not have given me over in my gray hairs."

⁊❧

Death balked Henry's plans for Wolsey, so he turned on all the clergymen who had recognized Wolsey's Papal authority. When they protested, Parliament—Henry's puppet—offered to drop prosecutions if the clergy confessed its "guilt" and paid a fine of 118,000 pounds.[9] Still protesting, the Church obeyed—and lost more ground.

Henry demanded to be named "The Protector and Only Supreme Head of the Church and Clergy of England." The clergy writhed in agony until the Archbishop Warham, 81, added "so far as the Law of Christ allows." So Henry replaced the Pope in England.

The regal boa constrictor then waited a year before applying more pressure. In 1532, acting through Parliament, he reduced Church death dues and transferred money from Indulgences and other Papal services from the Vatican to his treasury.

Meanwhile he forced Queen Catherine to return her Crown Jewels and gave them to Anne Boleyn. Catherine complained to her nephew, Charles V, who wrote the Pope. In turn the Pope sent Henry a rebuke. This exacerbated matters.

The English Bishops, aware of this correspondence, held a Convocation, prostrated themselves before the throne and begged to be released from vows of obedience to the Vatican. Henry VIII found this accept-

---

9. $150 million?

able, and from that day to this the Church of England became an arm of the State. Free of the Vatican, Henry VIII married the pregnant Anne Boleyn in January, 1533. In April the Bishops approved. In May the new Archbishop of Canterbury, Cranmer, declared the King's marriage to Catherine of Aragon null and void, and pronounced Anne a lawful wife. That information reached the Vatican with predictable results. Clement VII declared the new marriage null, its future offspring illegitimate, and excommunicated Henry VIII. At one time such a sentence would have shaken Henry's throne, but that time had passed.

?◆

France under Francis I was the largest and richest realm in Christendom with a population of 16 million to England's 3 million and Spain's 7 million. Its countryside was semi-feudal; peasants held their land in fief to seigneurs and chevaliers who provided military protection. The land teemed with cattle, butter, milk and fowl; the peasantry lived well. The cities did not live as well; inflation raced ahead of wages, illegal strikes were frequent. Paris, largest city in Europe, was home to 300,000 people; Lyon—a commercial center for Swiss and German goods—was second only to Antwerp in financial importance.

The Court of France glittered with luxury. Women were unusually influential in matters of State; especially the King's mother Louise of Savoy and his sister Marguerite of Valois who married, at 35, the King of Navarre (a courtesy title) who was 24.

In 1516 Francis obtained Vatican approval for the French Crown to appoint Bishops and Abbots. In effect, the higher clergy of France became dependent on the King. Thus France quietly achieved a political control of the Church that cost northern Germany a bloody struggle and what Henry VIII did not obtain for another fifteen years.

This politicalization of the French Catholic church deepened its already secular character. Devout priests and nuns existed, of course. But Brantome, a famous French writer, repeated a common saying: "Avaricious or lecherous as a priest or a monk."

This created the same discontent among the people as in Germany, Switzerland and the Low Countries. People demanded reform, a la Luther. As early as 1512, Jacques LeFevre published a Latin translation of St. Paul's *Epistles,* which expounded salvation not by works but by faith in the Grace of God earned by the redeeming sacrifice of Jesus. In 1523 LeFevre published a French translation of the New Testament and a year later, of the Psalms. Denounced as a heretic, he was protected by Marguerite, whose Reform sympathies were notorious.

Luther's books flowed across huge, literate France. His New Testament became a revolutionary catalyst on working class levels, who drew from the equality of souls the deceptive analogy of equality on earth. Some suffered hideous tortures for this: brandings, amputations of hands and noses, nipples plucked out by pincers, red-hot irons to the head; burnings alive.

The King's sister Marguerite protected Reformers and Humanists who found the new Catholic world a dangerous place. The satirists Rabelais, Marot, Desperier and others found protection under her. The King once found her on her knees, praying with Farel, the forerunner and later supporter of Calvin.[10] Rabelais dedicated *Gargantua* to her.

Francis I was, in contrast, militaristic. Alarmed at the Peasant's Revolt in Germany he ordered Protestantism stamped out in France. But his faith was so thin that he allied France with the Turks, in order to defeat Charles V.

In 1532, the same year that Henry VIII established his ecclesiastical controls, Francis I, irritated by the close bonds between Charles V and Clement VII, drew nearer to the Protestant Princes of Germany. A year later his relations with Clement improved, and he again promised severe measures against the Reform.

In that manner the Christian cause swayed in the winds of political power struggles throughout Europe. Divisions in doctrine led inexorably to divisions inside States and between States.

Jean Chauvin, born in 1509, was eight years old when Luther rose like a meteor. Jean's father was Gerard Chauvin, secretary to the Bishop of Noyon. Jean's mother died and his father remarried. Three sons were destined for the priesthood.[11]

---

10. William Farel, a small, red-bearded, itinerant preacher in France and Switzerland: anti-Papal, anti-images, anti-mass.

11. Two received benefices; one became a lifelong "heretic." Gerard himself was only narrowly permitted burial in consecrated ground.

When Jean entered the College de la Marche at the University of Paris he was registered as Johannes Calvin; it is as John Calvin that he is known to history. His schooling was Humanist, supported by a benefice obtained from the Cathedral through his father. To this was added a Curacy. He was educated together with a scion of the House of Montmor, a Noyon aristocrat.

Calvin's second College at the University was de Montaigue, from which Erasmus had graduated, and which Loyola entered in 1528. Whether they ever met is now unknown, which is a pity, because they came to represent the poles of the Reformation and the Counter-Reformation.

Late in 1528 his father ordered Calvin to Orleans to study law because, according to Calvin later, his father thought lawyers became rich. Obedient in this as in all other duties, he proved an apt pupil. "The law," said historian Will Durant, "seemed to him . . . the molding of man's anarchic impulses to order and peace."

That may at first have been true. Certainly Calvin's later use of Justinian's title *Institutes* provides tacit evidence of the law's influence. But at 22, when he received his Licentiate (or Bachelor of Laws) in 1531, Calvin had barely begun his intellectual journey.

It started, in true Renaissance fashion, with an immersion in pagan literature. In 1532, anxious for prestige among his fellow Humanists, he published a commentary on Seneca's *De Clementia:* a salute to mercy (after Cicero).[12] It revealed "a remarkable command of the whole mass of classical literature, a fine intelligence, and a serious interest in the higher moralities. . . . A great career as a Humanist seemed opening before him."[13]

Calvin sent the first copy of his book to Erasmus, the hero of all Humanists, together with a letter calling the older man the "second glory." "He was quivering with anxiety for the success of his book; he wanted to know how it was selling, whether it was being talked about, what people thought of it."[14]

---

12. Seneca was Nero's tutor: mute evidence that education is not character.
13. Benjamin B. Warfield, *Calvin and Augustine* (Philadelphia, PA: Presbyterian and Reformed Publishing Company, 1980), p. 4.
14. Ibid.

Then Calvin was converted. This Gift of God is beyond understanding to those who have never received it. Those so blessed have their lives and personalities so altered that they are never again the same. This experience does not arrive upon appeal nor is it a reward, and has distinguished as many whom the world judged to be unworthy as it has the worthy.

Saul of Tarsus, the heartless witness to the stoning death of St. Stephen, the Pharisee who wanted authority to persecute and murder more Christians, was converted by the appearance of a Jesus so radiant that Saul was left sightless for three days. He rose, after that experience, as St. Paul, the tireless missionary to the Gentiles.

The conversion of Aurelius Augustine came when he held the high post of Government Professor of Rhetoric in Milan, enjoying life among the elite. A good marriage would help his career, but the woman with whom he had been living for fourteen years was in the way. He got rid of her, "leaving a sore and wounded place in his heart where it had adhered to hers." A marriage to an heiress was arranged to take place in two years. In the interim he took another concubine. Then his conscience rebelled; "a horrible shame gnawed and confounded his Soul."[15]

The Holy Spirit touched him when he was in the depths of this remorse, and he emerged as St. Augustine, "incomparably the greatest man whom between St. Paul the Apostle and Luther the Reformer the Christian Church has possessed."[16]

"In the summer of 1505, Luther entered the Augustinian convent at Efurt and became a monk, as he thought, for his lifetime. The circumstances which led to this sudden step we gather from his fragmentary utterances which have been embellished by legendary tradition.

"He was shocked by the sudden death of a friend (later called Alexius), who was either killed in a duel or struck dead by lightning at Luther's side. Shortly afterward, on the second of July, 1505, two weeks before his momentous decision, he was overtaken by a violent thunderstorm near Efurt, on a return from a visit to his parents, and was so frightened that he fell to the earth and tremblingly exclaimed: 'Help, beloved Saint

15. Ibid., p. 363.
16. Ibid.

Anna! I will become a monk.' "[17]

Calvin later described his own conversion in a few terse sentences. "[W]hen I was too firmly addicted to the papal superstitions to be easily drawn out of such deep mire, by a sudden conversion He brought my mind (already more rigid than suited my age) to submission (to Him). I was so inspired by a taste of true religion and I burned with such a desire to carry my study further, that although I did not drop other subjects, I had no real zeal for them. In less than a year, all who were looking for a purer doctrine came to learn from me, although I was a novice and a beginner. . . ."

That was no more than the truth but also, paradoxically, less than the whole truth. One of the distinguishing features of conversion is its ineradicable sense of not only having sinned, but of remaining a sinner. After his conversion Calvin, previously proud of his scholarship and precocity, referred to himself as "by nature timid, mild and cowardly."

But it was true that others came to him. One was Nicholas Cop, Rector of the University of Paris and a favorite of Queen Marguerite's. Calvin helped Cop draft an address that called for a purified Christianity and stressed salvation through grace: in effect, the new theology. The Sorbonne boiled; Cop was charged with heresy. He fled, and barely reached Basel.

That revived the campaign against Protestants. Calvin, warned, took refuge in Angueleme in January 1534, where he wrote a treatise on the state of the soul after death and started another on Christian doctrine. In May he returned to Noyon, his early home, and surrendered the benefices whose income supported him, because he could not in honor live off a Church in which he no longer believed.

That was ethical but daring. While in Noyon Calvin was arrested twice and twice released. After these life-threatening escapes, this "timid and cowardly" man ventured back to Paris, talked with several Protestant leaders—and met Servetus.[18] At this juncture some zealous Protestants nailed more posters against the Vatican throughout the city. Francis I retaliated with a fierce campaign and Calvin—now known and marked by the authorities—ran finally from France.

---

17. Philip Schaff, *History of the Christian Church,* vol. VII, The German Reformation, Part I (New York, NY: Charles Scribner's Sons, 1910), p. 112.

18. Whom he would, memorably, meet again later.

ළ

While Calvin, in Beza's words, renounced "all other studies and devoted himself to God," Thomas Cromwell in England renounced all others for the sake of Henry VIII.

The son of a blacksmith, Cromwell wandered through Europe as a youth, returned to England to amass a fortune in textiles and money lending. Inordinately ambitious, he left commerce for politics and faithfully served Cardinal Wolsey for five years. He earned Henry's respect not only for his competence, but by remaining at Wolsey's side even after the Cardinal was disgraced.

In March 1534 Henry VIII made Cromwell Chancellor of the Exchequer, then Master of the Rolls, and in May, Secretary. As the King's right-hand man, Cromwell became Henry's instrument of unlimited power, and the most hated man in England.

Henry VIII, with Cromwell as point man, pressed Parliament into an Act of Succession declaring his marriage to Catherine invalid, making the Princess Mary a bastard, naming Elizabeth (Anne Boleyn's daughter) heiress to the throne (unless Anne had a son), and requiring a loyalty oath from all subjects. Only Bishop Fisher and Sir Thomas More refused; both landed in the Tower.

At the end of 1534, a new Act of Supremacy stated the King's authority over both Church and State in England, including power over morals, organization, heresy, creed and ecclesiastical matters formerly held by the Church. Bishops had to swear obedience. The line "so far as the law of Christ allows" was dropped. Henry VIII became the most complete despot England had ever before known—or would ever again know.

ළ

Henry VIII and Cromwell cut down anyone who disagreed with the new order. Some Carthusian priests who appealed to Cromwell were sent to the Tower, hanged, cut down, disemboweled and dismembered. Since the King had no argument with Catholic dogma, Protestants were prosecuted. Since he was against the Pope, Catholics who obeyed the Pope were also prosecuted.

When the Pope named Bishop Fisher a Cardinal, the King accepted the challenge and Fisher was put on trial. On June 17, 1535, the Cardinal-elect refused to take an oath to obey the King, and was sentenced to death. Later his head appeared on a pole at London Bridge; the King said it could go from there to get a red hat from the Vatican. Sir Thomas More remained adamant and was convicted of treason. Erasmus, who said, "we had but one soul between us," was horrified. The new Pope Paul III issued a Bull excommunicating Henry, interdicting all religious ceremonies in England and called for a Catholic rebellion. But neither Francis I, nor Charles V allowed the Bull to be published in their realms; neither believed in Papal supremacy over kings. Their attitudes—and Henry's—further diminished the Vatican.

ᘓᔎ

Cromwell had more power than Wolsey at his highest. He piloted England's policies abroad and at home. He watched the censored, licensed press; his secret police were everywhere. He personally put men on trial, and acted as prosecutor, judge and jury.

His only problem was keeping the King supplied with money. Knowing that new taxes were politically impossible, he looked at the monasteries: centers of secret disobedience. The monks had grown indolent, and failed to maintain hospitals and charities; the Bishops did not control them.

Europe provided precedents for their seizure: Zwingli had closed monasteries in Zurich; Lutheran Princes had moved against them. During the summer of 1535, Cromwell had the monasteries and nunneries inventoried; by early 1536 he was ready to move.

He was, briefly, delayed by the death of Catherine of Aragon who left a tender letter to Henry. He wept over it, for he was sentimental. Anne Boleyn was about to deliver again. If the issue was male, her position was secure, though the King was no longer charmed. He was, in fact, courting Jane Seymour.

On the day Catherine of Aragon was buried, Anne Boleyn delivered a dead child. Henry began to talk about an annulment and, darkly, of having been victimized by witchcraft.

Cromwell then organized two campaigns. One, against the monasteries and nunneries, listed their failures and recommended their closure to Parliament. The other, issued through the King's Council (which

Cromwell headed), charged the Queen with adultery with five men, including her brother Lord Rochford. In May 1536, the Queen and all five landed in the Tower, charged with adultery.

Within days a jury—which included Anne Boleyn's father, the Earl of Wiltshire—found all five and the Queen guilty and sentenced them to death. Archbishop Cranmer declared Anne's marriage invalid and the Princess Elizabeth a bastard.

A week after the sentence on May 19, 1536, Anne Boleyn was beheaded. On the same day Henry received a "dispensation" from Cranmer to remarry. On the following day Jane Seymour became secretly betrothed; on May 30, three weeks after Anne Boleyn's head and trunk were buried, Henry VIII married for the third time.

ह

Overall, 587 and 130 convents were closed. Over 6,000 monks and 1,500 nuns were dispersed. Twelve thousand persons whose livelihoods or alms depended on religious houses lost their incomes. The incomes from confiscated lands and institutions were sharply reduced, but the Crown added millions in treasure, coin, lands and buildings to its holdings.

Henry knew better than to sit alone on these new holdings. Many properties were sold at bargain prices to minor nobles or merchants or lawyers who supported the throne. Cromwell received or bought eight abbeys; his nephew Sir Richard Cromwell received seven. These properties and their incomes were the basis of a family fortune that benefited Richard's great grandnephew Oliver Cromwell in the next century.

A few monasteries were returned to the Anglican Church; small sums were set aside for charity. Money went to the Navy and to refurbish forts and ports; some went for war. Some was lost by Henry in gambling.

Meanwhile the English language gained in breadth and scope, making the Latin cultural monopoly increasingly tenuous; "a xenophobic hatred of priests and witchcraft, which merely waited an opportunity to vent itself, and above all, a rising consciousness among the English that they were a people somehow different to all others, called to a special destiny," began to rise.

"The English had come to believe they were the chosen people. They could thus answer the Continental Armory of faith and superstition with the vehement conviction of divinely inspired rectitude."[19]

Henry VIII was lifted by this widespread belief. The power of the Government, formerly held in check by the Church, was enormously expanded. The old feudal aristocracy, thinned by adventures, was further reduced by the King's pruning. A new aristocracy appeared. "New Men," rooted in commerce and industry, began to accumulate land and to gain entry into court.

In contrast to the Ages of Faith, when the nobility checked royal power, the New Men defended and expanded the throne. Catholics continued to be burned alive for denying the King's religious supremacy, Protestants for questioning Catholic theology. Dissent was treason.

England under Henry VIII seemed in the grip of evil enthroned. Yet, as though to illustrate the uncanny Ways of God, the Reform advanced.

Calvin lived quietly in Basel. Once ambitious for worldly fame, he now wrote under an assumed name—a form of anonymity. "I, who was by nature a man of the country and a lover of shade and leisure, wished to find for myself a quiet hiding place. . . ."[20]

He did not break that anonymity when *Christianae Religionis Instituto* (Principles of the Christian Religion) appeared to widespread praise in the spring of 1536. Warfield called it "at once an apology, a manifesto and a confession of faith." It was like a searchlight, illuminating a dark landscape.

It arrived when Reformers in France were being hideously persecuted. "I had no other purpose than to bear witness to the faith," Calvin said later. "I desired no fame for myself, I kept my authorship secret."

Then God impelled Farel to intervene, and changed the course of the world.

19. Johnson; *op. cit.,* p. 174.

20. Calvin, *Commentary on the Psalms,* Library of Christian Classics, vol. 23, Preface (London: SCM Press; Philadelphia: Westminster Press, 1958).

Chapter Four

GENEVA

———— ?❧ ————

A new heart will I give you, and a new spirit will I put within you.

— Ezekial

Geneva 1532 was a Renaissance scene of material prosperity and spiritual squalor. It had a Prostitute's Quarter, priests living with concubines, a corrupt Bishop in authority.

With the Reformation, resistance arose headed by *Eidgenossen* (Oath Comrades), which the French corrupted into *Huguenots,* and preacher William Farel.

Arrested for preaching against the Bishop's rule, Farel was released by the city fathers. When he was joined by Pierre Viret and Antoine Froment, the trio became so popular the Genevan priests fled. After further upheavals, Geneva emerged Bishop-free and allied with Berne— the strongest military power in Switzerland.

Protestantism became official in May 1536. The Small Council abolished the Mass, images and relics were removed from the churches,[1] education became free and compulsory. Genevans had to swear allegiance to the Gospel or leave.

All this happened before Calvin arrived.

?❧

Calvin was en route from France, where he helped settle his parent's estate. Accompanied by Antoine, their half-sister Marie and some

---

1. A campaign against images was, by this time, a continuing part of the Reformation.

others, he was headed for Strasbourg. Troop movements made a detour through Geneva necessary, and they rented rooms for a night at an inn.

Already famous as the author of the *Institutes,* Calvin traveled incognito. "Then a person," he said, ". . . discovered me and made me known to the others."

Farel appeared to ask him to stay. Calvin protested that "my heart was set upon devoting myself to my private studies, for which I wished to keep myself free. . . ." Farel grew indignant.

"God would curse my retirement and the tranquility of the studies I sought, if I should withdraw and refuse to help, when the necessary was so urgent. By this imprecation," Calvin said, "I was so terror-struck, that I gave up the journey I had undertaken; but sensible of my natural shyness and timidity, I would not tie myself to any particular office."[2]

He first spoke in the Church of St. Peter on the Epistles of St. Paul, and launched the most famous ministry since the Apostle.

၂ல்

Luther, 53, was suffering from several untreatable ailments. Medicine then was still caught in the non-cures of Hippocrates and Galen.[3]

These ancient practitioners stressed the "four humors of the ancients: blood, phlegm, black bile and yellow bile." Disease was thought to be caused by an imbalance or superabundance of the humors, and treatment consisted of bleeding and purging.

Medical historian E. M. Thorton said "The supposed activities of the humors—peccant, acrid, or putrid—took up the greater part of lengthy dissertations of stupefying verbosity and, as succinctly described by R. Kevran, "[T]he Latin language was used to confer majesty on this rigmarole, and all this was punctuated by quotations from Galen and Hippocrates."[4]

Exaggerated respect for ancient science had, in other words, frozen European medicine.

2. T. H. L. Parker, *John Calvin: A Biography* (London, England: Dent and Sons, 1975), p. 53.

3. Hippocrates lived from 460 B.C. to 377 B.C.; Galen from A.D. 129 to A.D. 199.

4. E. M. Thornton, *The Freudian Fallacy: An Alternative View of Freudian Theory* (New York, N.Y.: Doubleday, 1984), pp. 4, 5.

Luther had another ten years to live when Calvin appeared; Melancthon and Bucer were at their height of influence. Zwingli had been dead five years and Bullinger had taken his place in Zurich. Luther had broken with Zurich since the disastrous conference at Marburg (in 1529). Calvin took Luther's side, and had no doubt of Luther's superiority.

ॐ

Calvin later said that he found the Gospel in Geneva, but no Church. "There was as good as nothing around here," he wrote. "There was preaching and that was all."

Warfield says Calvin "would have found much the same state of things everywhere else in the Protestant world. The 'Church' in the early Protestant conception was constituted by the preaching of the Word and the right administration of the sacraments: the correction of the morals of the community was the concern not of the Church but of the civil powers."

Calvin was soon a pastor. That meant baptizing babies, officiating at weddings, conducting church services and preaching. This led him to create a Church discipline—a step that eventually led to a Church free of the state.

Neither Calvin nor Farel nor any other Reformer introduced the idea of monitoring morals in Geneva. The Vatican had done that, un-counted centuries before, and maintained that system for generations. But the Bishops grew lax in the late Middle Ages and indifferent during the Renaissance.

In the early years of the Reformation, censorship of manners and morals remained a settled, accepted part of existing, ancient police regulations not only in Geneva, but in all Europe.

Calvin believed that the Church's power to excommunicate was central to its discipline. He did not mean excommunication for political reasons, as was practiced by the Vatican during its decline, but excom-munication for persistent refusal to live according to Scriptural values.

But that was the limit of Church authority. If excommunication was accepted with indifference, he told the Genevan council, it's up to you to decide "how long you will endure and leave unpunished such contempt and such mockery of God and His gospel."

The distinction may seem merely technical. Europe had lived for over a thousand years with a combined Church and State. But the 27 year old Calvin proposed that only the Church *and not the Government* could define a heretic. The Church alone would protect its altars. That was new.

ᴈ❧

Other innovations met opposition in the Genevan council. Farel published a *Confession of Faith* and Calvin a *Catechism.* Both were approved in November 1536; all citizens were ordered to attend the church of St. Peter's and swear allegiance to Farel's *Confession.* That was more than some citizens wanted.

A faction calling itself the *Patriotes,* which included secret Catholics, called Farel and Calvin French agents and stoned the ministers' homes as a patriotic duty. Another faction, called *The Libertines* or Liberals, argued for complete freedom of conscience, worship and behavior.[5] These dissidents parties combined to gain Council control in February 1538.

The new Council ordered Farel and Calvin to retreat, but they said they would not serve the Lord's Supper until the city obeyed the new discipline. They were deposed for that, and given three days to leave. Farel left for Neuchâtel, where he remained for the rest of his long life. Calvin went to Strasbourg, and Geneva celebrated.

ᴈ❧

In Strasbourg Calvin pastored several hundred Frenchmen, preached or lectured every day; twice on Sunday. He and the congregation were both poor. He had to sell his library and board students. Adopting the Augustinian view that "there is no salvation outside the Church," he celebrated the Lord's Supper, introduced congregational singing, and lecturing on the Gospel.

He had persistent money problems. "I can't call a single penny my own," he wrote. "It is astonishing how money slips away. . . ."

---

5. Calvin gave the word *libertine* a new definition in his responses to their arguments.

His tests did not end there. The plague took Farel's nephew, whom Calvin had helped tend. Courald, his blind colleague in Geneva, died at Orbe in October 1538. Calvin grieved, and his depression was deepened by insomnia. "I am utterly exhausted by these melancholy thoughts all night long." Then his friend Pierre Robert died at Ferrara.

Finally Louis du Tillet, who had sheltered him, and who fled from France with him, who had shared the Genevan experience with him, suddenly returned to France and the Roman church.[6]

Tillet wrote to say that the banishment from Geneva was a sign of God's displeasure that had convinced him to return to the old faith. That touched a nerve; Geneva, which promised so much, had been a terrible failure.

Calvin's friends urged him to marry. He didn't take proper care of himself, he was overburdened. Calvin agreed, and various candidates appeared. Finally he married Idelette de Bure, the widow of a onetime Anabaptist with two children, a boy and a girl.

The marriage was happy. A year later Calvin published a second edition of the *Institutes* under his own name. Luther read it, and sent a message to Bucer: "Salute for me respectfully Sturm and Calvin, whose books I have read with special delight."

Meanwhile Calvin and Farel were succeeded by incompetents in Geneva. The city relaxed into its old ways. "Gambling, drunkenness, street brawls, adultery flourished; lewd songs were publicly sung, persons romped naked through the streets."[7]

Of the four officials who led the movement to expel Farel and Calvin, one was condemned to death for murder, another for forgery, a third for treason, and a fourth died resisting arrest. The businessmen who controlled the city began to regret the Genevan relapse. In May, 1541, the Council annulled the sentence of banishment and delegations appeared in Strasbourg to persuade Calvin, but not Farel, to return.

He hated the idea. Return to the city where his house was stoned, and where he was subjected to unforgettable insults? "Rather would I submit to death a hundred times than to that cross on which I had to perish a hundred times over."

6. Parker, *op. cit.*, pp. 69, 70.
7. Durant, *op. cit.*, p. 471.

He wrote Farel, "Whenever I call to mind the wretchedness of my life there, how can it not be but that my very soul must shudder at any proposal for my return?"

But delegations kept apologizing and pleading. He suggested that Geneva allow his fellow Reformer, Pierre Viret, to return. If that worked, then he might consider returning. Strasbourg protested: it did not want to lose its most famous resident.

By the summer of 1541, the idea of a visit to Geneva was dropped in favor of Strasbourg *lending* Calvin to Geneva for six months.[8]

His return in September 1541 was splendid. He had an escort, a wagon for his family and a good house, fully furnished. His salary was 500 florins, twelve strikes of corn and two casks of wine a year. People crowded around him so eagerly that he completely softened. He wrote Farel, "Your wish is granted. I am held fast here. May God give His blessing."

Geneva and Calvin had joined forever.

ॐ

In 1542 France declared war—again—against Charles V, and was joined by Sweden, Denmark, Gelderland, Scotland, the Turks (!) and the Pope. Turkish and French fleets combined to besiege Nice in 1543, a possession of the Emperor's, but the siege failed.

Charles V overcame these combinations. He made peace with the Pope, forced France to retreat and Francis I to abandon various territorial claims and to sign the treaty of Crepy in September 1544.

This denouement left Francis I nearly finished. He had inherited a large, populous, rich nation; he was to leave it bankrupt and on the edge of new wars. He had scuttled chivalry and betrayed Christianity by alliances with Turks. He had rebuilt Fontainebleau and spent fortunes on women. In 1538 disease had injured his uvula and left him with a stammer; he developed a persistent abscess. He grew wary and suspected that poisoners were after him—which might have been true, for his son's impatience to inherit was flagrant by the middle 1540s.

Finally Francis I died in 1547—but not quickly. His deathbed advice

---

8. Such was his popularity; a feature modern historians seem unable to grasp.

to his heir Henry II was, ironically, to not allow himself to be dominated by a woman—but Diane de Poitiers, twenty years his elder, had already ensnared the incoming King.

໖

In the 1540s Henry VIII subjugated Ireland and declared himself King and head of the Church. Reformers entered the Pale[9] to strip churches of relics and images. Henry spread some spoils among those Irish chieftains who accepted titles of nobility and abjured the Pope, but in reality nothing changed. The Irish remained Catholic, and added religious reasons to their political and cultural hatred of the English.

At home the King ordered a better English Bible translation after the Bishops suppressed Tyndale's. When this appeared[10] every home was "allowed the privilege" of reading it. As elsewhere, it soon became the inspiration for discontent as well as revelation. Amateur expositors appeared on all sides. Men came to blows in taverns; congregations wrangled. Henry then ordered Parliament to rule that only nobles and property-owners might legally possess a Bible, and only priests could openly discuss it or preach about it. But he was too late: the Reformation had arrived.

໖

His third wife, Jane Seymour, gave Henry VIII a son, but died herself twelve days later. Henry waited two years before remarriage appeared necessary. He had a legitimate heir; he now sought a strategic alliance. Cromwell was assigned the task.

Cromwell had become widely admired by European Reformers, who hailed him one of their own. He had steered England away from the Vatican, closed Catholic religious houses, and created a new, Protestant aristocracy.

At home Cromwell swam in a sea of hatred, protected only by the King. The English nobility, which had hated Wolsey as an upstart

---

9. The area occupied by the English in Dublin; the Irish were those "outside the Pale."

10. By Miles Coverdale.

clergyman, hated Cromwell even more deeply—and was joined in that
hatred by all Catholics and their priests.

Cromwell, however, was careful. Unlike Wolsey, he was neither
pompous nor conceited. His personal life was simple. He clutched at
money mainly to pay the army of spies he maintained and whose work,
said John Richard Green, "he surveyed with a sleepless vigilance."

More than fifty volumes remain of the great mass of his correspondence with all sorts of people: outraged wives, wronged laborers and
persecuted heretics. For all these Cromwell acted as a court of last appeal.
"His single will forced on a scheme of foreign policy whose aim was to
bind England to the cause of the Reformation while it bound Henry
helplessly to his minister."[11]

The King knew that Cromwell was unpopular. He also knew that
although rebellion had been suppressed, Catholicism remained alive in
many hearts. He began, adroitly, to reduce the Protestant presence. In
1539 he assented to *An Act Abolishing Diversity of Opinions,* reasserting
Catholic doctrines and usages under savage penalties.

Cromwell's choice for the king was Anne of Cleves, sister in law of the
Elector of Saxony and sister of the Duke of Cleves. The Duke was at odds
with Charles V. Cromwell hoped to unite England and the German
Protestant states. Henry wanted to know what Anne looked like and
Holbein was sent to paint her.

When Holbein's painting arrived it produced an impression of
beauty and of majestic height. This pleased the giant. A marriage
contract was signed, and presents distributed to the ambassadors.

Cromwell's hope was to push back Charles V and the House of
Austria because they alone could organize a Catholic reaction against the
Reformation. He hoped to unite the Princes of Protestant Germany
with France to bring Spain down. If that plan had succeeded, it would
have changed Europe. Southern Germany would have been pushed into
Protestantism; the Thirty Year's War would have been averted.

Unfortunately he was ahead of the times. The German Princes were
afraid to challenge Charles V; France would not surrender an already
captive Church. And he underestimated the conceit of Henry VIII.

---

11. John Richard Green, *A Short History of the English People,* vol. 1 (New York,
N.Y.: Colonial Press, 1899), p. 420.

When Anne of Cleves arrived Henry rushed forward but stopped dead when he saw her. Her features were coarse, she was fat, obviously not bright, and awkward. Cromwell said, "I am very sorry therefor." The King's comments were unprintable.

Cromwell had settled matters too well: the marriage had to be performed. The ceremony, conducted while Henry looked away, was held January 6, 1540. The next day Cromwell hopefully asked Henry how he liked the queen. "Worse than ever," said the King.

೭ฆ

Surprisingly, Henry VIII then made Cromwell Earl of Essex and Lord Chamberlain. A large section of the Essex properties swelled these gifts, as did additional manors and revenues. But behind the scenes, the Catholic Duke of Norfolk, the greatest peer in the realm and head of the Catholic party, was told to prepare a case against Cromwell.

On June 10, 1540, Cromwell attended, as usual, a meeting of the Privy Council. After preliminaries, he was startled when the Duke of Norfolk rose to level a charge of treason. Cromwell flung his cap to the floor with a passionate cry. "This then," he said hoarsely, "is my guerdon for the services I have done! On your consciences I ask you, am I a traitor?"

Amid a cacophony of insults and curses, Norfolk himself tore the Ensign of the Garter from Cromwell's neck. Someone called the guards, and Cromwell said bitterly, "Make quick work, and not leave me to languish in prison."

೭ฆ

Henry's Council announced, amid elaborate verbiage, that the marriage was invalid because it had never been consummated. The Princess was too embarrassed to return home; Henry was beyond embarrassment. He settled 4,000 pounds a year upon her and let her maintain a tiny court in a palace at Richmond.

The King had meanwhile been courting the young, beautiful Katherine Howard, niece of the Duke of Norfolk. His nuptials to Katherine were celebrated on 8 August, 1540, eleven days after Cromwell's head was chopped off.

The Catholic party rejoiced. They had seen three Protestant Queens: Anne Boleyn, Jane Seymour and Anne of Cleves. The Duke of Norfolk glowed as the King celebrated the Catholic liturgy, and honored Catholic holidays as of old. He even leaned toward a renewed alliance with Spain.

The power of Henry VIII was at its zenith when he turned on Cromwell—the man who made that power possible. Cromwell placed all England at Henry's feet. Constitutional forms had been kept, but expanded definitions of treason, new oaths of allegiance and "investigations"[12] had leeched the ancient freedoms of England.

౨●

Henry's swing toward Catholicism led to increased persecutions of Protestants. Even the Protestant Cranmer, Archbishop of Canterbury, was threatened.

Then evidence surfaced that the beauteous Queen had been promiscuous. Cranmer was sent to tell her this, and to prepare her for her fate. He left her in a state of agitation "so violent he feared she would lose her reason."

She landed, like Anne Boleyn, in the Tower. The men included Francis Derham, an officer in the house of Norfolk and several others. After harrowing hearings they were hanged, drawn and quartered. Lady Rochford, named as the queen's "accomplice," was condemned with her.

On February 12, 1541, six months after her marriage to Henry VIII, Katherine Howard, 20, was beheaded.

The King, however, continued to believe in marriage. In 1543 he married Catherine Parr, a woman twice widowed, and not only a Protestant, but one of learning and eloquence. But the Catholic party remained in power, because the King was against France and drifting toward an alliance with Charles V.

౨●

---

12. A term familiar to modern Americans.

Charles V had long believed the Vatican should reform, and encouraged what was called the "New Learning:" a reform movement inside the Catholic faith. Its adherents worked for years toward a reconciliation between the Catholic and Protestant parties of Europe. But from the start it did not seem likely that the Council of Trent, first convened in 1545, would accomplish much.

As Thomas Cromwell had seen, the time for reconciliation had long passed. Neither Pope Paul III, a member of the Farnese family, nor the Vatican hierarchy had the slightest intention of reforming—nor, for that matter, were Protestants anxious to return to the Catholic fold— no matter how much it swore to change.

In 1546 Henry VIII's health collapsed. An open ulcer on his leg refused to heal; he was so heavy he had trouble walking, and was usually helped. His temper grew uncertain. His geniality faded; he became a dark, brooding, antisocial presence.

His last Queen, beautiful, gracious and solicitous, was uniquely able to restore his spirits. Ardently Protestant, she held him in theological discussions. He enjoyed these; he was learned, liked to prove it and did not disdain discussion with a woman—in private.

One evening the King was with Wriothesley and Gardiner, two of the Catholic leaders, when Catherine joined them and began to discuss the need to reform the Church. The King was embarrassed, and "brake off that matter and took occasion to enter into other talk." Catherine was surprised.

After the Queen left, the Chancellor and Bishop expressed shock that anyone could question "unchallengeable wisdom." The King, caught on at once, and wondered if the Queen had ever violated any religious regulations—and the hunt was on.

Wriothesley and Gardiner soon prepared a case. The Queen suspected nothing until the night Henry signed an arrest warrant in his private apartment.

After the signing Chancellor Wriothesley snatched the papers, thrust them under his outer clothing and hurried away. In his rush, one paper dropped. A lady in waiting picked it up, grasped its importance and took it to the Queen.

She realized her peril at once and uttered, said a later chronicler, "loud cries and seemed to be in her death-struggle. . . . All her attentions, all her devotion to the King had availed nothing; she must undergo the common lot of the wives of Henry VIII."

Hearing of her distress, Henry's physician came and told Catherine how she had offended. The King, hearing that some problems had developed, had himself carried to her apartment. She rallied enough to say she had been grief-stricken at the thought of having somehow lost his love. He comforted her, but she was not deceived: she now knew that his conceit had no limits.

From then on, when the subject of religion arose, she looked humbly downward, and said the King's wisdom was irrefutable; beyond argument. That was all that was needed to save her life.

But Henry knew his time was growing short, and soon turned to the question of who would govern as Regent during young Prince Edward's minority. The Duke of Norfolk, uncle of the ill-fated Katherine, of royal descent, was head of the Catholic party. His heir, the Earl of Surrey, was suspected of Vatican contacts. The Seymours, on the other hand, uncles of Prince Edward, were advancing "in esteem and authority," and were Protestants.

In early December 1546, the King was warned that the Howards had claims on the Crown from before Edward's birth. The Duke of Norfolk's heir was said to aspire to the hand of the Princess Mary. If he should marry her, Prince Edward might lose the crown.

The evidence, gathered by the ever-treacherous Chancellor Wriothesley, seemed damning. The Duke of Norfolk and his heir were both thrown into the Tower. The King "had not long to live and he desired that these two great lords should go before him into the grave."

The King was now dangerously ill but still poisonous. Norfolk, surprised at being in the Tower, wrote begging letters.[13] On January 21, 1547, the Duke's heir lost his head. On the 24th, Parliament passed a Bill of Attainder[14] against the Duke; the King agreed to the Duke's execution on the 27th. Preparations were made, but the King lay dying that same night.

The fear he had created was so heavy his physicians were afraid to tell

---

13. All the condemned, as their last hour approached, fell into this pathetic exercise: even Cromwell.
14. A Bill against a single individual.

him, "because it was against the law to speak of the death of the King. One might almost have said that he was determined to have himself declared immortal by Act of Parliament."

A courtier asked if he needed a confessor, but Henry believed Heaven would respect his rank, and said "the grace of God can forgive all my sins."

Pressed again, he mentioned Cranmer, the Archbishop. But when the prelate arrived, Henry was beyond speech. He died at two o'clock in the morning on Friday, January 28, 1547.

Henry's will outlined the succession to nine year old Prince Edward, (the son of Jane Seymour) and a Council of Regency. His death, greeted with profound relief by many, threw England into the Protestant camp, for the boy King was an ardent Protestant, as were all the Seymours.

꙰

The deaths of both Francis I and Henry VIII in the same year 1547, underscored the turbulence of their generation. Luther had died the year before, in 1546, and nailed his challenge in 1517. The thirty years following Luther's challenge—a single generation—saw the Peasant's War, the Sack of Rome, the split of northern and southern Germany, divisions among the Cantons of Switzerland, the break of England from the Vatican, and more wars, battles, executions, massacres, arguments and new books, atrocities, ferment and fury than in any single generational rebellion in history.

In that single period Luther and Melancthon, Zwingli and Farel, Charles V and Henry VIII, Francis I and several Popes had contended for the heart, soul and mind of Europe. No strictly chronological description of these struggles is possible; the best historians can do is to look at first one, then another, and then another of these men, who virtually simultaneously, rose to attack or defend, judge or accept, a system that had taken over a millennium to evolve, and that had seemed, only three brief decades before, destined to last forever.

Chapter Five

CALVIN AND SERVETUS

———— ❧ ————

*Two parties are here present: he
hears but half who hears one
party only.*

— Aeschylus

Calvin believed that "the Church could not hold together unless a
settled government was agreed on . . . such as was in use, in the early
Church." He set forms that Reform churches would follow for centuries. Each was to be ruled by pastors, doctors, elders and deacons, and
operated according to ecclesiastical ordinances. Pastors were to preach,
doctors to teach, elders to monitor discipline and deacons to tend the
sick and the needy.

All Church officials were elected; laymen outnumbered clergy. As
usual, major opposition came from other theologians, whose objections
to Calvin were incessant and, usually, unpleasant.

Calvin never ruled Geneva. The city was not a totalitarian society, but
a Republic, with elections and dissent. Calvin held no civil office, could
neither arrest nor punish any citizen, appoint or dismiss any official. To
argue that his eloquence and logic constituted tyranny is to invent a new
standard.

Calvin worked as a pastor, preached twice on Sundays and once every
Monday, Wednesday and Friday. In late 1542, he was urged to preach
more often (!), but this proved too much, and he broke down. When his
health improved, his burdens increased. He spoke without notes and
directly from the Hebrew Old Testament and the Latin New. And he
prepared.

> If I should enter the pulpit without deigning to glance at a book, and
> should frivolously think to myself, "Oh, well, when I preach, God will

give me enough to say," and come here without troubling to read or thinking what I ought to declare, and do not carefully consider how I must apply Holy Scripture to the edification of the people, then I should be an arrogant upstart.

In 1549, the *Companie des estranger* hired a stenographer to take down and transcribe Calvin's sermons, delivered in a church unheated in winter and uncooled in summer. This arrangement lasted for the rest of Calvin's life.

The personality of this thin, short, frail man was complex, and suffered from the usual lack of comprehension that attends genius. He had a strong will and remarkable energy, but was often ill. Surrounded by lesser minds, he often lost his temper. And he had frightful migraines.

But he was not sour: his gift for making and keeping friends was extraordinary. Farel, Melancthon, Bullinger, Cop, Wolmar, Laurent de Normandie, Beza, de Montmorency, Knox and others remained close to him through all vicissitudes—and he to them. That speaks volumes.

He was not perfect. "Painfully sensitive" to criticism, he could hardly bear opposition. He had trouble believing that he could be wrong. In that, he was hardly unique among the theologians of his time. And Calvin was, as are all men, a man of his times.

He liked wine and bowling and indulged both even on Sundays; lived simply, slept only six hours a day, never took a holiday, refused increases in salary and raised money for the poor. He was musical, introduced singing at Strasbourg and had music included in the ecclesiastical ordinances of Geneva.

He spent hours reading and dictating: The *Institutes* were never really completed: they were enlarged, deepened and improved.[1] He lived surrounded with books, read and dictated daily. It was his dictations, more than his preaching and more than Geneva that created his fame in the world.

"The strength of that heretic," said Pope Pius IV, "consisted in this, that money never had the slightest charm for him. If I had such servants my dominion would extend from sea to sea."

But there was more to Calvin than that.

---

1. But his sermons were never revised; he did not, ever, review them.

ૐ

No good man has ever had a worse press; no Christian theologian is so often scorned; so regularly attacked. He is a devil-figure for anti-Christians and even for many imperfectly educated Christians. This is odd, for America does not ordinarily attack religious leaders or faiths. Even the Ayatollah Khomeini, inspirer of bloody purges, was not used as a peg to attack Islamic beliefs. But there has long been open season on Calvin.

This is especially strange because Calvin's doctrine is "just the Augustinianism common to the whole body of Reformers—for the Reformation was, from the spiritual point of view a great revival of Augustinianism. And this Augustinianism is taught by him not as an independent discovery of his own, but fundamentally as he learned it from Luther... in much detail from Martin Bucer into whose practical, ethical point of view he perfectly entered. Many of the very forms of statement most characteristic of Calvin—on such topics as Predestination, Faith, the stages of Salvation, the Church, the Sacraments—only reproduce, though of course with that clearness and religious depth peculiar to Calvin, the precise teachings of Bucer, who was above all others, Calvin's master in theology.

"Calvin did not originate this system of truth; as 'a man of the second generation' he inherited it, and his greatest significance is... that he was able, as none other was, to cast this common doctrinal treasure of the Reformation into a well-compacted, logically unassailable and religiously inspiring whole. In this sense it is as a systemizer that he makes the greatest demand on our admiration and gratitude. It was he who gave the Evangelical movement a doctrine."[2]

That such a contribution, and so God-centered a thinker should arise in the terrible sixteenth century to lift men's eyes from a frightful landscape toward eternity was among the greatest events of history.

ૐ

Calvin was not alone. The great value of the Reformation was that it

---

2. Warfield, *op. cit.,* p. 22.

reminded the world of the transcendental meaning of life. At 28 John Knox, an ordained priest and lawyer, heard George Wishart preach the Reformed doctrine and was heated by a religious fervor from which he never cooled.

At first his conversion seemed poorly-timed. In 1546 Wishart was captured by the Earl of Bothwell, turned over to Catholic authorities, condemned for heresy and burned at the stake.

That same year sixteen young men captured the Castle of Saint Andrews. Protestants including Knox poured into the castle. In July 1547 a French fleet appeared, and the castle was besieged. They surrendered and 120 were carried off to France. There they were held as prisoners of war. Knox landed in a slave galley chained to an oar, wearing the brown robe, canvas breeches and red cap of a galley slave.

Already famous for his preaching, Knox was traded to the English in a prisoner's exchange in 1549, after nineteen months of captivity. He was appointed a preacher in Berwick, a teeming border town, for England was by then officially Protestant.

ﻬ

Henry VIII had willed that after his death the Realm would be ruled by a Council of Regency. But the Earl of Hertford, brother of Jane Seymour[3] pushed the Council aside and took over under the ironic title of The Protector. He also elevated himself, or had the boy King elevate him, to Duke of Somerset.

Somerset sought popularity by repealing the Statute giving Royal Proclamations the force of law. As usual when an autocratic government weakens, its retreat encouraged resistance.

Meanwhile Protestantism flourished. "This year," said a contemporary in 1548, "the Archbishop of Canterbury did eat meat openly in Lent in the Hall of Lambeth, the like of which was never seen since England was a Christian country."

Sweeping ecclesiastical changes took place. The Catholic-oriented Six Articles were repealed, a royal command ordered all paintings and images removed from churches, priests received permission to marry,

---

3. Henry's fourth wife.

Communion replaced Mass, the English language replaced Latin, the English *Book of Common Prayer* was introduced. Gardiner, who protested that such changes were illegal, was sent to the Tower.

Protestant pamphlets flooded the land; German and Italian mercenary soldiers were imported to stamp out rebellions in several regions. The rebellion was suppressed, but its occurrence led to The Protector's fall. He was succeeded by the Earl of Warwick, who in turn made himself Duke of Northumberland.

Northumberland continued the Reform. A new Catechism appeared; stone altars were demolished and replaced by tables stationed in the middle. A revised *Prayer Book* appeared with forty-two articles.[4] Commissioners were appointed to oversee the new faith, and to apply penalties against heresy, blasphemy and adultery.

Archbishop Cranmer, ardent for Reform, sent resistors to the stake; Bishop Hooper refused to wear episcopal habits, calling them livery of "the Harlot of Babylon"—a term for the Papacy. Some priests threw away their surplices; the teaching of divinity ceased at the universities, student enrollments dropped and the impulse of the New Learning[5] faded.

Half the lands of every See were taken. And "while the courtiers gorged themselves with manors, the Treasury grew poorer. The coinage was again debased. Crown lands to the value of many millions of modern money had been granted away to the friends of Somerset and Warwick. Royal expenditures mounted in seventeen years to more than four times the previous total."

Calvin led a hard life in Geneva. Despite charges that he had grown wealthy, he wrote that he did not possess "one foot" of land, and had not enough money to buy one acre. "I am still using someone else's furniture. Neither the table at which we eat, nor the bed on which we sleep, is my own." The house in which they lived was owned by the Council.

---

4. Later reduced to Thirty-Nine.
5. Efforts to blend Catholicism and Reform.

His wife, Idelette, died in 1549. She had borne him only one premature child, which soon died. On her deathbed Calvin promised to treat her children as his own. Afterward he said, "I have been bereaved of the best friend of my life. . . ."

Meanwhile Geneva became the hub of the Reformation. Calvin spoke regularly to about a thousand persons. His output, and the works of his colleagues, spawned Europe's greatest concentration of printers and publishing firms. Around them clustered paper and ink manufacturers, editors, translators, salesmen, routes and lists, customers and authors. The Fuggers—international bankers[6]—provided the capital.

Calvin established an Academy that taught Latin, Greek, Hebrew and Theology. Graduates carried the Reform into France, Holland, Scotland and England. Many were from noble families; a majority from the bourgeoisie. Some of these young pastors, who left Geneva to travel secret pathways through the Alps, armed only with letters of accreditation and false papers, found martyrdom. In time the survivors planted Huguenot churches throughout France.

The resentment of Calvin's Genevan enemies never ended. As memories of their misrule faded, the Libertine Party revived. By 1552 it dominated the Little Council. Its leaders harassed the clergy by demanding lists of all the excommunicated—with explanations. The ministers refused. The Libertines then ruled that ministers could no longer serve on the General Council.

Calvin was baited till he asked to be relieved. The request was refused. His enemies didn't want to drive him away: they wanted to subjugate him. It was at that low point in Calvin's career, when he was in political decline, that Servetus appeared.

ॐ

Servetus holds a special status in anti-Calvinist legends. The death of this single individual, out of all the tens of thousands of deaths in the terrible sixteenth century, continues to arouse special indignation. But theologians know Servetus as a forerunner of Unitarianism, a pioneer in the "historical school" of Biblical criticism, a spreader of Judaic criti-

---

6. They also bankrolled Catholic Charles V.

cisms of Christianity and as one of the great theological disturbers of all time.

Born Miguel Serveto in Navarre, Spain in either 1509 or 1511, the son of a notary, he appears fully formed in history, his childhood a mystery. He studied law in Toulouse, where he saw his first complete Bible. Although he vowed to read it "a thousand times" he also seems to have read the Koran and an astonishing number of Jewish theological criticisms of Christianity, which influenced his views.[7]

Servetus early won the patronage of Juan de Quintana, confessor to Emperor Charles V. The Prelate took Servetus to Bologna and Augsburg in 1530, exposing him to Protestantism. Declaring himself a Reformer, Servetus then visited Oecolampadius at Basel, but soon began to argue against the Trinity.

In 1531 he published a book titled *Seven Errors about the Trinity.*[8] Dr. Jerome Friedman, author of several monographs on Servetus, says that Servetus repeated Jewish criticisms of the Christian concept of the Trinity as "polytheistic" and, later, as a "chimera" (that is, one third lion, one third goat and one third dragon).

After that first book Servetus left Basel for Strasbourg, where he quarreled with Bucer. Asked to leave Strasbourg, he returned to Basel, where he was ordered to retract his anti-Trinitarian arguments. He promised he would, but instead wrote a second book expanding his criticisms. That evoked an Inquisition order for his arrest, and Servetus vanished.

Shortly afterward Michel de Villenueve (his mother's name) appeared at the University in Paris as a lecturer in mathematics, mysteriously supplied with identity papers, introductions and sponsors.

He studied geography, astronomy and medicine as well as mathematics and dabbled in astrology. He dissected with the great Vesalius, and gained equal praise. He challenged the young Calvin to a debate, who risked his life to win a promising convert, but Villenueve/Servetus did not appear.

When the placards appeared, he left Paris at the same time as Calvin,

7. Jerome Friedman, "Michael Servetus: The Case for a Jewish Christianity," *Sixteenth Century Journal,* vol. 4, no. 1, April, 1973, *passim.*
8. *De Trinitas Erroribus Libri Septem.*

and resurfaced in Lyon. There he edited a scholarly edition of Ptolemy's *Geography*. Back in Paris he wrote a book on Astrology that was condemned and suppressed. Then he became the personal physician to the Archbishop of Vienne, whose friendship he had gained in Paris. Out of many candidates he was chosen to edit a Latin translation of the Bible by Santes Pagnini. That took three years, six volumes, and created widespread shock.

In the *Pagninus Polyglot Bible* Villenueve/Servetus stripped the Old Testament of all prophecies presaging the arrival and message of Jesus, and ascribed contemporary political meanings throughout. Using rabbinical sources, he disputed Christian interpretations from Genesis forward. At each stage and for each prophet, he argued, God appeared with a different name and a different message, aimed at contemporary understanding.

"In the process of reinterpreting major prophets within the context of their own times," wrote Dr. Friedman, "the Spaniard succeeded in ridding the Bible of much traditional Christian meaning."[9]

While this circulated, Villenueve/Servetus wrote letters to Calvin asking difficult questions. When Calvin sent serious replies, Villenueve/Servetus disputed the answers. Calvin answered at greater length and sent him a copy of the *Institutes*. Servetus returned the *Institutes* with criticisms scribbled throughout. He also sent Calvin chapters of a book he was writing, accompanied by a number of insults. Of the Trinity, he wrote "I have often told you that triad of impossible monstrosities that you admit in God is not proved by any Scriptures properly understood." Then, after other insults, Villenueve/Servetus said he would like to visit Geneva, and asked Calvin for a pledge of safe-conduct.

Although he knew by then that his correspondent Villenueve was really the notorious Servetus, Calvin did not expose him because he did not deal with Catholic authorities. But his anger was deep.

In early January 1553, Servetus published his collected works under the title *Christianismi Restitutio*.[10] *The Restitutio* was clearly aimed against Calvin's *Institutio*. This final effort revised his two books

---

9. Jerome Friedman, "Michael Servetus: Exegete of Divine History," *Church History*, vol. 42, 1974, p. 465.

10. The Restoration of Christianity.

attacking the Trinity, seven more books on faith and the kingdoms of Christ and Antichrist, apologies to Melancthon and thirty letters to Calvin. Printers in Basel refused to handle it, but Servetus, still known as Villeneuve, persuaded printers in Vienne.[11] This edition included, amazingly enough, a treatise on the pulmonary circulation of the blood, anticipating Harvey by over two generations, apparently because Servetus believed blood represented the soul.[12]

In the balance of the *Restitutio,* "[a]ccepting the Jewish criticism of the Trinity as essentially valid, Servetus . . . used not only Kimchi's[13] commentary on the Psalms, but his criticism of the Trinity and his wording of the latter's anti-Christian polemical works as well."[14]

Although issued anonymously, sophisticated readers recognized Servetus' style. Calvin discussed these with his friends but not publicly—because he did not want to help float heresies. But Guillaume de Trie, Bude's son-in-law and Calvin's friend, wrote a cousin in Vienne that an arch-heretic lived in Vienne and was employed by the Archbishop. "He is a Portuguese Spaniard named Michael Servetus in his real name, but he calls himself Villenueve at present. . . ."

Trie's cousin alerted the authorities who asked for proofs, which de Trie sent. But he added:

> I tell you one thing: I had the greatest difficulty getting them out of M. Calvin. Not that he wants such execrable blasphemies to go unreproved, but because it seems to him that his duty, as one who does not bear the sword of justice, is to convict heresies by doctrine rather than pursuing them with the sword. . . .

Villenueve was arrested and questioned. Shown some missing pages he had sent Calvin, describing infant baptism as a "demonic monstrosity" he denied believing that, and said he couldn't tell whether the missing notes were his or not.

---

11. These men, brothers in law, were Genevans. One was a member of the Libertine Party who had been forced to flee Geneva to escape punishment for various crimes.
12. A Judaic belief.
13. A famous Jewish rabbi and polemicist.
14. Jerome Friedman, "Servetus and the Psalms: The Exegesis of Heresy," *Histoire de l'Exegese au XVI Siecle* (Geneva: Droz, 1978).

Shown a "letter" on free will he wept, said it was part of letters written when he was a youth of fifteen or seventeen, just after he read "a book printed in Germany by a man named Servetus, a Spaniard—I do not know what part of Spain he came from or where he lived in Germany . . . and after I read the book in Germany, being very young . . . it seemed to me to be good, in fact better than others."

He wrote to Calvin, he said, repeating questions Servetus had asked, and for purposes of the correspondence had taken the name of Servetus. . . . When he saw that Calvin became angry, he broke off the correspondence. On infant baptism he had changed his mind and now wished to keep in step with the Church. As for the 'letter' on the Trinity, that merely expressed the opinion of Servetus."[15]

After that, more mystery. The official explanation is that Servetus sent his servant to collect some money due him. The jailer gave the prisoner a key to a small garden, located, apparently, at the prison. Servetus climbed over a wall and vanished. Improbabilities abound in that explanation, but Servetus' life was replete with mysteriously charmed circumstances.

෴

The boy King of England, Edward VI, had grown, by 1550, into "a slight, delicate youth of thirteen who carried one shoulder higher than the other and had to squint to see any distance. To his doll-like beauty was now added an incongruous pose of rough majesty—a wholly unconvincing imitation of his hearty, burly father [Henry VIII]. He put his hands on his hips and strutted about on his thin legs, frowning with dissatisfaction and piping out 'thunderous' oaths . . . [that] contrasted oddly with the religious doctrine that streamed so readily from his lips. He was very much an unformed boy, but he had the makings of a fastidious, pedantic king, impressive yet unappealing. And his frailty had become alarming."[16]

This made Emperor Charles V uneasy. The men in authority in England knew they would rue their rule if the King lived to his majority.

---

15. Parker, *op. cit.,* pp. 119, 120.
16. C. Erickson, *Bloody Mary* (Doubleday, 1978), p. 270.

To escape a day of reckoning, they might well kill Edward and his elder sister Mary, who was the official heir to the throne—and an ardent Catholic.

Madrid was weighing an invasion of England to place Mary on its throne and restore it to Catholicism when news arrived that young King Edward was seriously ill. His weight dropped; in 1551 he had measles and smallpox. In early 1553, he showed signs of advanced tuberculosis.

Rumors of poison floated, for the Renaissance was not over, and such steps were not unknown in England. Physicians warned the Council that Edward was in danger. The possibility that Mary, whom the Protectorate had mistreated might come to the throne, sent shivers around the Council table.

Northumberland and others clustered around the young King's bed at Greenwich and propped him up with pillows while he wrote, at their dictation, a document altering the succession.

Its substance was too intricate for a sick boy to fathom. In effect, the succession would pass to Lady Jane Grey who would marry Northumberland's son; their eldest son would inherit and the House of Dudley would link into royalty.

No word of this was made public. When the Grey-Dudley wedding was held, the Duke pretended great cordiality toward Mary. Meanwhile he placed followers in main castles and strongholds in the event of rebellion. The King was fading, there would be a struggle—and the Duke intended to win.

The King's condition, however, worsened too quickly. There would be no time for Lady Jane to bear an heir. The Duke then made a slight alteration in the will Edward had written, to read: "Lady Jane and her heirs male."

ॐ

On June 17, 1553, the Vienne tribunal, aware that M. de Villenueve was really Servetus, sentenced him in absentia to "be burned alive in a slow fire until his body becomes ashes. For the present the sentence is to be carried out in effigy and his books are to be burnt."

Servetus, now wanted by all Catholic authorities and with both Spanish and French warrants out, wandered for three months. He decided to go to Naples—a city then, as now, notorious for the power of its criminal underworld. But first he headed for Geneva.

No explanation of that strange decision has ever been discovered. One possibility is that Calvin represented what Servetus jealously wanted to be: an internationally respected scholar whose interpretations and books made him a world figure. Servetus apparently hoped for a debate, with Calvin's followers as audience, in which he—Servetus—would emerge triumphant.

He was in Geneva, under still another assumed name, for a month without being detected. He probably attended Calvin's weekday or Sunday sermons during that time, since his years-long fascination with Calvin is a matter of record. He was reckless enough to stay in Geneva even after he had arranged for transportation to Zurich.

On the fifth Sunday his long string ran out. He was recognized in Calvin's church, Saint Pierre, listening to Calvin, and was arrested.

ॐ

The final days of young King Edward VI were ghastly. He withered into immobility, emerging only to cough up "a livid black sputum that gave off an unbearable stench," and died July 6, 1553.

Two days before Edward's death the Princesses Mary and Elizabeth were summoned to his bedside. Neither answered that summons; both knew that their lives were in danger.

Lady Jane Grey would have become Queen if Northumberland had been able to control events, but that is a power not granted to men. He was shaken to discover that Mary eluded capture and had raised an army of her own—an army he had to leave London to confront.

En route to that collision, the Duke's forces quarreled and melted, for he was hated—and Mary was popular. The Duke sent envoys to ask France for help, but events moved too fast.

The Council members changed with the new wind. The Treasurer carried the content of the Privy Purse to Mary; the others abandoned the Duke, and even offered a reward for his capture. They appeared in the streets of London to proclaim Mary Tudor Queen of England. That created astonishment, for to openly favor Mary the day before had meant death. Then enormous joy erupted; people rushed into the streets, bells rang, people threw coins out of windows, groups danced. That night bonfires appeared, drinking and banqueting continued.

Northumberland—arch manipulator and iron-fisted ruler—surrendered without a fight. His closest companions rushed to surrender and
to plead for pardon on their knees.

Mary, surrounded by supporters, waited until all the rebels had been
collected and their leaders imprisoned. Then, gorgeously attired, she
entered London August 3, 1553, escorted by thousands, to receive a
tumultuous welcome.

Protestant ministers watched these proceedings with dismay. Mary's
biographer Erickson said, "Along the roads between Framlingham and
London she had seen time and again the same ancient, blasphemous
slogan at every crossroad; it was repeated in the placards and banners
that decorated London... *Vox populi, vox Dei*—the voice of the people
is the voice of God."[17]

᠅

Servetus was allowed paper, ink and all the books he cared to buy.
Calvin lent him several on the early Church fathers.

Nicolas de la Fontaine, Calvin's secretary, was in the same prison
under a Genevan law that placed an accuser in prison as well as the
accused until he could provide proofs. Calvin drew up an indictment of
thirty-eight articles supported by quotations from Servetus' writings,
which de la Fontaine submitted.

The first hearings on August 14, 1553, established questions to be
proven. Were certain writings heretical? Did Servetus write these? Did
he intend to distribute such views for sale? Had he communicated them
earlier to M. Calvin, M. Viret and M. Poupin? Finally, was heresy a
criminal offense?

The Libertine judges held long technical discussions to avoid recognizing Calvin and his fellow ministers[18] as equal judges of public
morality. The arrival of Servetus embarrassed their campaign to reopen
the brothels of Geneva and to eliminate sumptuary laws. To openly side
with the most notorious heretic in Europe would not help such plans.

On August 17 and 21, Calvin appeared at the trial as the accuser and

17. Erickson, *op. cit.,* p. 296.
18. Known as the Venerable Company of Pastors.

Servetus shouted at him. This was not as brave as it seemed: his jailer had told him he had the sympathy of the civil judges.

The Little Council then sent to Vienne to ask why Servetus had been jailed and how he had escaped. It also wrote to Swiss churches and cities for their opinions. They hoped to base a decision on an international consensus, rather than from Calvin's opinion.

On September 1, 1553, two more of Calvin's enemies joined the judges in the trial and argued with Calvin. Inside the larger General Council, both Libertine and Patriot members openly raged—not against Servetus—but against Calvin.

On September 3, 1553, Servetus' reply to Calvin's thirty-eight charges answered each point, questioned Calvin's right to be involved in the trial, and accused him of being a disciple of the criminal, Simon Magus. Calvin answered in twenty-three pages. These were given to Servetus, who returned them with margin comments reading "liar," "impostor," "hypocrite," "miserable wretch." Durant the historian, an anti-Calvinist sympathetic to Servetus, speculates that imprisonment and strain had broken him, but invective was habitual with Servetus.

Calvin's enemies then asked Servetus if he would like to continue the trial, or be returned to Vienne. "He threw himself on the ground, begging with tears to be judged here, and let Messieurs do with him what they would, but not let him be sent back there."

By October 18, 1553, replies arrived from the Swiss cities. All condemned Servetus. Perrin, a Libertine judge, then tried to transfer the case to the Council of Two Hundred. That was rejected.

On October 26, 1553, the Little Council passed a sentence of death by being burned alive on Servetus. Calvin, who was present, said, "he moaned like a madman and . . . beat his breast, and bellowed in Spanish *"Misericordia! Misericordia!"* In a painful last interview, he asked Calvin, who came to see him, for mercy. But when Calvin asked if he would retract his heresies, Servetus refused.

Calvin and the other ministers, however, agreed to Servetus' last request for a quicker, less painful death by beheading. The Council refused. *It was determined that Calvin would not decide a single detail.*

Farel, who accompanied Servetus to the stake, charged Calvin with softness.

ॐ

The men of Calvin's time united in approving the sentence. Melancthon wrote Calvin and Bullinger thanking God for the "punishment of this blasphemous man" and called the execution "a pious and memorable example to all posterity." Bucer said that Servetus deserved to be disemboweled and torn to pieces. Bullinger agreed that civil magistrates should punish blasphemy with death.

But matters did not rest there; in fact have not rested since. The rulers of Vienne have not been condemned, either by historians or theologians, for sentencing Servetus to death in absentia. Their names are not indissolubly linked to Servetus in arguments against Catholicism.

What seems difficult for secular moderns to grasp is that all Sixteenth Century governments believed the Biblical teaching that a nation religiously divided against itself cannot stand.[19]

It was, after all, not a nationalistic period, but "a period when people were united only by the bonds of religious belief." In no region was this better understood than in Spain, "which had no room for Erasmianism[20] or for the doubtful *converso*[21] any more than for the Protestant."[22]

Repeated denunciations of Spain for expelling those who refused to adopt Christianity and abjure Judaism "does not entirely satisfy," wrote the Marxist historian Fernand Braudel. "He sees[23] only one side of the tragedy... not recognizing those of the Spain of different periods, which were in no way illusory, fictitious or diabolical. A Christian Spain was struggling to be born. The glacier displaced by its emergence crushed the trees and houses in its path. And I prefer not to divert the debate . . . by saying that Spain was amply punished for her crimes, for the expulsion of 1492. . . . Some have said that these crimes and passions, cost her her glory. But the most glorious age of Spain began precisely in 1492 and lasted undimmed until . . . 1643 or even 1650. . . ."

In other words, the example of Spain—a land violently divided by

19. Mark 3:25.
20. The overly-praised tolerance of Erasmus was really timidity.
21. False converts.
22. Fernand Braudel, *The Mediterranean,* vol. 2 (New York, N.Y.: Harper and Row, 1973), p. 825.
23. Referring to Jewish historian Leon Poliakov.

religion for centuries—as well as the examples of internal strife provided by the rise of various heretical movements inside Christianity through the centuries provided both the theorists and rulers of the Sixteenth Century with ample evidence that toleration of religious dissent could have, and indeed often had, frightful results.

Calvin's rejection of Servetus was based on more serious grounds than mere scholarly dispute. The anti-Trinitarian arguments of Servetus, his insistence that God was not triune, constituted a rejection of the Divinity of Christ and was, therefore, clearly anti-Christian. Nor was Servetus alone.

Unitarian ideas were floating, especially among Italian refugees in Geneva. Matteo Gribaldi voiced anti-Trinitarian opinions even during the trial of Servetus, for which he was later banished. Gentile, another Italian refugee from Calabria, was examined in Geneva after expressing Unitarian views, and recanted. He went to Lyons, was arrested by Catholic authorities, and freed when he said he only wanted to refute Calvin. In Bern, however, he was convicted of perjury and heresy, and beheaded.[24] Unitarianism, in other words, had seeped into Protestant strongholds to undermine the faith. Arguments disseminated by Servetus had, obviously, an effect in his own time. His "historical" approach would have an even greater effect later.

There is also another dimension, customarily ignored by academic historians and by modern intellectuals. That is the Christian. The Christian view of history does not surrender all that occurs to "the blind forces of instinct and human passion. . . . God has not abandoned His creation."[25]

Christians believe that heresy is an attempt to misdirect God's Plan, and Servetus was more than a simple heretic: he was a scholar who, *while pretending to be a Christian,* attacked the foundations of Christianity. He was a dangerous enemy of the faith. Left unchecked, Servetus would have unhinged both the Reformation and Catholicism, and left Europe bereft in the ashes of its faith centuries before that situation was actually realized.

---

24. Yet the ministers of Bern are not today held aloft for scorn.
25. Christopher Dawson, *The Christian View of History,* cf. God (Oxford University Press, 1977), p. 36.

The confrontation between Calvin and Servetus, therefore, was one of the high moments of history; heavy with not simply earthly, but eternal significance.

᠎ℰ

The Libertine leaders controlling the city government of Geneva were furious because the Servetus trial reinforced the city's clergy. Their revenge took the form of an onslaught against ministerial authority: they claimed the right to approve—or cancel—any excommunication ordered by the Church.

In this the Councilors confused religious and political rights. Because a citizen in a republic could dissent and still remain a citizen, they argued, why could a man not dissent and remain inside the Church?[26]

Calvin and his fellow ministers nearly despaired of convincing the Council that to allow dissent equal footing with faith inside the Church was to subvert the faith; to not only foster schisms, but to desecrate sanctuaries. Calvin prepared, once again, to leave Geneva.

Then the Council of Two Hundred, the city's top body, gave way and, in Calvin's words, "allowed the Church to defend its altars."

B. B. Warfield later pinpointed the significance of that victory when he wrote that it made the Church,

> absolutely autonomous in its own spiritual sphere. In asking for this he [Calvin] was asking for something new in the Protestant world.
>
> Of course Calvin did not get what he asked for in 1537, nor did he get it when he returned from his banishment in 1541. But he never lost it from sight; he was always ready to suffer for it . . . and at last he won it.
>
> In the fruits of that great victory we have all had our part. And every church in Protestant Christendom which enjoys today any liberty whatever . . . owes it all to John Calvin. It was he who first asserted this liberty in his early manhood . . . it was he who first gained it in a lifelong struggled against a determined opposition; it was he who taught his followers to value it above life itself, and to secure it to their successors with the outpouring of their blood. And thus Calvin's great figure rises

---

26. This argument has recently resurfaced inside the United States, and is a part of a growing politicization of religion.

before us not only in a true sense the creator of the Protestant church, but the author of all the freedom it exercises in its spiritual sphere.

Although they did not understand the full significance of what Calvin had achieved, the Libertine party leaders knew they suffered a setback, and renewed their attack. Their next demand was that Calvin submit all his writings to them for approval before publication.

In a temper he said, "If I live for a thousand years I will never publish anything else in Geneva," and wrote despairing letters to Farel.

Then the citizens came to his rescue. In 1555 the Libertines, to their great surprise, lost the elections. They were indignant, and some made feeble alcoholic efforts at rebellion. That failed and several fled. Others were arrested and, in the custom of the times, tortured. After that, Geneva settled down.

Chapter Six

ENGLAND

—————— ❧ ——————

The changes and chances of this mortal life.

— Book of Common Prayer

When Mary Tudor was crowned the reigning Queen of England, people assumed that England had become her dowry, and would pass to her husband when she married. For a woman to rule her husband was unnatural; to rule a realm unlikely.[1]

This was paradoxically believed even though Margaret Tudor, sister of Henry VIII, had ruled Scotland as a Regent for her son years earlier, and Mary Hapsburg ruled Flanders as Regent, and Catherine de Médicis was a de facto sovereign in France.

But Henry VIII had created a gentry that served the Crown. In his new State the sex of the monarch was less important than in earlier times though it would never become unimportant.

The first issue that arose was Mary's marriage. An offer had arrived from Charles V, that she marry his heir, Prince Philip, and accept, together with the Prince, 60,000 pounds a year. That prospect, which included the clear possibility of becoming an Empress and sharing the greatest position in Europe, delighted the new Queen.

But the English people were outraged. They hated foreigners and the idea of a foreign King was insupportable. A rebellion erupted. Mary was astonished because it was led by the Duke of Suffolk, father of Lady Jane Grey, whom she had pardoned for his earlier treason.

To general surprise she appeared at a throng at Guildhall, promised to abandon the marriage if the people protested, and spoke so well her

---

1. Matilda, daughter of Henry I, ruled briefly but was forgotten.

agents were able to muster an army. (Armies were small then; arms were privately owned and universally possessed; there was no standing army.) Suffolk was arrested and so was his daughter; his associates went into hiding.

After that, Mary Tudor forgot about mercy.

Suffolk was beheaded; so was his daughter Lady Jane, 16, and her husband, 17. About a hundred of their followers were executed, and Queen Mary set about dominating her kingdom as efficiently as had her father Henry VIII.

Nor did Mary stop there. She was determined to marry Prince Philip and to suppress dissent. Descended from hard rulers, she proved as adamant as her ancestors.

੨৶

The blond Catholic Philip arrived July 1554, aboard an elaborate galley accompanied by a fleet of 125 ships. His land escort included twenty of Spain's top nobility with their wives and servants and a bodyguard of several hundred. Twenty carts carried 96 chests loaded with £3 million in gold ducats for his expenses.

Mary waited eagerly. Half Spanish and half English, slender, auburn-haired, magnificently dressed, with rosy cheeks, she was learned in Greek, fluent in Latin and French. But her Spanish was a different dialect than Philip's; they had to converse in French, in which Philip was not fluent.

Matters appeared to go well at first. The wedding was suitably elaborate; the Spaniards arrived with money. But the situation was more complex in reality than it appeared, for it was a period when women deferred to their husbands, and Mary quickly fell deeply in love with Philip. On the other hand Philip[2] was not King of England, although the customs of the time caused many to assume that he was.

That honor had to await official steps, and these were not forthcoming. Mary was Queen, and not anxious to recede from her power. She did, however, share State papers and decisions, and Philip began to assume a commanding influence—inside the Palace.

---

2. Who had been elevated to King of Naples by his father.

Suddenly sunshine penetrated this murk: it was announced in October that the Queen was pregnant. We know now that this was a terrible medical error: retrospective medical opinion is that she suffered from ovarian dropsy, which would have prevented her from carrying a child to term even if she conceived.

Mary's doctors were misled by her amenorrhea. Perhaps, being palace physicians, they were unaware that this had been a recurrent problem for several years. In any event the news that the Queen was pregnant created joy in dynastic circles in both England and Spain.

Meanwhile there remained the supremely important issue of Catholicism. Mary sent for Reginald, Cardinal Pole, who had broken with Henry VIII over the Boleyn marriage and had been in exile for twenty years.[3] During those years Henry had the entire Pole family executed (except the cowardly Geoffrey Pole), and Reginald Pole yearned for revenge.

It was in exile that Reginald Pole became a Cardinal; he failed to become Pope in one election by only two votes. A leader in the Counter-Reformation, his greatest desire was to see England return to Catholicism.

He arrived November 20, 1554, bearing with him not only an appointment as Papal Legate (ambassador) but permission from Pope Julius for English Protestants to retain lands taken from the Catholic Church under Henry VIII.

That barrier fallen, Mary's first Parliament fell in line. A formal request was made to return England to Catholicism. Huge celebrations were held when royal assent was granted; Pole granted the nation "absolution" in St. Paul's Cathedral.

By December the return of England to Catholicism was made complete by a Second Statute of Repeal. All barriers to Papal authority in England were erased, all clergy ordained and promoted since the schism were confirmed in their orders and benefices, all judgments of the Church courts upheld, all marriages performed by schismatic clergy

---

3. Pole's lineage was royal; his mother was a niece of Edward IV and Richard III.

upheld. The Church was, once again, to receive "first fruits" and tithes. Philip was declared Regent in the event Mary died in childbirth. He expected to be declared King but that, to his great disappointment, was not done.

"More ominous was the revival, soon after the absolution was declared, of the medieval statutes prescribing how heretics tried in Church Courts were to be handed over to civil authorities for execution;"[4] but since that procedure had also prevailed under Protestantism, it seemed merely part of overall change.

Overall, it was a typically English blend of principle with materialism. The Lords and Commons were willing to rejoin the Catholic Church as long as they could keep what they had stolen from it.

The English spirit dominated, in other words, over all lesser arrangements. Philip, "who had certain myths of his own, must have been outraged to hear, at his first court sermon preached in England, by no less a Papist than Cardinal Pole, that England was 'prima provinciarum quae amplexa est fidem Christi'—the first country to receive the faith. Moreover, went on Pole, 'the greatest part of the world fetched the light of religion from England.' Mary nodded her head vigorously; she believed it too."[5]

This supranational spirit was to impede Philip in all his dealings in England. His companions and servants were jostled in the streets of London; veiled insults were soon unveiled. Where thieves in Spain worked at night, or invaded empty houses, the Spaniards discovered frightening English highwaymen. In the first week of Philip's arrival his company suffered many robberies and one of the Prince's own household chests was taken.

"They rob us in town and on the road," one Spaniard wrote. "No one ventures to stray two miles but they rob him and a company of Englishmen have recently robbed and beaten over fifty Spaniards." The Spanish complaints were ignored. "As far as the English were concerned, the hated Spaniards were only a temporary curse, to be endured with hostile indifference until Philip had served his purpose as the father of Mary's children."[6]

---

4. Erickson, op. cit., p. 391.
5. Johnson, op. cit., p. 176.
6. Erickson, op. cit., p. 383.

ⰆⰮ

But hearts are not changed by fiat. Books by Calvin, Luther and other Reformers had penetrated England's mind and could not be forgotten. Protestant emigres, beyond reach in Europe, shipped back a river of pamphlets against Catholicism.

A covert religious rebellion soon appeared. Small groups met in cellars, ruined churches, cemeteries, private homes. Priests were mysteriously attacked; seditious ballads appeared. English Protestants in Europe included blacksmiths, farmers, laborers, and merchants inspired by leaders like John Knox, the Bishops Ponet and Hale and John Foxe.[7]

These leaders, meanwhile, found havens and support in Geneva, Frankfurt and Strasbourg. Their campaign against Mary Tudor found its most effective expression in the writings of Knox, who had been warmly received by Calvin, with whom he shared deep affinities.

ⰆⰮ

But the restoration of Catholicism enabled Mary to have men and women executed for dissent with Rome. She did not lack for judges— nor for prisoners. Among these were John Hooper, former Bishop of Worcester, jailed for having married, and for refusing to "put his wife aside."

The Queen, already under Catholic criticism for leniency, was assured by her beloved Philip, by Gardiner (Bishop of Winchester), and by Cardinal Pole that religious unity was indispensable for national survival. Gardiner had already, in fact, announced his intention to burn three Protestant bishops—Hooper, Ridley and Latimer—unless they recanted.

In early February, 1555, Hooper was burned at the stake together with four others, in an especially gruesome way. Gardiner's health broke soon afterward, and Bishop Bonner then headed the persecutions.

These applied against ordinary as well as extraordinary people. Horror, fear and resentment grew proportionally; so did rebellion. Extra guards had to be stationed to protect the Queen, who turned 39 in

---

7. Already compiling his Book of Martyrs.

February, and was nearing the final weeks of her confinement.

News of her delivery was broadcast on Tuesday, April 30, 1555. Huge rejoicings erupted. Church bells rang in Antwerp; ships at anchor fired their guns—the celebrations were premature.

Mary's physicians said their timing was off, and set a later date. She remained in her apartment, and was only occasionally glimpsed. Meanwhile the weather turned bleak and sunless, cold even at midday, though it was still summer. Rain fell constantly; fields turned into mud and grain grew stunted. Philip chafed.

In this lowering atmosphere there were riots when more burnings were ordered. By July the Queen agonized. Her prayer book still survives, with the pages bearing a prayer for the safe delivery of a woman with child especially worn and stained.

When it finally became obvious that Mary had never been pregnant, Philip left. Once in Brussels he plunged into dissipation—a rare excess that betrayed his relief.

A bitter Queen resumed her duties. Had she borne an heir, history would have taken a different course. Her humiliating failure destroyed her marriage, crushed her personal prestige and much of her self-confidence, dashed her hopes and the hopes of Madrid as well. Like her mother, she was left, essentially, with only her faith to sustain her. She unleashed her bitterness upon an England that refused to follow her wholeheartedly into that, as into her marriage.

In September 1555 Cranmer, the Archbishop of Canterbury, was "questioned" by Catholic judges. Former head of the Reformation in England, he had dissolved the first marriage of Henry VIII and the Queen's mother Catherine of Aragon, had married Henry and Ann Boleyn, replaced the Mass with the Book of Common Prayer, had prosecuted dissident Catholics and had tried to enthrone Lady Jane Grey.

Pressed, he refused to recant. He was found guilty of heresy, but execution was delayed pending an order from the Pope. Then Ridley, 65, former Bishop of London, was tried and stood his ground. Finally Latimer, former Bishop of Worcester, 80, ". . . a man grown quite careless of life, dressed in an old threadbare gown, his white head covered with a cap upon a nightcap over a handkerchief, his spectacles hanging from his neck, a New Testament attached to his belt," appeared.

On October 6, 1555, Latimer and Ridley were burned simultaneously. Each was chained to an iron post with a bag of powder around
his neck to shorten his agony. When the fire was lit Latimer looked
toward the younger man and said in words that still ring through the
centuries, "Be of good cheer, Master Ridley. Play the man. We shall this
day light such a candle, by God's grace in England, as I trust that shall
never be put out."

ॐ

In December 1555 the Pope approved of Cranmer's death sentence.
The author of The Book of Common Prayer, one of the greatest English
works ever created, weakened. He sent several entreaties to Cardinal
Pole from the Tower, recanting his Protestantism and expressing a new
faith in Catholicism.

Such recantations had saved others, but the Queen, who had hated
Cranmer from her childhood, insisted upon his death. Bound, finally,
to the stake, Cranmer said,

> Now I come to the great thing, which so much troubleth my conscience
> more than anything that I ever did or said in my whole life, and that is
> the setting abroad of a writing contrary to the truth; which here and now
> I renounce and refuse . . . as written for fear of death . . . and that this,
> all such bills and papers which I have written, I have written or signed
> with my hand since my degradation . . . and forasmuch as my hand
> offended, writing contrary to my heart, my hand shall first be punished
> therefor, for . . . it shall first be burned. And as for the Pope, I refuse him
> as Christ's enemy and Antichrist. . . .

And as the flame rose around him, he held out his hand.[8]

ॐ

The majority arrested for religious reasons were humble people.
Many were sentenced to death. So many that "the executions became
commonplace, but not mundane; those who watched the Protestant
men, women and children die the slow death by fire found it difficult

---

8. His place as Archbishop of Canterbury was taken by Cardinal Pole.

to forget. . . . The spectacle of a man dying in the flame, singing a psalm 'until his lips were burnt away,' was a haunting image, as was the sight of a sixty year old widow bound to the stake, or a young blind woman, a ropemaker's daughter, sentenced to death by a bishop she could not see. . . ."[9] Resistance increased and even Cardinal Pole developed reservations, the Queen remained adamant.

But events undermined her efforts. The new Pope, Paul IV, was an amazingly energetic 80 year old. In youth he saw Ferdinand of Aragon (Mary's grandfather) conquer Naples and later recalled the Sack of Rome by Charles V (Mary's father in law). He hated Spain and burned to reunite Papal Italy. To do this, he allied the Vatican with Henry II of France. Catholic Spain found itself once again pitted against the Vatican and France. Mary, married to a Spanish heir, was asked to join with Madrid in a war against France and the Pope.

She had never expected such a nightmare choice. Her temper as well as her health began to suffer, and she sent beseeching letters imploring Philip to return. She also asked Charles V for advice on how to deal with rebellious Protestants: a problem he had never solved.

Mary's pleas came when illness was finally closing on the Emperor. He had, in his career, sent over 30,000 Protestants to terrible deaths, but by 1555, he despaired of ending the Reformation. "Old at thirty-five, he was afflicted at forty-five with gout, asthma, indigestion and stammering, he was now half his waking time in pain and found it hard to sleep. . . ."

In the autumn he ceremoniously turned the Netherlands over to Philip. The gift was enormous but loaded with burdens. Protestantism had swept the Netherlands, fueled by the symbiosis between Catholicism and the Spanish overlords. Philip's first steps were to deepen the suppression of the Dutch people by fire and sword.

With the Libertines out of power, Calvin was busy with pastoral visits, sermons, his immense correspondence and assisting various refugees. John Knox of Scotland was one of these. In 1555 Calvin helped

---

9. Erickson, *op. cit.*, p. 450.

Knox obtain an English-speaking congregation in Frankfurt, but he was too severe, and had to return to Geneva, which he described, as "the most perfect school of Christ that ever was on earth since the days of the Apostles."

But Knox did not forget Scotland. That nation, allied with France and menaced by England for generations, was ruled by the Regent Mary of Guise, widow of James V.[10] The Regent ruled in the name of her daughter Mary Stuart, who was in France.

Knox returned to Scotland to visit Mrs. Elizabeth Bowes and to marry her daughter Margaret. He also rallied powerful Protestant nobles including Mary Stuart's illegitimate half-brother the Earl of Murray. That aroused the Catholic authorities, and Knox barely managed to escape arrest, leaving the ecclesiastical court to burn him in effigy. That action was too late: Knox had become the leader of the Reformation in Scotland.

Back in Geneva, Knox pastored an English-speaking congregation where his authority was unquestioned. One of his precepts was that governors as well as the governed should obey the Bible. This doctrine, at a time when Luther had announced that rulers were divinely appointed and due an obedience sanctioned by God, was to shift Protestantism into more political positions.

Knox's writings, like Luther's, were alternately denunciatory and beatific. Papists were "pestilent Mass-mongers," and priests were "bloody wolves." When Mary Tudor married Philip of Spain, Knox called her "an open traitoress to the Imperial Crown of England." But in a "Letter to his Brethren" in Scotland, he said,

> . . . my hope is that ye shall walk as the sons of light in the midst of this wicked generation; that ye shall be stars in the night season, who yet are not changed in the darkness; that ye shall be as wheat among the cockle . . . that the coming of the Lord Jesus, whose omnipotent spirit rule and instruct, illuminate and comfort your hearts and minds in all assaults now and ever.

❧

---

10. James V was defeated at Solway Moss by the English, deserted by his nobles and died of shame. Henry VIII then invaded Scotland, sacked Edinburgh and looted the Lowlands in 1544.

In early 1556 Charles V completely abdicated and handed the Crowns of Castile, Aragon, Sicily and the Indies over to Philip II. The title of Emperor of Germany had gone to his brother Ferdinand. With a young new King, the Spaniards, hopeful at first, asked for the restoration of their ancient liberties, but Philip II was even more rigorous than his father.

ॐ

His war with France and the Vatican persuaded Philip II to seek a rapprochement with his wife, Mary Tudor. He was irritated with her because the English Parliament had failed to name him King of England, but with Philip duty came before emotion. He sent some warmer letters; her replies became hopefully ardent. By January 1557 he persuaded her to join England with him against the Vatican. Nothing could better prove his hold than that, which pitted a fervent Catholic against the Pope.

Before Mary would send troops she wanted Philip's return. Before he would return, he wanted to see English soldiers in the Netherlands. He won, and Mary sent foot and horse soldiers. The French, watching closely, wondered if Mary could retain her Crown after this unpopular step.

But that was only an initial payment. Philip said that he would return only if England declared war against France. Mary gave the messenger 100,000 pounds but said only his master's presence would gain another step.

Philip arrived March 18, 1557, without his former pomp, and joined Mary at Greenwich the next day. Both found the other greatly changed. Philip had become a young old man, serious to the point of solemnity. Mary had become a gaunt, middle-aged woman: thin-lipped and determined, her eyes staring.[11]

Her hold on her throne was slender; there were numerous plots against her life. Her effort to restore Catholicism had rested from the start on having a Catholic heir; her barrenness made that impossible. Her efforts to balance the national budget led her to increase taxes to the

---

11. This was partly myopia; her vision was so poor she had to hold papers very close to read them.

edge of rebellion; her personal popularity vanished in the flames of her persecutions.

Her feelings for Philip were intense, but she knew she had married a man whose responsibilities would keep him always away. Her distress was not lessened when he brought his current mistress (and cousin), the Duchess of Lorraine, to England with him.

But she brought Philip to Council meetings to exhort the members to approve a war with France. The members demurred in Latin so Philip could follow the argument. When the vote was negative, she had the Councillors brought to her apartment individually, where she threatened "some with death, some with the loss of their goods and estates, if they did not consent to the will of her husband." The Council succumbed in June 1557.

The following month was Mary's last brief taste of happiness. Philip was pleased; the Duchess of Lorraine was sent away. It was not exactly a second honeymoon; they spent their time pouring over military plans. Mary also had to secure the Scots border, outfit the fleet, raise money for Philip and sell Crown property for cash. Their days, divided between State business, hunting or hawking, vespers and compline, raced past.

Philip did not delay to please Mary: he waited for men, money and ships from Spain. When these arrived on June 10, 1557, he at once prepared to leave. Mary traveled with him for the four days between London and the coast, sharing his bed. On July 6, 1557, they said goodbye, and she watched him board a vessel for Calais—they never again saw one another.

Chapter Seven

CHANGE AT THE TOP

————— 🖎 —————

Princes are like to heavenly bodies, which cause good or evil times.

— Bacon

By the middle of the Sixteenth century, the Vatican had realized its mistake in hesitating over Luther and the rebellious Swiss, and gathered its formidable international resources for a full-scale war against the Reformation.

Burnings, tortures, censorship and expulsion increased dramatically under Mary Tudor and under Catherine de Médicis of France and Mary of Lorraine in Scotland. John Knox, watching as horrors mounted under the rule of the "gentler sex," issued an enraged *First Blast of the Trumpet Against the Monstrous Regiment of Women.* It was a blast against persecution rather than women, but the title piqued women then and since.[1]

Knox compared Mary Tudor's policy to Jezebel's, who had introduced the worship of Baal. The reaction of the English Queen was to outlaw his book, and make it a capital offense to own a copy. In midsummer 1558, Knox again attacked with *An Appellation to the Nobility and Estates of Scotland* urging an uprising against the Regent, Mary of Lorraine. Knox argued that Christians should not accept governance by Pagans, a category in which he placed Catholics.

Reform Scots, watching Catholic processions in which effigies of the Virgin and the saints were carried and even kissed, agreed with him. The open alliance between the hated French, the Regency and the Vatican

---

1. By coincidence, Philip II replaced his aunt at about the same time Knox's book appeared.

increased Protestant fervor. One result of Knox's exhortations was that the image of St. Giles was taken, forcibly, out of the Mother Kirk (Church) in Edinburgh and later burned.

A "Common Band" of Protestant nobles—Argyll, Glencairn, Morton, Lorne and Erskine—met at Edinburgh[2] and signed the "First Scottish Covenant." They termed themselves "Lords of the Congregation of Jesus Christ" as opposed to the "Congregation of Satan," (i.e., the Vatican), called for "a reformation in religion and government" and demanded the liberty to "use ourselves in matters of religion and conscience as we must answer to God." They vowed to establish reformed churches in Scotland and announced that the Book of Common Prayer, used in England under Edward VI, was to be adopted by all congregations.

In response, Archbishop Hamilton ordered the burning of Walter Milne,[3] an elderly priest who had left the Church, married and adopted the Reformed faith. The people were outraged, and when another Reformed preacher was summoned for trial, armed men forced their way into the Regent's presence to warn her they would allow no more trials, no more burnings over religion.

Scotland was still fierce and semi-feudal; the warning was not to be taken lightly, especially when the Lords of the Congregation sent word to the Regent that they stood behind it. Meanwhile, word was sent to Knox that his safety was guaranteed if he returned to Scotland.

૨૭

Knox's *Blast* circulated widely in England, where it joined a flood of pamphlets attacking the Queen. She was called "Traitorous Marie" and "Mischievous Marie," but the tag that stuck was "Bloody Mary."

Philip II, solicitous at a distance, sent reassuring letters and the Count de Feria to keep Mary and Cardinal Pole company—but neither was in condition to be appreciative. The Archbishop of Canterbury, aware that his efforts to restore England to the Catholic faith had been defeated, was estranged from the Vatican and was deep in a tertiary fever. The Queen, her belly distended with terminal dropsy, stricken by intermit-

2. In December, 1557; Knox probably didn't get the news until weeks later in 1558.
3. In April, 1558.

tent fevers and wayward mental states, had sunk into involutional melancholia.

≈

Charles V's final residence was a mansion inside the monastery of St. Juste, where he continued his lifelong gluttony, gulping huge quantities of Estramadura sausages, eel pies, pickled partridges, capons, "rivers of wine and beer." He also read reports and dictated dispatches to Philip in the Netherlands, recommending brutal measures against Protestants. To the end he regretted having allowed Luther to live.

In August his gout turned into fever, and for a month "he was racked with all the pains of death before he was allowed to die." That finally occurred September 21, 1558.

≈

News of the Emperor's death reached England in October 1558, at a time when Mary herself lay dying. Her courtiers had fled. Pressed by her Council and the Count de Feria, the fading Queen agreed to name her half-sister, Elizabeth, the heir.

Philip sent an envoy saying that he would marry Elizabeth as soon as Mary died; the French suggested she marry the Duke of Savoy. The slender red-haired Elizabeth, waiting at Hatfield, scornfully dismissed both offers, saying she would be "foolish" to marry a foreigner.

Mary died of her fever in early morning, November 17, 1558. Twelve hours later Cardinal Pole, Archbishop of Canterbury, was carried off by the same fever in Lambeth Palace. Both left soundlessly.

Elizabeth waited. On the day of her sister's death she walked alone a short distance from the Palace, taking a few books, hoping for a calm interval. She had just settled herself at the base of an oak when she heard a noise, glanced up and saw William Cecil running toward her, waving something in the air.

He reached her as she rose, fell to his knees, and said, *"Your Majesty,"* that her sister was dead, and that he offered his poor homage.

Overcome, she said in Latin—a language as familiar to her as English—*Domine factuum est istud, et est mirabile in oculis nostris!"* (It is the Lord's doing; it is marvelous in our eyes.)[4]

ॐ

The new year 1559 opened with Charles V silent in Spain's Escorial; with his sister Mary, former Regent of the Netherlands, dead; with Mary of Lorraine, Regent of Scotland, pursued by the Lords of the Congregation, with Bloody Mary gone and the Protestant Elizabeth Tudor crowned in England.

John Knox, who had issued his *Blast* against women rulers only six months earlier, wrote a letter exempting Elizabeth from his criticism, and arrived in Edinburgh on May 2, 1559. The next day he preached at Perth and set off a revolution.

His sermon against idolatry so inflamed his listeners that they poured out and gutted three monasteries. The Regent's brother, Cardinal Lorraine, advised her to cut the Protestants down in Scotland as Bloody Mary had in England, but the Lords of the Congregation made that impossible. The Regent, ill and pursued by the Lords, signed a truce three weeks later.

Knox then moved to St. Andrews, where his exhortations led crowds to strip all images from all the churches of the city. The Archbishop fled to Perth, but the Congregation, on the grounds the Regent had violated the truce by using French funds to pay her troops, moved against that city, captured it, and sacked and burned the Abbey of Scone.

The Regent, fatally ill, retreated to Leith and sent to France for help.

ॐ

Elizabeth's spontaneous quote from the New Testament did not reflect piety but education, for she was a complete creature of the Renaissance, and regarded religion with private incredulity. She set the date of her coronation[5] only after many consultations with Dr. John Dee, her astrologer.

---

4. "And Jesus saith unto them, Did ye never read in the scriptures, the stone which the builders rejected, the same is become the head of the corner; *this is the Lord's doing, and it is marvelous in our eyes?*" (Matthew 21:42)

5. January 15, 1559.

Fluent in Latin, French and Italian, well-read in Ariosto and Tasso, familiar with the Greek Testament as well as Sophocles and Demosthenes she combined the methods of Machiavelli with a deep femininity. Her Court would glitter with luxury, entertainment, art, music, drama and poetry, while her private Council sessions were marked by an arbitrary will and a strident manner.

As ruler, her first move was to have Parliament void the statutes that had clouded her legitimacy. Then Parliament approved an Act of Supremacy, which restored to the Crown "the ancient jurisdiction over the state ecclesiastical and spiritual . . . abolishing all foreign power repugnant to the same."

These were basic steps. Her right to the Crown had been denied by Parliament only five years earlier; the Vatican officially declared her illegitimate. The entire Catholic world believed the legitimate heir was Mary Stuart, Queen of the Scots and great granddaughter of Henry VII. Mary Stuart was a cousin of Elizabeth's, but one of impeccable descent. Elizabeth had inherited the throne only through her sister's Will, amid doubts that a Crown could be a bequest.

In France during childhood, Mary Stuart had signed a treaty with the French agreeing that if she died without issue, Scotland would become a French possession. At 16 she married Francis, the *Dauphin* (heir) of France. They added the arms of England to their own, and styled themselves "King and Queen of England and Ireland."

Elizabeth, meanwhile, refused a Papal offer to recognize her legitimacy if she retained Catholicism in England. That was against her instincts, which were remarkably keen. Her father Henry VIII and her brother Edward VI had created a Protestant core that would defend a Protestant Queen, and not even Catholics wanted a civil war.

But with the entire Catholic world against her, and only a tenuous alliance with Spain to protect her, she played for time, pretended to consider offers of marriage and accepted a Papal Legate at Court.

2❧

She needed time, for Bloody Mary had left a bloody mess. Successive currency degradation had crippled commerce. Huge governmental loans at ruinous rates burdened the Crown. Tens of thousands of paupers roamed the land. Mary, obsessed with religion, had allowed the

Navy to rot and left the army ill-paid and ill-fed. The French had landed troops at Leith to help Mary of Lorraine, and the threat of invasion loomed over England.

William Cecil, Elizabeth's principal advisor, left Cambridge to become a lawyer. Cecil[6] had served the Protector Somerset, and Somerset's enemy Northumberland; had helped crown Lady Jane Grey, then switched to Bloody Mary and become a Catholic in the process. Such dexterity led many, then and now, to consider him unprincipled; his notes reveal Cecil to be an English politician. His abilities were enormous, which earned him the usual envy and hatred from all but a handful who, fortunately, included his Queen.

Cecil's second wife, Mildred Cooke, was an ardent Reformer. That was an important element in Cecil's life, in the future direction of England and the English-speaking world. Despite all the twists of Elizabethan policy, Cecil always swung it, somehow, in directions that fit the Protestant cause.

ॐ

The new Queen economized and ruthlessly reduced the bureaucracy. Taxes on the nobility and the Church were increased. In six months governmental costs were cut by 60 percent. Sir Thomas Gresham, Elizabeth's financial advisor, noted that England's credit, once derided, was now "that of all other princes."

But those steps paled beside the way the new Queen approached the religious turmoil she inherited.

Her deviousness appeared when the religious exiles, who rushed home in eager expectation of seeing Calvinism restored, arrived by the thousands. Although they cried that the time had arrived "for the Walls of Jerusalem to be built again in that kingdom where the blood of so many martyrs, so largely shed, may not be in vain," the new Queen was silent.[7]

Nobody denied their sufferings. Although the majority of the English had traditionally been cool toward religion, and had tended to regard

---

6. His father was a clerk of the wardrobe to Henry VII.

7. Mary M. Luke, *Gloriana: The Years of Elizabeth I* (New York, N.Y.: Coward, McCann & Geoghegan, 1973), p. 35.

execution "as a fair professional hazard" for the ardent, contemporaries were struck by the sheer scale of Marian persecution. There had been nothing like it seen in England before; it had the flavor of Continental excess. In over three years[8] Mary burnt nearly 300 people (about 60 had been executed during the first 20 years of the [English] Reformation),[9] and destroyed the credibility of a Catholic government.

Elizabeth, however, had no liking for Calvinism either, no matter what its believers endured. When they poured across the English landscape "to sow abroad the Gospel more freely, first in private homes and then in churches and people . . . began to flock toward them in great numbers and . . . wrangle among themselves and with the Papists,"[10] her suspicions seemed justified.

It was then that the new Queen issued the Proclamation that established her famous Compromise.

England was directed to use the Lord's Prayer, the Ten Commandments, the Apostles Creed, the Epistles and Gospels in English. But the remainder of the service was to be in Latin. Preaching was forbidden, but Cranmer's earlier and later edition of the Book of Common Prayer were allowed. (One followed the Catholic doctrine of transubstantiation; the other denied it.) England, in other words, was to be both Catholic and Protestant.[11]

It is doubtful if such a policy would have been possible in Scotland or Ireland, where religion was deeply and passionately held. English zealots, they were always in a minority; most of the people preferred form over substance.

೨‌ও

By the end of 1559, a navy and an army were created—not a moment too soon. French troops in Scotland were on the verge of crushing the Lords of the Congregation when an English fleet appeared in the Firth, and forced a French retreat to Leith. A short time later Mary of Lorraine

---

8. Mary reigned 5 years, 5 months and 21 days.

9. Johnson, *op. cit.*, pp. 158, 159.

10. Ibid.

11. The Compromise reflected Elizabeth's agnosticism, which John Knox described as "neither good protestant nor yet resolute papist."

died. Then Henry II died, and young Francis II, husband of Mary Stuart, inherited the French crown.

These changes forced France to make a treaty with England, ending the war into which Philip had dragged Mary Tudor. France agreed to leave Scotland; Francis II and Mary agreed to leave the Government of Scotland to a Council of the Lords—and acknowledged Elizabeth as Queen of England.

The Scots Parliament listened raptly to John Knox, and made Calvinism the official religion of Scotland. This was the first victory of Calvinism, accomplished over the objections of a Government and an Established Church, launched and inspired by the teachings of Calvin and Knox, rooted in the Bible—lifted into reality by political tides.

The Calvinist victory in Scotland improved Elizabeth's position and cemented William Cecil as her chief advisor. Cecil wanted her to become leader of Europe's Calvinist diaspora, but she refused. Her resistance to the Vatican was not rooted in belief, but in an aversion to sharing authority.

ॐ

Elizabeth's accession marked the fourth time that the English people were ordered to change their religious beliefs in twenty-eight years. That they obeyed in each instance was consistent with Christian tradition.

Ever since Constantine, the Christian Church and State had been partners in unity. Kings punished schismatics and heretics as a matter of duty. The Renaissance, however, witnessed a long, two-hundred year struggle before Henry VIII in which princes sought the power to appoint bishops, to curb ecclesiastical courts and to limit Vatican authority.

In France the Crown achieved independence of Rome through political means; in Spain Philip II controlled the Church. "By merely extending the power of ecclesiastical supervision that they already possessed, the Princes of reformed countries, or town councils of the cities[12] were eminently fitted to become the virtual and, if necessary, the titular governors of their churches."[13]

---

12. As, for instance, in Geneva.
13. Perry Miller, *Orthodoxy in Massachusetts 1630–1650: A Genetic Study* (Harvard University Press, 1933), p. 4.

All men then agreed that a State had to be united. Diversity was seen as division, division as disorder, disorder as leading to civil war. Although the great unity of all Western Europe had been shattered, its individual states retained this basic concept.

Calvin's great, hard-won victory was to halt the Genevan Council's authority at the door of the church, but it was to be many years before the significance of that victory was realized and expanded.

Not that it was completely unnoticed. Cecil advised Elizabeth to become not "Supreme Head" but "Supreme Governor" of the church. Cecil said this showed that the Crown "was not challenging the authority and power of ministry of divine offices in the church," and should be acceptable to Catholics as well as to Protestants.

Elizabeth ordered all persons to attend church, and forbade "all vain and contentious disputations in matters of religion." When a petition asked permission to launch greater reforms, she said, "It was not to her safety, honor and credit to permit diversity of opinions in a kingdom where none but she and her council governed."

៛▰

The College at Geneva was the intellectual center of the Calvinist diaspora. Its graduates were sent to various places, often in France. These were dangerous missions, for to be a Reform minister in a Catholic realm was to be automatically guilty of treason.

In time the Calvinists created networks of secret churches and congregations which sent information back to Geneva. Services were held in private homes behind heavily curtained windows; sometimes in barns and fields. Men were assigned to take the pastor's place in the event of a raid; there were instances of daring rescues.

Setbacks paradoxically inspired congregations and brought new recruits. When Ann du Bourg, a member of the Paris Parliament, was arrested for protesting Calvinist persecutions, he wrote a protest in prison against a Ruler who forced subjects to live "contrary to the will of God."

That statement made a deep impression in the Calvinist world, even after du Bourg was burned for heresy and sedition. Huguenots increased, and nobles joined them. These were men unaccustomed to suffering wrongs patiently, and some plotted to kidnap the young King, to force him to change the official religion.

Calvin, contacted, advised against force. He argued that rulers are to be obeyed even when they are unjust. Since rulers are surrounded by ministers, nobles and Parliaments, Calvin thought resistance should be limited to constitutional means. (Calvin may have had the example of John Knox and the Lords of the Congregation in mind.)

In France, however, the three estates of clergy, nobles and commoners had not met for 50 years. Meanwhile many nobles had become Huguenots. Two were Princes of royal blood: the King of Navarre and his brother the Prince of Conde.

But the Queen Mother, Catherine de Médicis, blocked the King of Navarre by enlisting the support of the Duc de Guise and his brother, the Cardinal of Lorraine.[14] The Guises, head of the Catholic party in France, led Huguenot persecutions.

The plot against the Crown, known as the Conspiracy of Amboise, failed. But it reminded the Calvinist world of the arguments of Beza, as presented in his book *On the Authority of Magistrates.* Written originally as a defense of the burning of Servetus, Beza argued that heresy could be suppressed by force—if applied by proper, legal authorities. In fact, he went further, and said that *local authorities could defy even higher national authorities on religious grounds.*

ॐ

Francis II died in 1560 and the Crown of France passed to his younger brother Charles IX. The young king's mother, Catherine de Médicis, ruled as Regent. Francis II's widow, Mary Stuart, decided to return to Scotland to claim her crown.[15]

Shortly afterward a massacre of Huguenots by the Duke of Guise and his brother the Cardinal of Lorraine aroused the Prince of Conde and Admiral Coligny to arms, and France became embroiled in the first of several internal religious civil wars that pitted two million Huguenots against 20 million Catholics.

The Catholics were led by de Guise and the Archbishop who—with the secret help of Catholic Spain—hoped to wrest the Crown from the

---

14. It was their sister, Mary of Lorraine, who had died defeated in Scotland.
15. See Otto Scott, *James I* (Vallecito, CA: Ross House Books, 1988).

Queen Mother and Charles IX. The Huguenots fought against persecution and for religious rights. Philip II of Spain wrote to his sister-in-
law Elizabeth in England that, "Religion is being used as a cloak for
anarchy and revolution."

Catherine de Médicis feared both sides, and believed that either one,
victorious, would unseat her. Elizabeth, advised by Cecil and with an eye
to her faithful core, sent funds to help the Huguenots.

The first French civil war ended in 1563, with a crushing defeat of the
Huguenots at Dreux, where they signed a peace Calvin thought
humiliating. Mutual toleration remained, but neither Calvinists nor
Catholics could accept an answer that seemed so divisive, so untraditional,
so deeply opposed by both theologians and statesmen.

ಎ

Similar pressures rent the Netherlands. The Northern Provinces
turned toward Lutheranism and Calvinism, despite savage penalties.
Philip II, although also Duke of Burgundy, was steeped in the traditions
of Spain, where national unity and religion were indissolubly welded.
The diversities of the Provinces were, to his eye, simultaneously heretical, treasonable and unreasonable.

Although his father had allowed the Netherlands nobles to rule via a
Council of State, Philip put his half-sister the Duchess of Parma, and a
Council of Three in authority. They were told to repress Protestantism
and to reorganize the Church in the Netherlands along more efficient—
i.e. Spanish—lines. That worsened an already unstable situation.

ಎ

A France dominated by the Guises meant a France able to assist Mary
Stuart in Scotland. At a time when England still harbored an ardent
Catholic minority, that was a real danger. Most of the magistrates and
all the clergy were Catholic. Calvinists were dominant only in London
and England's south, their ranks swollen by refugees from the Conti-
nent.

Although a minority in numbers, Calvinists were a majority in spirit.
In 1563 an English translation of John Foxe's *Book of Martyrs* appeared
to ignite the Reformers with indignation for at least a century.

Its depiction of the Calvinist martyrs under Bloody Mary can still stir indignation but it also crystallized ideas expressed in the second year of Elizabeth's reign (1560) by Aylmer, who wrote in *An Harborow for Faithful and True Subjects* that England abounded in all good things, and God and the angels fought on her side against all her enemies.

> God is English. For you fight not only in the quarrel of your country, but also and chiefly in defense of His true religion and of His dear son Christ. [England says to her children:] "God hath brought to me the greatest and excellentest treasure that He hath for your comfort and all the worlds. He that would out of my womb should come the servant of Christ John Wyclif, who begat Huss, who begat Luther, who begat the truth."[16]

Foxe's *Book of Martyrs* seethed with similar sentiments, and sold 10,000 copies "despite its size and expense" before the end of the century; enough for every parish church in the country. It gave, said one observer, "a complete rationale for all the characteristic features of Elizabethan England: the Queen herself, a national church . . . the spread of printing, education, and the use of the vernacular as the language of culture and science."

Foxe argued that the English were divinely appointed to safeguard true religion. But such warfare, he said, was waged not by rulers alone but by all classes of the chosen race. He cited from English history to claim that one essential test of a people's fidelity to God was their willingness to rebel when rulers were misled by corrupt advisors. . . ." Religion was thus a leveller of classes, indeed, of the sexes; all should be united in the national work of God."[17]

In Scotland, Mary Stuart's Catholic advisors had other ideas. Beautiful and learned, the former Queen of France created a small Renaissance court which drew the Scots nobility, whose eyes were fixed upon the Crown Matrimonial, which exceeded all other prizes. She hoped to sever the connections between the Scots Calvinists and Elizabeth; to unite her realm and then attract English Catholics.

She charmed George Buchanan, Scotland's great poet (and a Calvinist convert) but John Knox remained unmoved. He saw, he said, "a

---

16. Johnson, *op. cit.,* pp. 176, 177.
17. Ibid., p. 177.

proud mind, a crafty wit and an obdurate heart."

ᘔ᙮

In 1563 Elizabeth's theologians emerged with England's new creed. It stressed predestination, justification by faith, Calvin's definition of the Eucharist as a spiritual rather than a physical communion with Christ. Mass was abolished, but the clergy was instructed to wear white surplices in reading the service and copes in administering the Eucharist. Communion was to be in two forms of bread and wine received kneeling. Confirmation and ordination were retained as rites but not viewed as sacraments; confession was encouraged only in the face of death. Many Catholic prayers were retained. Thirty-nine Articles embodying the new creed were made obligatory on all the clergy of England.

In other words, a theological muddle—but a muddle that had behind it the authority and power of the State, monitored and enforced by a Court of High Commission, created for the purpose. The Vatican, which had, like the Catholics of England, rejoiced at the defeat of the Huguenots in France, was outraged.

The Pope issued a Brief, saying that the proposal to join Catholics and Calvinists in the Common Prayer was schismatic, and forbade the attendance of English Catholics at the new English service. Government agents entered existing churches to remove images and destroy them. Crucifixes were forbidden.

Resistance flared. "There has been enough words," said Sir Francis Knollys, a minister of the Crown, "it were time to draw the sword." A Test Act, mandating an oath of allegiance to the Queen and a renunciation of the temporal power of the Pope was demanded from all officeholders, lay or spiritual—except peers. This placed the entire infrastructure of Government in the hands of the Queen. The Crown applied this Test carefully against the laity, but more rigorously against the clergy, and the High Commission, with the Archbishop of Canterbury at its head, was instructed to be thorough. It was a time when the clergy's power and influence were too strong to be lightly treated.

ᘔ᙮

In Calvin's time physicians killed more than they helped, and suffering was unrelieved. Although Calvin's output, like that of Luther and others, was prodigious, life spans were short and illnesses calamitous.

In 1564 Calvin was only 55, but the Fifties were considered old age. Charles V had died, racked with pain, at 58; Henry VIII died a rotting hulk at 56; Francis I, famed for his energy in youth, was spent at 55. Even Luther, a physical marvel, died ancient at 63.

Calvin's condition makes painful reading. He had gout, the stone, piles and hemorrhages; could not ride a horse, suffered from tuberculosis, had to be carried first on a chair and then on a litter. Even lying in bed was painful; food was distasteful and he complained that "the taste of wine is bitter." No wonder he began to pray for death.

People appeared to say good-bye. The Syndic appeared with 25 crowns which he refused, saying he would not accept pay when he was not working. Between visits he dictated letters; in April 1564, he made his will. "There was," said one biographer, "not much to leave."

Toward the end he reviewed his life. "I am quite different from other sick people," he said. "When they come near their end, their senses fail and they become delirious . . . but it seems as if God wants me to concentrate all my inward senses."

His last words were reminders of his experience in Geneva.

> I have lived here amid continual strifes. I have been saluted in derision of an evening before my door with forty or fifty arquebus shots. Just imagine how that frightened a poor scholar, timid as I am, and as I confess I have always been. . . . They set dogs at my heels, calling out "Wretch! Wretch!" and they snapped at my gown and my legs . . . and what is more, all that I have done is worth nothing.

Then he rallied and gave instruction regarding his Catechism and discipline, and begged them to keep what he had systemized. He remained lucid to the end. He watched Death appear and knew when it bent down and touched him at eight in the morning of May 27, 1564.

So died the man who gave the Evangelical movement its theology; whose principles were those of Augustine and Luther and whom Warfield considered the creator of the Protestant church and its freedoms. No Christian leader has ever been so often condemned by so many. And the usual grounds for condemnation are the execution of Servetus and the doctrine of predestination.

Yet Servetus was only one of tens of thousands who went to their deaths in Calvin's time, and none of their judges ever received the denunciations heaped upon Calvin—who had no civil authority, and was not a judge in Geneva. Men of the twentieth century, who have witnessed without moving a finger the arbitrary murders of tens of millions have no ground upon which to stand and judge John Calvin.

What is widely misunderstood is that Calvin did not give first place to predestination, but to the Grace of God. "Where the Romanists placed the Church," said Warfield later, "Calvin set the Deity." To argue that God does not constitute Providence is, to a Christian, to argue from an impossible position.

Perhaps, however, it is precisely that argument that set so many teeth on edge. Calvin made clear what all men fear: that God cannot be escaped. In that lies the secret of Calvin's continuing unpopularity and even hatred among the enemies of Christendom—and in his survival among the Godly.

Genevans put his body on display but the processions grew so long they began to fear they would be accused of creating a saint. They stopped the processions, and buried him on Sunday, May 28, in the common cemetery, without a tombstone, as he had requested. Time would prove that he would not need one.

Chapter Eight

ELIZABETH AND MARY STUART

———— ❧ ————

The daughter of debate that discord aye doth sow.

— Elizabeth I

Calvin's death ended the pioneer period of the Reformation. Notable figures appeared later, but the foundations were laid, the theology erected and the Calvinist structure completed, except for a tower added by the incomparable John Knox.

The "Reformation Parliament" of 1560 had worked with John Knox to mandate a Calvinistic Scotland. But the Reformers did not plan on Mary Stuart. As Queen she refused her assent to the new order, and Scotland remained legally Catholic. Catholic priests still held their benefices; half the nobility remained loyal to the Vatican, and John Hamilton, a kin of the royal Stuarts, remained the Catholic Primate.

Mary Stuart did not announce her position, but she held Mass in the castle. That led to several meetings with John Knox, whose arguments met with an indignant response. Romantic writers have repeatedly portrayed these as encounters between a tolerant and beautiful Queen and an old bigot. But sympathy more properly belongs to the lined, diminutive Knox, whose authority consisted of only his faith, intellect and courage, and not with the six foot, imperious Queen at a time of absolute monarchy.

Scotland was a divided nation, which could not long endure in the sixteenth century. The 19 year old Queen, advised by the Guises in France, Philip II in Spain and the Vatican, seemed in a strong position, for she was heir to England's throne if Elizabeth died.

Her chief appointments were Lord James Stuart, 26, (the Earl of Murray), her illegitimate half-brother and William Maitland of

Lethington. Maitland wanted to unite England and Scotland—an old goal shared in London: the snag was over which nation would rule the two.

Meanwhile cousinly letters passed between Elizabeth and Mary Stuart that created an officially neutral climate between the two realms. Murray and Maitland ruled while Mary held dances, masques and conversations inside Holyrood Castle.

Beyond the political rewards of her position, Mary had an aristocratic disdain for the Spartan Scots Reformers and their "severe manners." She overlooked the fact that Calvinism was interlinked with learning; that Knox with his advanced education[1]—was in that respect no exception.

Some historians also glide past the fact that the Scots were familiar with events in the Netherlands: where people were being tortured, beheaded, hanged, drowned, burned and buried alive by the Vatican's heavy hand; where they had recently witnessed burnings at the behest of Catholic prelates at home, and had known of the horrible executions under Bloody Mary in nearby England. The Scots had every reason to fear that their own Queen would, if she could, renew fearful persecutions.

๖ะ

The question of who would marry the Queens of Scotland and England obsessed both realms and much of Europe. Rumors appeared that Mary Stuart would marry Don Carlos, the son of Philip II of Spain.[2] Knox preached a withering sermon saying that "an infidel—and all Papists are infidels" would "banish Jesus Christ from this realm."

That led to another summons from the Queen, another confrontation and another famous exchange. In effect, Knox argued that the Queen could not impose Catholicism upon Scotland. Each time he pressed the argument he increased Calvinist ranks.

In 1563 a Reform crowd protested a Mass in the royal chapel, and frightened away the priests. The Queen ordered two Calvinists, leaders of the mob, to go on trial for invading her premises. Knox ordered his followers to attend the trial; the Queen decided that was treason. Knox

---

1. He was a lawyer and at one time a Papal knight.
2. Before it became known that Carlos was insane.

was ordered to stand trial. He dutifully appeared, but his supporters crowded the Council chamber. He defended himself so well he was acquitted.

？❧

If Elizabeth married a Catholic prince, the Calvinists would erupt. If she married a Calvinist the Catholics might rebel. In Scotland, Mary Stuart had a similar problem. If she married a Catholic the Scots Calvinists would combine with England which might invade again. In such an event France would send another army to assist her. Civil war is a high price to pay for a decision.

Mary Stuart thought to strengthen her position by asking Elizabeth to name her heir to England's throne. But the Queen of England, surrounded by deadly plots, was not to be lured into such danger. "I am not so foolish," she said tartly, "as to hang a winding sheet before my eyes."

But she did allow Henry Stuart (Lord Darnley) to go to Scotland.[3] Lord Darnley is today only recalled for his associations; his actual name is barely remembered. He is usually called Lord Darnley, even after he became King Henry of Scotland. When he went to Scotland, Elizabeth called him "the long lad" for he was well over six feet; an unusual height in his time. He was important because he was next in line for England's throne—after Mary Stuart. His family obeyed the new English worship, but its Catholic sympathies were well-known.

By marrying Lord Darnley, Mary Stuart hoped to unite the Catholics of England and Scotland. This transparent design infuriated Elizabeth and even alienated the Earl of Murray. The marriage was seen as an open challenge to the Calvinists. The Earl of Murray and other Calvinist nobles awakened from their illusion that Mary Stuart was a helpless female, and tried to raise a rebellion, but Mary Stuart was ready for them.

Personally leading a Catholic army, she drove Murray and his close companions across the border. Philip II, who had frowned at Mary Stuart's initial policy of Toleration as well as her French connections, was enthusiastic. "She is," he said, "the one gate through which Religion

---

3. Government permission was then needed to travel; we today live under similar rules.

can be restored in England. All the rest are closed."

Elizabeth raged, plotted assassination, threatened to send an army to Scotland and blamed Cecil—as usual. As usual, he counseled patience. England watched Mary Stuart's efforts, but saw no need to move until more immediate threats appeared.

&

Mary Stuart's neat plan did not last long. Her young husband proved dissolute, arrogant and jealous. He alienated the Queen's Council and accused the Queen of adultery with her private secretary, David Rizzio.

When the Queen became pregnant he named Rizzio, and gossip spread. Years later Henry IV of France said that James I, Mary's child, must be "the modern Solomon [because] his father was the harpist David."

Lord Darnley[4] (now King Henry) then foolishly joined in the murder of Rizzio on March 9, 1566.

June 15, 1566, Mary Stuart delivered a son: James Charles Stuart. The news shook Elizabeth. "The Queen of Scots is lighter of a fair son," she said bitterly, "and I am but a barren stock." (The fine-boned Elizabeth suffered, as had her half-sister Mary Tudor, from amenorrhea [absence of menstruation].)

With a male heir, Mary Stuart's position soared. Her Ambassador in England wrote, "Your friends are so increased that many whole shires are ready to revolt, and their captains named by election of the nobility."

An alarmed Commons, dominated by Calvinists, nagged Elizabeth to marry. She promised she would, then forbade any further discussion of the topic. But for a few month's Elizabeth's crown—and the future of Calvinism in both Scotland and England—trembled. Then Mary Stuart, already sinful, slid into evil.

&

Mary Stuart could not forgive her husband for his suspicions—and his loose tongue. She turned to the swashbuckling Earl of Bothwell, who himself had designs on the Crown Matrimonial. His hopes soared when

---

4. He had contracted syphilis. See: Scott, *op. cit.,* passim.

Mary Stuart descended to a liaison. Knox, outraged, openly called her a whore.

In October 1567 Bothwell arranged, with the Queen's assistance, the assassination of King Henry. Mary Stuart first coaxed Henry to Edinburgh, and lulled his suspicions. Then the small house where the syphilitic was placed shook under a charge of gelignite.[5] People rushed to discover the structure in ruins and King Henry's corpse lying beside it.

꙳

The Scottish court claimed the murder was committed by the Queen's half-brother, the Earl of Murray. But the claim was quickly drenched by a flood of evidence that pointed to Bothwell—and to the Queen.

Elizabeth wrote that, "Men say that instead of seizing the murderers, you are looking through your fingers while they escape; that you will not punish those who have done you so great a service."

To allay suspicion the Scots Queen had Bothwell stand a mock trial, at which he was acquitted. The Scots Parliament, bowing to the combination of the Queen and Bothwell, gave him Dunbar Castle— and distributed a variety of lands and benefices to other nobles associated with him. He obtained a divorce of his own—and word spread that he soon would marry the Queen.

This news disgusted both Catholic and Protestant circles. Knox protested that such a marriage would be unlawful in the eyes of God, and was again hauled before the Queen's Council. There he confronted the fierce Bothwell, whom he charged with adultery, complicity in murder and rape—and walked away.

Bothwell married the Queen in a Reform ceremony conducted by the Bishop of Orkney in mid-May, 1567. That Mary Stuart consented to such a ceremony made her a lost soul in Catholic eyes. The Catholic clergy of Scotland grew aloof; the Calvinistic clergy, now convinced she had helped murder her husband, called for her to be deposed, and the people turned savagely against her.

---

5. The forerunner of dynamite.

If that were all, the tale would hardly be worth recalling. What lifts the case of Mary Stuart aloft for centuries to regard was what John Knox saw in it, and forced others to see as well.

Knox demanded that the Queen stand trial for murder and adultery, both listed as capital crimes in the Bible, with no exceptions for worldly rank. His argument convinced other Calvinist ministers—and their congregations.

That alarmed Elizabeth. She believed a monarch was not only above the law, *but was the law.* The idea that subjects could put a monarch on trial brought horrid memories of the fate of her mother, Anne Boleyn. She sent word that England would invade and punish anyone who harmed Mary Stuart. The response was chilling: if a single English soldier crossed the border, Mary Stuart's white throat would be slit.

Meanwhile Mary Stuart was forced to abdicate. A scattering of Calvinist nobles conducted a makeshift coronation of the infant James. At its conclusion Knox, from the pulpit, described how the boy Joash had been anointed and crowned while the Queen Athaliah cried treason from her palace. He read aloud the ancient story of how the nobles had proceeded from the coronation of Joash to kill Athaliah, to tear down the temples of Baal and to restore the rule of the prophets in the land.

Despite this Biblical precedent, Knox did not call for rebellion; he called instead for the trial of Mary Stuart.

Mary Stuart, however, escaped and found refuge with the Hamiltons. Within a week a force of 6,000 Catholics gathered to protect her. Confronted by disciplined Protestants under Murray (who had returned to become Regent), Mary's army melted. She fled Scotland altogether and after a wild ride of three nights—crossed into England to throw herself upon the mercy of her cousin and rival, Elizabeth.

♦

Elizabeth had no time to enjoy the fall of her rival; Europe was boiling. The Duke of Alva had fallen upon the Calvinist rebels of the Netherlands with fire and sword: a great revolt was underway against Philip II. Its effects spread into France, where the uneasy truce maintained by Catherine de Médicis between Calvinists and Catholics collapsed. The Duke of Guise and the Prince of Conde reorganized for another, larger war.

English Calvinists wanted intervention against Alva, but his initial successes cheered English Catholics. Meanwhile Mary Stuart's presence in England created uneasiness. If Elizabeth allowed Mary safe passage to France, her relatives the Guises would invade Scotland to replace her on her throne. To allow her to circulate about in England was to enable her to organize both English and Scottish Catholics and to threaten Elizabeth's throne.

Cecil advised that Mary Stuart be held tight. Elizabeth was privately horrified that a monarch could be confined; she feared the precedent. She suggested that Murray forget the charges against Mary, that Mary should return to Scotland and allow Murray to rule in her name. Both refused.

The war in the Netherlands, the looming civil war in France and the divisions in Scotland exacerbated arguments inside England. Elizabeth did not dare to declare war against mighty Spain on behalf of Calvinists. But she did lend money to the Calvinists of France and encouraged the harassment of Spanish shipping.

The Duke of Norfolk plotted with Spain to rally the northern English earls. Discovered, Norfolk landed in the Tower, and Mary Stuart to the custody of Lord Huntington. Then news arrived that a Papal Bull excommunicating Elizabeth was on its way. That inspired a Catholic uprising led by the Earls of Northumberland and Westmoreland in late 1569:

> The Bible and Prayer-book were torn to pieces, and Mass said once more at the altar of Durham Cathedral, before the Earls pushed on to Doncaster with an army that soon swelled to thousands of men.[6]

Their intention was to rescue Mary Stuart and make her Queen of England first, and then to return to her the throne of Scotland. The Queen of the Scots was hastily transferred to tighter custody at Coventry, the northern Earls wavered and their armies melted.

The end of the squall did not lessen Elizabeth's outrage: she ordered summary executions and that "the bodies not be removed, but remain

---

6. John Richard Green, *op. cit.*, vol. 2, p. 52.

till they fell to pieces where they hung." Six hundred so executed were left hanging across the English landscape as grim proofs of her fear and her rage.

꙳

The suppression of Catholic rebellion in England was matched by the rise of Calvinism in Scotland after Mary Stuart's flight. The Earl of Murray acting as Regent, summoned the Scots Parliament and installed Calvinism as the triumphant religion of the land. Knox had the deep pleasure of seeing all the Reforms of 1560 finally and legally ratified, and Papal authority in Scotland outlawed.

In the custom of the times, new laws barred Catholics from holding office. Future rulers of Scotland were to swear to uphold the Reformed doctrine. The revenues and properties of the old Church were to be transferred to the new Kirk.

The Scots Parliament then crossed an important meridian by charging the nation's Queen and the Earl of Bothwell with conspiracy to murder King Henry. The Scots, following the reasoning and instructions of John Knox, had assumed the right to put a ruling prince on trial.

꙳

Mary Stuart in elegant confinement, surrounded by her priests and ladies in waiting, blamed the Earl of Murray for driving her out of Scotland—and keeping her from her throne. Froude, the nineteenth-century English historian, believes that she inspired a plot against Murray that drew the Catholic Hamiltons into murder. One well-aimed shot, in early February 1570, was enough. Murray was 35, and his death plunged Scotland into civil war.

Murray's death left Knox vulnerable; he was continually harassed. Nor was that all. In late 1570 Knox suffered a stroke that deprived him, for a time, of speech. He recovered his tongue but not his strength, and had to be helped to the pulpit. Young James Melville watched him struggle and begin to speak in a low tone. After a time, Melville, said later, Knox's voice rose, and he seemed to grow so vigorous that Melville feared he would pound the pulpit to pieces and, literally, fly away.

But shadows gathered. The Scottish nobility lusted for the riches of the Church. Murray had prevented open looting, but Murray was gone. The Kirk wanted revenues to operate schools and hospitals, and the nobles did not dare to seize all benefices outright. But they transferred bishoprics and other livings to ministers, who made over the major part of such incomes to nobles.

Knox watched this dilution of his great victory without surprise: he had always known the grasping needs of an impoverished people. But Knox himself had "not made merchandise of the Word of God."

That Scotland became Calvinist was his great victory. The Earl of Murray was dead, but his successors were sworn to uphold the Reform; the infant King James VI—a Calvinist Prince—had been installed, and his education was entrusted to George Buchanan, Scotland's greatest poet and most famous (next to Knox) convert.

Knox had humbled a reigning monarch, toppled a government, ousted a hierarchy, converted a people and could regard, toward the close of his life, a landscape transformed by his efforts and the teaching of his mentor, Calvin.

Knox's triumph in Scotland was crucial to both England, Scotland and the British colonial world to come. But it was, at the time, a limited, local victory in a backward European outpost, of importance mainly because it severed a tentacle of France and lessened a threat to the Reformation of England.

꿏

In the larger world, the great struggle in 1571 was not between Christians but between Christianity and Islam: between the European West and the Turks.

The struggle was marked by intense savagery; its outcome was in doubt for generations. As usual, the West was weakened by internal arguments. Francis I of France had, in his efforts against Charles V, allied Catholic France with the Mohammedan Sultans, a policy continued under his successors. Nothing could more plainly indicate the squalid moral depths of the Renaissance.

In 1571 the Turks reigned from Hungary and the Ukraine to Egypt and Persia, from close to Gibraltar to the Caspian Sea. Constantinople under the Turks was more populous than ten of Spain's largest cities combined. Turks harassed Christian shipping from their north African

Protectorates, and clawed at the coasts of Italy and Spain from bases in Algiers, Tripoli, Bizerte, Tunis.

Venice, the great maritime Republic, was weakened by successive Turkish onslaughts. By 1561 the Turks exacted tribute from the Venetian colony of Ragusa and pillaged the coast of Adriatic Italy as far as Trieste. Then Cyprus fell, in 1571.

The Papacy, under Pius V, was inflamed. Pius, who spurned rich vestments, was forceful, severe and austere. He banned nepotism and favoritism, herded Roman prostitutes into ghettos, cleansed the convents and expelled the Jews from the Papal States. He thought Christianity's greatest enemies were heretics and Turks. But his efforts to persuade Spain to help Venice failed—until Cyprus.

The Turks won Cyprus only after a long siege. Five thousand Greek and Italian Christians resisted so fiercely that they managed to kill 30,000 attackers. Surrender came only after supplies were exhausted and they faced plague. Decent terms were extended by General Mustapha Pasha.

The Christians emerged to full military honors. Ships were available for their departure. On the last day, the Christian general Bragadino visited Mustapha Pasha to say good-bye, and the Turk casually asked what guarantees he had that his ships would be returned. "The word of a Venetian gentleman," said Bragadino.

The Turk, however, demanded a hostage. When that was refused, he ordered all the Venetians executed. The rest of the garrison was shipped to Constantinople as slaves. Bragadino, however, received special treatment. His nose and ears were sliced off, his teeth broken, he was whipped daily, forced to do humiliating labor and kiss the ground trodden by Mustapha Pasha. On August 17, 1571, he was flayed alive in the central square of the city as he recited the *Miserere mei.* His skin was stuffed with straw, dangled from the topmast of Mustapha's flagship and flaunted along the Cypriot coast.

That enraged Philip II of Spain, who turned his formidable power toward the creation of a joint naval force.

The Turks, alerted, placed the bulk of their fleet near Corfu. That island was laid waste; only its great fortress remained intact. The Turkish fleet then fanned out, to await the allies.

The Christians were led by Don John of Austria, the illegitimate half-brother of Philip II, who managed to coordinate all his allies and to resolve all their objections, qualms and resentments.

The two fleets met at sunrise in the Bay of Lepanto on October 7, 1571. The Christians had 208 warships; the Turks had 230. Unlike many naval battles, this was not one of movement; the Christian forces moved to grapple with the enemy. Spanish infantry flowed onto Turkish vessels, and hand-to-hand combat prevailed, almost as on land.

In the end the Turks were badly beaten. Their losses were estimated at over 30,000 dead and wounded, and 15,000 taken prisoner. The Christian forces lost 10 galleys, 8,000 men killed and 21,000 wounded. The sea around them ran red; Cervantes, who lost the use of his left hand in the engagement, thought it was the greatest and yet most frightful event of all time.

⁊ꙮ

Many historians disagree. No territory changed hands; the Christians did not follow up their victory with an assault on Constantinople[7] and the Turks remained a menace for centuries.

That retroactive judgment misses the mark. Lepanto was a great turn in human history. It ended a fear of the Turks that had spread, like a noxious gas, throughout Europe. "The Christian victory," wrote the Marxist historian Braudel (no great friend of Christianity)[8] "halted progress toward a future which promised to be very bleak indeed."

Lepanto was a miracle of deliverance: bought in blood and money, planned by Philip II, led by Don John. It is no wonder that church bells tolled and prayers of thanks were recited by millions, or that the faithful saw the Hand of God in the event. Only God could have saved so divided a Europe against so determined and savage, rich and heavily armed a foe. After Lepanto the Turk remained a menace, but not an unconquerable one.

⁊ꙮ

But 1572 was not over. An uneasy truce prevailed in France. In reality

---

7. They were prevented by bad weather.
8. Fernand Braudel, *op. cit.,* p. 1103.

more than a truce: a trend toward reconciliation and even tolerance. The impulsive Charles IX, anxious for peace, granted the Calvinists freedom of worship except in Paris, eligibility to public office, and the right to rule four cities for ten years. His mother Catherine de Médicis offered her daughter, the Princess Marguerite, to Henry Bourbon of Navarre, the titular head of the Calvinists. Never had any power come so close to tolerance.

The prospect filled the new Pope, Gregory XIII, with horror, and deeply disturbed Philip II. One saw heresy enthroned; the other feared a unified, invigorated France.

❧

The true political leader of the French Calvinists was the aristocratic Admiral Coligny. The King was frail and vacillating, and had long been under—and long chafed under—the influence of his mother, Catherine de Médicis.

In less than a year Coligny became commander of the fleet, was made a member of the King's Council and chaired it during the king's absences. The King began to call him "mon père" and to consult him on policy matters.

This alarmed Catherine de Médicis and angered Henry the Duke of Anjou, the King's dissolute younger brother. News reached Madrid that the Calvinist Coligny supported a war by a unified France against Spain. With the Netherlands in rebellion, Coligny argued, a strong push could bring Flanders into French hands.

Catherine saw Coligny a King by proxy; the Duke of Guise—head of the Spanish-funded Catholic League—watched his own influence diminish.

In June 1572 Henry of Navarre arrived in Paris with 800 Calvinists and Coligny. Four thousand more Calvinists arrived while the Catholic clergy of Paris foamed with rage. Nevertheless the wedding took place on August 18, 1572, without Papal dispensation.

The city seethed. On August 22, two shots from a window ripped a finger off Coligny as he walked the street, and ravaged one arm to the elbow. The King was deeply angered, and Catherine de Médicis said the Court was indignant. The Guise faction remained silent.

Behind the scenes, however, Catherine and Anjou, and the Duke of

Guise, continued to pressure Charles IX. They complained that Coligny pressed war despite the financial straits of the kingdom. Contrary pressures were placed on Coligny: his men advised him to kill the Guise leaders, but he resisted.

Later the Duke of Anjou, when he became Henry III, admitted that he and the Duke of Guise agreed that the Calvinist leaders had to be assassinated. The next step was for Catherine, Anjou and Guise to convince Charles IX that the Calvinists plotted rebellion. Thirty thousand, they said, planned to seize and carry him off. His choice was between his mother's life and the lives of six Calvinists.

He asked why a trial could not be held, and was told it was too late. His mother said she would leave France and return to Italy. Finally the thin 23 year old King of France shouted, "By the death of God, since you choose to kill the Admiral, I consent! But then you must kill all the Huguenots in France, so that not one shall be left to reproach me . . . Kill them all! Kill them all!"

೭ꣲ

The massacre began at three in the morning on St. Bartholomew's Day, August 24, 1572. Men behind Henry of Guise burst into Coligny's lodgings, murdered the guards, ran the Admiral through and threw him out the window. He landed dead at Guise's feet. Guise spat on the body, turned and told his men to spread the word that the King commanded the death of all Huguenots.

Horrible slaughter, rare even in war, followed. Coligny's head was cut off and sent to the Louvre; the genitals and hands offered for sale, the cadaver hung by its heels. "The populace rejoiced at the freedom given its suppressed impulses to strike, to inflict pain and to kill."[9]

Nearly five thousand Calvinists were murdered in Paris alone; husbands and wives took advantage of the disorder to get rid of unwanted mates, merchants were killed by competitors, a jealous professor urged the death of the philosopher Ramus, homes were sacked on the pretext of searching for Huguenots; mothers, children and even embryos were not spared.

---

9. Durant, *op. cit.*, vol. 7, p. 351.

Inside the palace the King of Navarre and the Prince of Conde were spared, but their men were murdered, one by one. "As I write," reported the Spanish ambassador, "they are killing them all, they are stripping them naked . . . sparing not even the children. Blessed be God!"

❧

Provincial cities followed suit. Lyon, Dijon, Tours, Troyes, Rouen, Toulouse and others indulged in similar orgies. In the end, which took several days, the total was over 30,000—an immense number in those days.

When the news reached the Cardinal of Lorraine (a Guise) at Rome, he gave the bearer a thousand crowns. Pope Gregory XIII and his Cardinals attended a solemn high Mass of thanksgiving. A special medal was struck and Vasari was commissioned to paint the massacre over the words *Pontifex Colbni necent probat* (the Pope approves the killing of Coligny).

❧

The effects of the massacre spread wide. The Calvinists launched a fourth rebellion two months later that lasted nearly a year. At its conclusion Charles IX signed another treaty guaranteeing freedom of worship. In political terms, it seemed as though St. Bartholomew's Day had ended nothing, decided nothing.

But the St. Bartholomew's Day massacre permanently altered Protestant thinking. The Calvinists turned from acceptance of the "divine right" of kings, to questioning the entire institution of monarchy. Francois Hotman, who fled to Geneva during the disorder, published *Franco-Gallia,* citing the election of kings during the Middle Ages, and saying that "To the people alone belongs the right to elect and depose kings."

The effect in England was especially deep. The Catholic cause, already strained by Bloody Mary, was now indelibly identified with bestial persecutions.

Chapter Nine

KNOX, MARY STUART
AND ELIZABETH

———— ?❧ ————

And, behold, this day I am go-
ing the way of all the earth.
— Joshua

In mid-November 1572, two friends dropped in on John Knox. He insisted that they stay for dinner, and joined them at the table. He ordered a hogshead (a barrel) of wine in his cellar to be pierced, "and with a hilarity which he delighted to indulge among his friends, desired Archibald Steward to send for some of it as long as it lasted, for he would not tarry till it was all drunk."[1]

That was his last convivial evening. For the next nine days he remained in bed, while visitors trooped through his house. Once he awoke from a troubled sleep, and described a dream in which Satan had appeared to him in the form of a lion, to remind him of his sins, and to tempt him to despair. Knox resisted, but,

> [n]ow he ... attacked me in another way; the cunning serpent has labored to persuade me that I have merited heaven and eternal blessedness, by the faithful discharge of my ministry. But blessed be God who has enabled me to beat down and quench this fiery dart, by suggesting to me such passages of Scripture as these: What hast thou that thou hast not received? By the grace of God I am what I am; Not I, but the grace of God in me. Being thus vanquished, he left me.

Like Calvin, Knox did not presume to anticipate God's judgment.

———————————

1. Thomas McCrie, *The Life of John Knox* (Edinburgh, Scotland: Nelson and Sons, 1905), p. 260.

When he was interred in St. Giles' churchyard in Edinburgh, the Regent[2] said simply, "There lies he, who never feared the face of man." He was 66.

ॐ

John Knox's vision of the Devil reflected not only his piety but also a Devil-conscious period; one often misunderstood.

Although acceptance of the reality of Satan[3] and witches is part of the Bible, "[W]itch trials were generally unknown until the final centuries of the Middle Ages."[4] Through most of the Middle Ages churchmen generally thought that "anyone who believed women went flying about at night was a victim of superstition."

This attitude slowly changed after the twelfth century, and accelerated after the plague in the fourteenth century, which some thought was Satan's victory. Dissent, death and the devil became intertwined in the popular mind. By 1450 the idea of evil actions by humans allied with the Devil gained general acceptance. In 1486, at the peak of the Italian Renaissance, *Malleus Maleficarum*[5] appeared, authored by two Dominicans who had, over local resistance, presided over witch trials and executions in southern Germany.

That book became a witch-hunter's manual for the next two centuries. The *Malleus* was an instance of rare ecumenical agreement between Catholics and Protestants. Although after 1521 it sank for nearly two generations, from 1576 onward it became the scholarly guide in a tide of witch trials.

Recent scholars have discovered that the history of witch trials has been tainted by forgeries. Norman Cohn and Richard Kieckhefer, working independently, have discovered forged accounts of large-scale witch hunts in fourteenth-century France and Italy.[6]

Contrary to myth, it was not Christianity but the revived Paganism

2. The Earl of Morton.
3. Known in Hebrew as The Adversary.
4. Dr. Joseph Klaits, *Servants of Satan: The Age of the Witch Hunts* (Bloomington, IN: Indiana University Press, 1985), p. 19.
5. The Witch's Hammer.
6. Klait, *op. cit.,* p. 48.

of the Renaissance and the political drive for centralized authority that created a climate favorable to witch trials and executions after 1560.

The Renaissance exhumed ancient works which led to the revival of ritual, ceremonial and experimental magic. Astrology came into vogue and "magic became a serious, learned undertaking" that anticipated the role of science today. A belief emerged in "white" magic or its counterpart, "black" magic, especially among the Renaissance Humanists.

These worshippers of antiquity spread the theories of Plato, the Kabbala[7], and Hermetic writings.[8] Neoplatonism was taught by the Florentines Marcilio Ficino and Giovanni Pico della Mirandola, among others. They believed that Man is both the slave and master of cosmic forces; that through study one could unlock the secrets of the universe, control nature and foresee the future.

The Reformers, however, led a great spiritual rebirth. They reminded people that "deterministic" magic, such as astrology, was not only forbidden in the Bible, but by its theory that human life is controlled by the stars, conflicted with Christianity.

A time of reawakened faith, therefore, placed the Humanists in an invidious position. They argued that white, or "natural" magic was beneficial, while black magic was criminal. This fine distinction might have sunk the Humanists had it not been for the political situation.

The turbulence of the Reformation (and the Counter-Reformation) led rulers and governments to stress conformity and unity. This led to new, written legal forms that expanded monarchial rule over aristocrats, municipalities and centuries-old feudal traditions. The king's law took precedence over traditional loyalties to clan, region or customs.

A new judicial system and criminal law procedures, drawn from examples of the Italian city-states, combined old Roman law and Church canon law in new secular courts. In these tribunals the prosecutors were also judges. The accused faced secret charges from anonymous sources.[9]

Even more ominous was the new, expanded use of "judicial" torture.

---

7. Jewish mystical writings.
8. Platonic second-century writings.
9. Much like our Congressional Nomination Hearings and Governmental Clearances.

This practice, applied by the medieval Church only in rare cases of heresy, became a regular, ongoing element in criminal procedure. Torture was especially favored in witch trials, and seldom failed to elicit confessions. Introduced in Germany by Charles V, it was allowed "whenever there was probable cause to believe the defendant guilty," and was known, in honor of the Emperor, as the Carolina.

Because witchcraft was both loathed and feared, the new rules facilitated its extirpation, and also served to suppress local irregularities and customs that, as in using a huge painted phallus for Maypole dancing, offended religious sensibilities.

These and other examples carried courts and the Crown into areas once reserved for the Church, though the Church was never in charge of crime but only of sin. When the definitions of crime were expanded, as in the case of witches and warlocks, the Humanists moved—as jurists—into regions once dominated by the clergy.

Witch finders were especially numerous in Germany, where half of all the witch trials were held. These were conducted "by learned doctors trained in Roman law and inquisitorial procedure," appointed by the rulers, who bypassed local authorities. "Authority," wrote Klaits, "was placed in the hands of professional jurists whose university backgrounds had exposed them to the values of spiritual reform characteristic of learned elites."

In this manner the Humanists spread from the universities into the legal system as officials of a new type, separate from the churches, and steadily—almost, it seemed, inexorably—more influential in the machinery of Government. Humanism became inextricably entwined with politics and Humanists began to displace the clergy from positions of political power.

One remarkable aspect of the Humanist entry into the Judiciary is not only the cruelty created during the witch craze, but that the Humanists later escaped onus for witch trials by blaming Christianity through repeated misrepresentations and even forgeries that circulate to this day.

꒒

Despite the St. Bartholomew's Day Massacre and the misgivings about monarchy that it evoked among scattered Protestant intellectuals, the "divine right" belief in kings continued to hold sway.

The Pope, after all, had claimed to be God's Regent on earth for centuries. From there to the claim of rulers to be divinely appointed in a world governed by God was a nearly inevitable sequence. If Luther had not drawn that conclusion, the Reformation may have had only a brief life, and Lutheranism might not have survived its earliest stages.

The switch from Pope to secular monarchs was not restricted to Protestant regions: the rulers of France, Spain, England and other realms were able to expand their authority over both the religious and secular sectors not simply through logic, but because people longed for stability—and because stability seemed possible only in unity. Hence, monarchs in Europe became as totalitarian as was possible.

The people, however, remained divided among Catholics and Protestants. In France this led to a continuing series of religious-cum-political wars; in the Low Countries to rebellion against Catholic Spain.

Under Elizabeth the Church of England remained divided throughout her reign. Catholics, forced by law to attend mandated services, remained Catholic in their outlook and attitudes. Puritans who wanted the purified services of Calvin were not allayed by the official Calvinism of the English Church, because the Crown ruled the Church, selected the Bishops and approved every ecclesiastical detail.

The English clergy did not enjoy the "defense of its own altars" that Calvin had so arduously won in Geneva. This led to "a paralysis of Church machinery and Church action and to an infinite amount of petty tyranny. When the Bishop of Ely was reluctant to obey an order to give the gardens of Ely House to Christopher Hatton, the Queen screamed at him by letter 'by God I will unfrock you.'"

The English clergymen, however, feared that only Elizabeth stood between them and a return to Catholic reaction, with all its burnings and Inquisitions. Those who protested against the Vatican were in one boat, with the Crown steering.

ຂ❧

Mary Stuart, as heir, imperiled Elizabeth. One assassin could bring down the government, and no authority would exist until Mary ascended the throne. That prospect threatened civil war, especially because Mary made no secret of her intention—with (if necessary) the help of Spain, the Vatican and Catholic France—to reestablish Catholicism in England. Her threat was underlined by the Papal Bull which excommunicated Elizabeth and gave all Catholics a religious basis for defiance.

Elizabeth regarded religion as politics wearing an ecclesiastical mask. "The Queen feels no great interest in any faith or sect, but that she has no other thought than to keep herself on the throne in whatever ways she can, and by means of that religion which may best serve her purpose."

In 1580 the first Jesuits—Fathers Edmund Campion and Robert Persons—arrived. An army bearing Papal banners invaded Ireland. In 1583 a Catholic plot was uncovered that involved great English noblemen, the Duke of Guise in France, Philip II of Spain and Mary Stuart. Lists of Catholic priests in various hiding places throughout England and a Spanish plan for invasion were discovered.

Troops and special agents made widespread arrests. Before it slackened an estimated 11,000 people were under some form of confinement, the Spanish ambassador was expelled, and England and Spain were close to war.

All this occurred shortly after Elizabeth had made John Whitgift the Archbishop of Canterbury. They were ideally suited. The Queen considered dissent unlawful, and Whitgift was a dedicated authoritarian, intent upon enforcing obedience to whatever the Queen approved.

Both considered Calvinists as traitors only slightly less dangerous than Catholics; neither could understand Puritan demands that the liturgy of the Church of England be "purified."[10]

Elizabeth put Whitgift in charge of a Commission that had such sweeping powers that it became known as the High Commission. Its authority stretched to include "heretical opinions, seditious writings, contempts, conspiracies, false rumors and slanderous words." Whitgift set about examining all printers and books, ministers and "disordered persons." In company with "a dozen bishops and a score of deans, archdeacon and civil lawyers," he intended to examine, punish, fine or imprison any and all dissent from the Queen's Church.

To refuse a High Commission summons meant fines or jail; a

---

10. It was these demands that spawned the term Purists.

summons included an oath to answer all questions truthfully. Refusal to swear meant a guilty verdict. A Puritan or a Catholic could not deny his opposition to Church of England practices without denying his faith, but a truthful answer meant conviction and punishment. The accused were not allowed lawyers. Whitgift headed, with Elizabeth's support, an English Inquisition.

When Cecil protested, Whitgift replied sharply that he served as the Queen chose; if Cecil had objections, let him voice them to the sovereign.

Cecil retreated but arguments arose that the Magna Carta protected Englishmen from being forced to testify against themselves. This impressed many, for during the time of Bloody Mary (as Foxe's *Book of Martyrs* attests), Calvinists had refused to answer questions about their beliefs—and had gone to the stake to defend their right to remain silent.

Undeterred, Whitgift proceeded to "deprive" a number of ministers of their posts, and to "suspend" more. When the High Commission used spies, the Puritans turned, in 1584, toward Parliament for help. Their chances seemed good because the Spanish threat loomed. Their hope was to create a national Synod a la Geneva, to govern the church and enforce uniformity of ceremony and doctrine. Some in Parliament tried to make this movement official, but failed. But Parliament did allow Petitions asking the Lords to approve a withdrawal of the High Commission's practices against the Reform, on grounds that ancient rights were being denied.

Elizabeth decided that Commons was out of hand. She had the Speaker roused from a sickbed to tell the House that the Queen forbade any further interference or discussion. Shortly afterward the Parliament of 1584–85 ended, leaving Whitgift triumphant.

But sparks had been kindled. Men began to talk about the Magna Carta and English liberties. Some even wondered whether their beloved sovereign should be obeyed in all respects, particularly when she trod on the House of Commons.

ॐ

But the Puritan minority was small and fragmented. It included Presbyterians who wanted a Knoxian eminence, Reform Episcopalians who wanted liturgical austerity, and Separatists who wanted churches independent of the Government. All these groups appeared fanatical to more worldly circles. This was especially true among the Anglican clergy, which had repeatedly changed its position in response to every royal command since the reign of Henry VIII.

Elizabeth called Archbishop Whitgift her "little black husband" and was so pleased with his feverish support of her unlimited power that she gave the High Commission permission to use torture. Despite this dread power, underground pamphlets and even books sprouted, denouncing the oppression of the Reform. Parliament again tried to intervene, and was again reprimanded by the Queen.

༄

When another plot involving Mary Stuart was discovered, Cecil moved to end the threat forever. Some believed his fears exaggerated, because the English did not like Mary's French-Scottish heritage, her reputation as an adulteress and a murderer. But relations with Spain were growing strained, and Mary Stuart represented Spain, the vast Catholic international and the Guises of France.

She was placed on trial at Fotheringay Castle before the English nobility, but an irresolute Elizabeth stopped the proceedings. Parliament intervened and found Mary Stuart guilty of treason (although England was not her country), and sentenced her to death. Elizabeth, pressured, signed the death warrant on February 7, 1587, saying as she did so, "There are more seemly ways for a Queen to die."

But she was realist enough to know that nobody could relieve her of responsibility, and she ordered that the sentence be carried out "in the Hall, rather than the green or the courtyard." Elizabeth wanted as little public stir as possible.

Cecil wasted no time. Mary Stuart's head was chopped off on February 12, 1587. That left the youthful James VI of Scotland, the son of Mary Stuart and Darnley, de facto heir to the throne of England.

༄

Mary's execution convulsed the Catholic world. French Catholics denounced Henry III for being too lenient with Huguenots. But Henry was privately pleased, because Mary Stuart had been related to the Duke and Cardinal de Guise, whose Catholic League was funded by Spain, and which contended with the Crown for control of France.

No event, however, could make Henry III popular. A transvestite with a whitened face, surrounded by giggling but deadly "mignons," seized by alternate frenzies of public dissipation and private remorse, the King of France was universally despised.

Yet the mystique of monarchy was so strong that even this weakling could ignore and cheat his Estates Generale, hold stately audiences, issue edicts and speak and write as if his realm were united.

Pope Sixtus V hoped that Mary Stuart's death would spur the King of Spain into action against England. Unlike his predecessors, Sixtus believed Philip II was essential to a restored Christian unity. It was English gold and support, in Scotland and the Netherlands, that bolstered the anti-Vatican cause.

In Spain, Philip II bent over his papers in the Escurial: his Church-Palace. Alone, he scanned reports from Castile and Aragon, Portugal, Naples, Sicily, Milan, Belgium and Mexico, Peru and Brazil, Goa in India and Sofala in Africa. All asked for directives only Philip could provide.

By 1587 Philip was well along in his plan to invade England. His conquest of Portugal had expanded Spain's Atlantic power. His admirals thought that a formidable armada could successfully assail England. In the Netherlands the Duke of Parma, an able and successful commander, proposed to ship a land army across the English Channel on barges.[11]

ع‌‌ﻭ

On the eve of the Armada, the High Commission unearthed a nest of Separatists in London.[12] Both Presbyterians and Puritans believed in one state and one church, but Separatists saw religion as a private relationship between Man and God. They did not believe that secular power could make a church or maintain the Gospel; they considered a church a Covenant between the elect and God: they did not believe it could encompass an entire nation.

---

11. An approach that later occurred to Napoleon and Hitler.
12. Leonard Levy, *Origins of the Fifth Amendment* (Oxford University Press, 1971).

The Separatists—like the Catholics, Presbyterians and Anglicans—also believed that it was the duty of the Government to suppress any beliefs contrary to the true religion, because heresy meant that souls could be damned. That was a firm sixteenth-century position, considered self-evident and incontrovertible by all factions.[13]

"From the viewpoint of a national establishment of religion, committed to a single form of worship under one sovereign," wrote Leonard Levy later, "Separatism represented a threat that could not be ignored." The Separatists denied Elizabeth's right to dictate their religion.

When the High Commission arrested Henry Barrow, "a gentleman lawyer" and a Separatist leader, Barrow wanted to know why he was arrested. Archbishop Whitgift said he'd be told after he took the oath.

Barrow said he'd be willing to swear, on certain conditions. When Whitgift reached for a Bible, Barrow said he would not swear *ex officio* by the Bible, whether his hand was on it or off it. Nor would he swear if his hand was on the table, or holding the Archbishop's hand. He would swear with his hand held toward Heaven, but *only if not commanded.* Then he said he would not swear at all, until he was told why he was arrested.

Whitgift, giving way, said Barrow was arrested for not attending church, for rejecting its services, and for being disobedient to the Queen. Barrow said, "These are reports. When you produce your evidence, I will answer."

The Archbishop assured him that his answers under oath would be believed, for oaths then were to God, and carried an awesome significance. He asked again if Barrow would swear. "I will know to what I swear before I swear," Barrow replied.

Whitgift said, "First swear, and then if anything be unlawfully demanded, you shall not answer."

"I have not learned to so swear," Barrow said. "I will first know and consider the matter before I take an oath."

Whitgift then abandoned the oath, and tried direct questioning. He asked Barrow when he had last attended church, and Barrow replied that it was none of the Archbishop's business. The Archbishop of Canter-

---

13. This seems difficult for later generations to grasp. Inability to respect a different viewpoint is a feature of contemporary intolerance.

bury then lost his temper and called Barrow various names. When he recovered he asked Barrow if he had ever spoken against the Church of England.

"When you produce your witness I will answer," Barrow said. "But upon your oath I will believe you," the Archbishop pleaded, and Barrow said, "I will not accuse myself."

He was sent to prison and then, eight days later, recalled. He later described the Commission as a group of "well-fed priests," similar to those who governed the Vatican. Questioned again, he again refused to swear, and won his point. Whitgift showed Barrow the charges against him, based on a pamphlet (which Barrow had actually written), that described the Church of England in withering terms. Barrow then refused to answer all questions.

Whitgift exploded. "Where is his keeper?" he shouted. "You shall not prattle here. Away with him! Clap him up close, close, let no man come at him; I will make him tell another tale, yet I have done with him."

ᏋᏇ

A full scale hunt for Separatists ensued. Barrow, sending a Pastoral Letter from prison, said he was imprisoned for refusing to take an oath to testify against himself.

His defiance emboldened others. Puritan objections to the oath spread; so did arrests and penalties. The Commission said the innocent need not fear oaths or the truth, and that witnesses were in no danger of life or limb. Meanwhile, roundups led to torture, torture led to confessions and names, names led to more arrests.

By 1588 the Puritan movement was in retreat and disarray; its ministers were driven underground. Influential Puritans at Court were thinned by death, and more compliant men began to appear. Archbishop Whitgift was assisted by a new Lord Chancellor who created a network of "spies, informers and pursuivants." Mails were intercepted and files of known or suspected Presbyterians, Separatists, Puritans or Catholics were created. Elizabeth, who had never really believed that the Reform protected her, prepared to meet the Spanish onslaught, while Whitgift and the Commission made it plain that dissent was treason.

ᏋᏇ

In 1588 when the Armada sailed toward England, France was torn by civil war. Three armies were in the field. One was led by King Henry III, one by Henry, Duke of Guise and one by Henry of Navarre, a Protestant.

Henry of Navarre, the hope of the Huguenots, was assisted by a force led by Count Dohna. Henry III and his forces, encountered by Dohna, were being defeated when Guise arrived to turn the tide. Henry III fled in disgrace.

Guise, who headed the Madrid-funded Catholic League, emerged with heightened prestige and popularity. Even the Queen Mother Catherine de Médicis turned to him. Henry III, thwarted and humiliated, finally dismissed men who had governed in his name since he was born, but who had always secretly obeyed his mother.

The King then convened the Estates Generale, the rarely summoned Parliament of France, in order to raise money. The members cheered his speeches but refused his requests. The King blamed Guise.

Guise, however, was also displeased. Without new taxes France could not raise new armies. Meanwhile both the King and the Duke were together in Blois Castle, where the Duke's men outnumbered the King's. As Grand Master, the Duke could enter any room—even the King's—with armed men at his heels.

჻

The failure of the Spanish Armada is well-known. A tempest wrecked Spanish plans, Parma's barges could not be used, and English tactics created confusion. Most of the Armada actually withdrew unscathed, but was buffeted by continuing storms and encountered nearly final disaster off the coast of Ireland while trying to get home.

Mattingly's history of the event[14] dispels the myth that the Irish murdered Spaniards washed onto their shores for their clothes, arms and jewelry, and "the legend, persistent in the west, that black eyes and hair, aquiline profiles and swarthy cheeks show the blood of Spaniards who came ashore . . . and stayed." In reality short, stocky, swarthy types have been known in Ireland, Scotland, Wales and England forever. Knox was one.

---

14. Garrett Mattingly, *The Armada* (Boston, Mass: Houghton Mifflin, 1959).

The Irish sheltered the Spaniards and helped several hundred to escape to Scotland. Many Spaniards did, however, drown on the Irish coast; others were hunted down and murdered by English soldiers under orders from the Lord Deputy, Sir William Fitzwilliam.

ॐ

When news arrived that the Armada had failed, the King of France made new arrangements. On the morning of December 23, 1588, Guise was roused from bed by a summons to an early Council.

Inside the Council chamber he found only his brother the Cardinal de Guise and the Archbishop of Lyon. Guise pushed into the King's apartment and some King's men fell in behind him. Guise whirled about, was struck by a dagger and his arms were seized. As the thrusts rained, he swayed and fell. In his clothes they found a letter to Madrid he had started, that said, "To keep up the civil war in France will cost 700,000 *livres* a month."

Guise can be counted among the Armada dead. So should his brother, the Cardinal de Guise, who died on the pikes of the King's guard. Other King's men arrested Catholic Leaguers in the Estates session.

Henry III did not savor his victory long. The Catholics of France were outraged—and they were the overwhelming majority. Paris rose against him as did other influential cities. Henry was forced to accept the support of the Protestant Henry of Navarre. But "when the dagger of the assassin Jacques Clement ended Henry III's life (seven months later), he was able to hand on his inheritance intact."[15]

ॐ

Some historians said the defeat of the Armada marked the decline of Spain and the rise of England, but that did not occur for generations later. At the time it marked the start of the Spanish Navy, and despite the efforts of Drake and Hawkins, more treasure flowed from the New World to Spain for the balance of Elizabeth's reign than ever before.

In fact, the war between England and Spain itself dragged on for another fifteen years, until after James I succeeded Elizabeth—and

---

15. Ibid., p. 385.

neither side could claim a victory.

Had the Armada succeeded, however, today's world would be different. Spain led the Catholic cause; England the Protestant in 1588. All Europe feared Spain in war: it had rolled over all adversaries—even the Turk. Catholic nations hoped Spain would crush Protestantism by striking down its most distant and fortified center. The Reformers hoped, in mirror-image fashion, to see Catholic Spain founder on English rocks, and the Vatican cause to collapse.

In an age of all or nothing, both sides hoped for all. When the Armada failed, the mystique of Spanish invincibility vanished. In that loss, Spain lost more than England. The right of smaller nations to maintain their own versions of unity was verified, and the national state, as opposed to medieval supranational unity, was strengthened.

The English understandably made a national legend of the event. But it remains one of the great ironies of Christian history that Spain, which had saved all Christendom at Lepanto, suffered a defeat in the English Channel that ensured the future division of Christendom.

Legend has it that England lived in bliss under "Good Queen Bess" after the defeat of the Armada; the reality was different. Elizabeth, who kept a crucifix and candles in her bedroom and privately clung to many Catholic attitudes (such as, for instance, clerical celibacy), set out to end religious dissent—no matter how muted.

In 1590 she wrote her heir, James VI in Scotland, that it was best to "stop the mouths" of those who claimed religious differences while weakening the throne. One result was the Puritans and Presbyterians, although still critical of Elizabeth's compromises, grew relatively silent. The Crown then targeted Separatists such as Barrow (who ended on the gallows) and others.

This led James Morice, a Puritan lawyer and Member of Parliament to introduce two Bills. One was against "unlawful Oaths, Inquisitions and Subscriptions." The other was based on the idea that to deprive a minister of his spiritual office was to "dispossess him of his freehold and to deny his liberty."

His Bills were significant, because they shifted opposition to the High Commission from religious to political grounds. After debate, Commons tabled both bills, but Elizabeth was outraged because they had been introduced.

Elizabeth's instincts in this instance were, as usual, accurate. To separate religion from the power of the Government meant reducing the sweep of Government—a reduction Elizabeth could not accept. In that she reflected her time, for it was an absolutist period. Calvinism in such hands was more severe than its founder, who lived in a republic where authority was diffused.

In a time when religion was as real as the weather, English Calvinism regarded the realm as a new Israel; preachers were prophets and the Devil was real.[16]

This belief was reflected in wills, was taught in the universities, distinguished the Church of England. Nicholas Tyacke, a modern British scholar who studied sermons, wills and literature of the period spanning the reigns of Elizabeth I and her successor James I, also described the rise of Calvinism in England as coincident with its international position.

At first, he said "the existence of . . . English Catholics lent credence to the identification of Protestants with the elect. Later, when relations with Spain deteriorated, Calvinism was transferable to the international plane and Englishmen were . . . portrayed as chosen by God to do battle for the true religion."[17] But as the Spanish threat faded, national unity eased, and the way opened for undermining Calvinism from within.

It first took the form of Arminians *avant la lettre* at Cambridge University in the 1590s, and came to flash point in 1595, when William Barrett, the college chaplain, publicly challenged the doctrine of predestination. Archbishop Whitgift intervened, and after consultations approved rulings known as the Lambeth Articles. They were unequivocally Calvinist. They displeased Elizabeth, but not enough to move her into action.

"This," said historian Tyacke, "may surprise those brought up to regard Calvinists and Puritans as one and the same. Such an identification, however, witnesses to the posthumous success of the Arminians in

16. Nicholas Tyacke, *Anti-Calvinists: The Rise of English Arminianism c. 1590–1640* (Oxford: Clarendon Press, 1987), Introduction.

17. Ibid., p. 4.

blackening the reputation of their Calvinist opponents; until the 1620s, Puritan, as a technical term, was usually employed to describe those members of the English Church who wanted further Protestant reforms in liturgy and organization."[18]

In 1601, during Elizabeth's last Parliament, laws against resisting the Church of England—either silently or aloud, in retreat or in the open— remained savage. "The High Commission reigned over religion as a branch of the English Judicial system: a sort of Star Chamber for Ecclesiastical Causes."[19] In that climate Puritans, Calvinists, Separatists, Presbyterians and other "dissenters" in England remained as officially stifled as Roman Catholics.

੭ੴ

The closing decade of Elizabeth's long reign[20] was marked by floods of change. "Stress on the divine nature of the printed word, the imperative command to disseminate the truth as rapidly and widely as possible, brought the medieval values and defenses tumbling down. Religion was the Word—the Bible—and the Word was English. The national language swept Latin away as the vernacular of doctrine and piety, and rapidly began to invade other spheres hitherto protected from public intrusion by the dead culture."[21]

"Extraordinary energies were released," observed historian Paul Johnson, "most strikingly in the theater, but in every other branch of literature and knowledge." The government issued or inspired pamphlets explaining and defending its actions and criticizing its enemies at home and abroad; Cecil himself wrote some. Puttenham's *Arte of English Poesie* promoted the abandonment of Latin. England, in these outpourings, was hailed as Eden. "A third of Shakespeare's plays concentrated on historical themes; some on Roman history reconstructed for English purposes, ten on English history alone."[22]

Discoveries in navigation were printed in English, and Johnson

---

18. Ibid., pp. 7, 8.
19. Levy, *op. cit.,* p. 203.
20. 45 years.
21. Johnson, *op. cit.,* p. 178.
22. Ibid.

credits Walter Raleigh's monumental *History of the World*—in English—with breaking new ground. These changes ushered in instrument-makers and special craftsmen who laid the basis for the industrial revolution.

These were all changes attendant upon the Reformation of religion and were true in Amsterdam and other parts of northern Europe. But England, safe from invasion, was the more concentrated arena. Its changes were relatively free from interruptions. The religious fervors of the Reformation[23] lifted the faith and the people from the decadence of the Renaissance into higher levels.

If the bright side shone brighter, however, the dark side was darker. England under Elizabeth lived under religious suppression, and the High Commission ruled every vagrant thought a crime. There were also temporal problems. The Crown income failed to match inflation, and the Queen had to regularly sell Crown lands. "At her death the monarchy was much weaker financially than at her accession."[24]

That made the Crown more dependent upon Parliament, and on several occasions Elizabeth had to become conciliatory. Bad weather, bad harvests, the expensive war with Spain were further handicaps. Huge transfers of property, launched and continued after the time of Henry VIII also altered society. Elizabeth kept the nobility small and in check; gentry had appeared in the countryside and in Parliament.

While dying on April 23, 1603, she was asked about her successor. When James VI of Scotland was mentioned, she clasped her hands around her forehead in the shape of a crown. She was 69.

---

23. Though many English writers like Johnson cannot admit it.
24. Ibid., p. 180.

Chapter Ten

SHAMIE JAMIE

———— ❧ ————

By blood a king, at heart a clown.

— Tennyson

James was the first of four Stuart kings. He was succeeded by Charles I, Charles II, and James II. All damaged the realm and the faith.

James was prematurely crowned in the wake of his mother's flight from Scotland. John Knox hoped that James would become a leader of international Calvinism, and chose George Buchanan, Scotland's leading poet and a Calvinist convert, as the boy-king's tutor.

That was ironic. Knox, after all, had forced Mary Stuart out of Scotland; Buchanan published the evidence against her in the murder of James' father. To expect the mature James to forgive men so deeply involved in the ruin of his mother was unrealistic.

Nevertheless, James received an excellent education in Greek, Latin, French, Spanish and Italian, Calvinism and the Bible. It was not, however, an education in the new tides of his time, for Buchanan was elderly and Knox died when James was only six.

Buchanan died when James was 14. By then the old tutor (who had taught James Knox's position that Kings are under the law), knew that the boy was bright, devious, cowardly—and hated Calvinism.

To prevent James from committing the mischief he foresaw, Buchanan published *Laws for the King of Scotland*.[1] *Laws* argued that all political power resides in the people, that society is a network of social contracts limiting both rules and ruled. Majorities should prevail, he argued, and if ruling minorities or kings resist, they should be overthrown. The

———

1. *De Jure Regni Apud Scotos.*

argument for tyrannicide poured from underground presses in Edinburgh and London, spread throughout Europe, fueled Calvinist sermons everywhere and was required reading at St. Andrews for years.

Buchanan preceded Hobbes by a full century and Rousseau by two and lit imaginations everywhere. The mature James banned the book and contended against it all his life.

When James' deviance first appeared, however, it was neither religious nor openly political but sexual. At 14, the year of Buchanan's death, the young King began a homosexual relationship with a cousin from France. That cousin, the Sieur d'Aubigny, was a French agent intent upon restoring the "Auld Alliance" linking France and Scotland.

That effort to swing Scotland back to the Catholic orbit failed when Presbyterian nobles chased d'Aubigny out of the land.[2] James then settled down to wait.

At 20 James was silent when his mother was executed in England, and continued sending letters to Elizabeth begging for money. Some have called this baseness shrewd.

~

Although Scotland was far behind England culturally, some of the learning that lifted the Elizabethan age in England trickled to the Scottish Lowlands. James, anxious to shine as a scholar,[3] attached his name to books created by his staff.[4] His first took predictable issue with Buchanan, and was titled *Basilikon Doron.* In it James cited the Old Testament to argue the divine right of kings. He also claimed to write a tome on demonology, a subject in which he considered himself an expert, having presided for a decade over a horrid series of witch trials and burnings.[5]

His presumed authorship gave James a lasting reputation for erudition.

Melville, head of the Kirk, accurately analyzed the *Basilikon* as

---

2. Scott, *op. cit.,* pp. 116–117.
3. A term then synonymous with "intellectual" today.
4. He anticipated the patrons of modern ghostwriters.
5. Eight thousand witches were burned in Scotland between 1500 and 1600; in the last 10 years James led the hunt.

"Anglican, Episcopal and Catholic." He saw that James wanted a national church replete with bishops, vestments, incense and obedience to a Pope-King.

Later James found all that in England, despite its national claim to be a Protestant power.

࠹

At first the English welcomed their new King. He was 37, an experienced monarch, Protestant, married and with two sons. Not only would England have its first mature male on the throne since 1547, but the succession appeared clear for decades to come. That alone was a relief after the long years of Elizabeth's ambiguities.

A new age appeared to be on the horizon, with new men at the top. Henry of Navarre, Huguenot victor of the French civil wars, calmed religious strife in France by the Treaty of Nantes, which granted French Calvinists freedom to worship and political rights in certain areas. But he did that only after switching to Catholicism. "Paris," he said, "is worth a Mass."

The mighty Philip II, who had tried to conquer England through marriage and war, died and was succeeded by Philip III, a weakling manipulated by advisors.

But the greatest changes were underway in the Low Countries,[6] where dissension had been boiling within Calvinist ranks for a decade or more, in the wake of Arminius.

Jacob Harmensen (Jacobus Arminius in Latin) was born in 1560, and was 43 (and still embroiled in controversies) when James VI and I inherited the Crown of England. A brilliant student, he learned some grim realities about the world when most of his family were murdered by Spanish troops in the sacking of Oudewater. In 1576 he studied at the new Calvinist University of Leyden, founded in part as a reward for the town's heroism in successfully maintaining a long siege in the War of Independence.

After Leyden, Arminius studied with Beza in Geneva, and from there was called to become a minister in Amsterdam, the greatest commercial center of the United Provinces. Ordained in 1588, the year of the

6. Holland in the Dutch language.

Armada, by 1591 he publicly denied the irresistibility of God's Grace, and preached that some could reject it and go to Hell if they chose. The corollary was, of course, that others could choose to accept God's Grace, and could go to Heaven.

It seems in retrospect almost inevitable that someone would bring forward this argument, for the Calvinist position on the inevitability and mystery of God's Grace was too stark for rebellious hearts to obey.

It is no mystery why Arminius' teaching became popular: he said what most people wanted to hear. And he was especially effective, because he persisted in claiming that he was not contradicting Calvin or Calvinism.

He was a master of the soft answer as well as the soft doctrine. Despite growing Calvinist opposition, he was made a Doctor of Divinity at the University of Leyden,[7] and given a chair in 1603, the year James VI became King of England as well as Scotland.

৽৶

Arminianism, as it became known, created enormous political troubles within the United Provinces. By 1603 it had become increasingly obvious that the North would not regain the southern Provinces. The United Provinces were swollen with Calvinist refugees from the Catholic South, and the North's stout resistance of Spain had been inspired and strengthened by orthodox Calvinism from the start.

The Low Countries were a tangle of council-directed towns, cities and provinces that had resisted centralized government since earliest times. That tradition of independence inclined the people toward the Reformation in the first instance and led to impatience with religious control by Reformers in the second.

This impeded Dutch Calvinists in their efforts to have church synods bring Arminius to book for his views; every effort in that direction led to disputes about jurisdiction between Church and Civil authorities. These deadlocks left Arminius free to gain adherents, and the United Provinces, once firmly bound against Spain, began to divide into increasingly hostile religious factions that soon seeped into the political.[8]

---

7. Arminius was the first to be so honored by the University.
8. No means of separating these have ever been discovered, despite widespread American illusions.

❧

Cecil, Lord Burghley, died before Elizabeth. His place as first minister was taken by his second son, Sir Robert Cecil, a clever, diligent hunchback, who became the Earl of Salisbury.

He found the new King grasping, difficult and peculiar. James spoke rapidly but thickly, using odd, unexpected terms. His wit was the jeering style known today as homosexual camp. His language was so filthy English historians still refuse to cite it. He hid from the people, wore padded clothing (against assassins), drank incessantly and openly panted after handsome young men.

Before Elizabeth's death, James had courted both Catholics and Puritans. Since his Queen was a Catholic convert, Catholics had special hopes. But after Elizabeth's death, when asked about his promises to that minority, James said, "Na, na, we'll not need the Papists now." Catholicism did not worry him.

His major worry was Calvinism, the movement that had saved him from certain death in infancy at the hands of Bothwell. The Calvinists were, at first, unaware of this; James' reputation was as the Presbyterian King of Scotland.

They learned differently at the Hampton Court Conference convened in mid-January, 1604. It was, essentially, a Conference to reconcile differences between the Church of England and the numerous "dissenters" who had appeared, and which Elizabeth's severities had failed to extirpate.

The official Churchmen at the Conference were represented by the Archbishop Whitgift and his chosen prelates. As a group they wanted, as always, more authority. Their ecclesiastical position was for more Sacraments and an expanded liturgy. The Calvinists inside the Church regarded only the Lord's Supper and Baptism as Sacraments—the orthodox Calvinist position.

Persons unlearned in theology are apt to dismiss such disputes as trivial. But as Max Weber later said, "Every consistent doctrine of predestined grace inevitably implies a radical and ultimate devaluation of all magical, sacramental and institutional distribution of grace, in view of God's sovereign will."[9]

---

9. Tyacke, *op. cit.*, p. 10.

In other words, Calvinists left Salvation to God; the Bishops said the clergy could arrange Salvation through suitable church forms. That was essentially a Catholic/Arminian position.

King James listened and smiled at the Bishops, because they acknowledged the king as divinely appointed and, as the Head of the Church, the final arbiter in all ecclesiastical matters. (James' favorite aphorism was No Bishops, No King.) That was the Lutheran position. Because this Arminianism *avant la lettre,* as it later became known, claimed to be traditionally Protestant, the Bishops preserved the semantics of the Reformation while weakening its positions.

Timid Puritan dissent was presented at the Conference by four Calvinist ministers toward whom the King was rude and threatening. The Separatists, illegal and in exile, sent a Petition to the Conference. It was ignored.

A decision to create a new translation of the Bible was the most beneficial result of the Conference. The fact that this translation became known in the United States as the King James Version remains an unwitting but grotesque joke.[10]

The worst decision of the Conference—urged by Archbishop Whitgift and his chosen prelates—was to retain High Commission controls over the mind of England.

In effect, the new King, expected to introduce new views, had, instead, embraced Elizabeth's.

But England had changed. The Spanish threat had declined. Puritanism had increased, Separatism had risen and been driven underground, and the English had grown tired of tyranny. After Hampton Court even Archbishop Whitgift worried about Commons and country. He did not say that the King was over-persuaded, but he did say he hoped, citing his advanced age, not to live to see the new Parliament.

God granted that wish. Toward the end of February, 1604, Whitgift was on his deathbed. James visited, but the old man could only whisper, time and again, "Pro ecclesia Dei; pro ecclesia Dei." But he did not leave behind a church headed by God, but by James I.

---

10. This was the most powerful and effective translation in the history of Christendom.

Reports of the King's rough handling of Puritans influenced the Parliamentary elections. Puritans rallied to the polls. Extra seats had to be placed for James' first appearance.

It proved to be a shambles. He arrived to announce a Union between Scotland and England which "God hath in my person bestowed upon you." He called himself "the husband, and the whole isle . . . my lawful wife. I am the head and it is my body. I am the shepherd and it is my flock."

After these transparent blasphemies, James denounced Puritan dissenters and read aloud his proclamation to the Bishops, who had been ordered into a great Convocation to unify the doctrines of the Church of England.

The members heard nothing about the Huguenots of France, the Dutch rebels or the Calvinists of Geneva. They learned instead that James had "no desire" to prosecute Papists, that he was actually the "Prince of Peace" and that peace with Spain was imminent.

After he left leaning on the arm of a handsome young courtier, Commons huddled in shocked anger.

James' first Parliament set the tone for all its successors during his reign. Although he remained sequestered among his courtiers, the English learned about his homosexuality through his favorites. The English people have always despised that vice in their public men; James was no exception.

The vice and corruption of the Crown soured all its relations with Commons, which grew increasingly important. James shortsightedly dealt serious blows to the nobility by first selling "baronetcies" (or Little Baronies) for a set amount of money, and then selling the higher titles for larger sums.

James was learned, "but it was the antique learning of the medieval world . . . he was bitterly and vengefully disappointed when it failed to cut any ice with the exponents of the sophisticated new learning he found in England."[11]

---

11. Johnson, *op. cit.,* p. 184.

"His Majesty rather asked counsel of the time past than of the time to come," noted Bacon.

The King's most highly regarded companion, outside his homosexual bedmates, was the Spanish ambassador Count Gondomar, "who had a similar schoolman's background, and with whom the King muttered lengthily in Latin syllogisms."[12]

This infuriated the English, who had grown more xenophobic with each passing year. The King's foreignness was held against him because it led to the elevation of Scots nobles. Not any Scots nobles, but those with whom he had liaisons, or were from Catholic houses that had supported his mother Mary Stuart.

James also offended on deeper levels. Although Elizabeth approved of religious suppression, she did not assent to the censorship of works of learning, education or science, "Under James . . . it became increasingly difficult to get anything new (officially) published. Some of the central works of Raleigh, Bacon and Coke had to wait until the parliamentary insurrection of 1640. . . . James failed to stop Raleigh's *History of the World* which became, to his fury, a best-seller; but he confiscated many of Raleigh's manuscripts."[13]

Above all, James went against the English grain. Peace with Spain was hailed, but a Spanish marriage between the Prince of Wales and the Infanta that involved concessions to Catholics was deeply unpopular.

Yet James pursued this course to the ludicrous extent of allowing his favorite and bed-partner the Marquis of Buckingham[14] and the Prince to actually go to Madrid, presumably incognito, to plead for such a marriage in person.

A perfect rain of scandals appeared. The wife of favorite Robert Carr was convicted of murder by poison and merely exiled to the country (with her husband); Lord Audley was executed for "sodomy, unnatural adultery and incest." The Lord Treasurer and the Lord Chancellor (Bacon) were convicted of corruption; Judges were dismissed for decisions against the Government's wishes.

The King regarded the Church and its Bishops as his private estate

---

12. Ibid.
13. Ibid.
14. Later raised to a Dukedom.

and approved when they created regulations so stringent that no man with a qualm could remain. He had similar difficulty understanding the right of Parliament to conduct debates. Hearing of views with which he disagreed, he sent angry rejoinders and even made speeches in response. Throughout his entire reign, James was at odds with Parliament.

People began to look back to the time of Elizabeth with longing; it became, in retrospect, a Golden Age.[15]

Her accession day, November 17, was celebrated with increasing fervor; her last, moving speech to Parliament recalled and reprinted. Theatrical references, songs, recollections increased; an Elizabethan industry, remarkable and still alive, emerged.

ഇ

But James did not forget the Kirk of Scotland. James sent a favorite (Chancellor Dunbar) to rule in his stead. In 1606 Dunbar convened the Scots Parliament, which obediently declared the King head of Church as well as State—and restored Bishops. Melville and seven others were summoned to James in London. He announced his Supremacy; they pleaded for their Church on their knees—in vain.

A month later Melville was physically forced to kneel before the Archbishop of Canterbury. When the guards released him he rose, seized the ornate lawn sleeves of the Archbishop and shouted, "Romish rags—and part of the Mark of the Beast!"

Guards came running but his shouts could be heard in the corridor as he was led away to the Tower, where he was imprisoned for four years. After that, he was exiled—and never again saw Scotland.

ഇ

"The King," James said, "is above the law." He asserted that Kings were not only God's "lieutenants upon earth, and sit upon God's throne, but even by God himself are called Gods."

James relied on the Church of England to protect these claims, which reflected the politics of Spain, France and the Vatican. He did not understand that in England the common law competed against eccle-

15. And remains one for many.

siastical law, and had done so for centuries.

Sir Edward Coke, Chief Justice of the Court of Common Pleas, did not believe that the Courts of the Church should have greater power than the Common Courts of England. Therefore when an appeal from a High Commission ruling came before him, he decided that Parliament could review the High Commission's behavior.

Although cowardly and depraved, James I was not stupid. As a child of the Scots revolution, he knew what could happen to a monarch whose agents were overruled. In early 1609, Coke's habit of issuing "prohibitions" against High Commission rulings, fines and imprisonments led to a confrontation between the King, his Bishops, and the Chief Justice.

Coke cited the Magna Carta which, he said, gave the Courts of Common Law the right to provide justice "from the highest to the lowest."

James replied angrily that if he chose, he could dispense justice himself, because he "had reason and could judge." Coke said the King could reason, but didn't know the law. He also added that the King was "under God and the law."

At that James flew into a rage. The issue he thought buried forever, drilled into him by Buchanan, that had led his mother to death, had risen inside England and the citadels of his power.

Coke apologized; the Bishops soothed the monarch, the meeting ended, but nothing changed. The Court of Common Pleas continued to clip the High Commission; underground presses continued Puritan arguments and even irreligious men began to chafe at the presumption of a body legally charged with controlling their faith—and their minds.

This struggle has often been described in purely political terms. Yet the argument that the king is under the law was presented to the people of James' time by the Calvinist Buchanan and his associates. It was a religious argument that marked the difference between Calvinism and Arminianism and Lutheranism among others.

With so clear a heritage it is difficult to understand why so many refuse to credit the Calvinists with establishing their freedoms.

॰

In 1609 the United Provinces obtained a 12 years' truce in their struggle against Spain that was guaranteed by Henry IV of France and the Emperor Rudolf II of Germany. Arminius died in the same year, but his arguments continued to disrupt the Dutch.

While Arminius lived, his caution prevailed. But after he died his supporters began to openly confront orthodox Calvinists. In 1610 they published a Remonstrance addressed to the States General of the United Provinces.[16]

That challenge brought the issue of *resistible* Grace into the open, and raised the question of where ecclesiastical and civil authority divided. The United Provinces had neither Pope nor King, and clergy and congregations began to line up sides.

By 1615 the United Provinces were on the edge of civil war. The Church alone could not resolve the argument, so the politicians intervened. One was Prince Maurice of Nassau, military leader of the struggle against Spain. The other was Johann van Oldbarnevelt, an anti-Calvinist. The two had quarreled over the Twelve Years' Truce, which Oldbarnevelt had negotiated and which the Prince had opposed (for it abandoned the Southern Provinces to Catholicism and Spain).

In 1618 Nassau staged a successful military coup against Oldbarnevelt's supporters. A few months later a national synod of the Reformed Church was called to resolve the theological issues among Reformed groups. Swiss, German and English clergymen were invited, and the Synod of Dort was the most representative Reformation gathering ever held.

The necessity for such a Synod was rooted in the assumptions of the time, in which everyone (without exception) accepted the Biblical observation that a House (religiously) divided against itself cannot stand. Dort was expected to resolve the issues raised by Arminians vs. Calvinists—once and for all.

₹⋫

King James had, of course, closely followed the religious disputes in the United Provinces. Both Dutch Calvinists and Arminians had traveled to England.[17] One result, was to awaken the English clergy to Continental Calvinist tides.[18]

---

16. After that, Dutch Arminians were known as Remonstrants.
17. The two countries were allies.
18. One observer said, "From a deep sleep."

At the time, however, James' political instincts dominated his ecclesiastical beliefs (assuming he had any). Oldbarnevelt was anti-Calvinist and anti-English, and leaning toward Catholic France. Maurice of Nassau was Calvinist and leaned toward England.

Paris, aware that the French Calvinists (Huguenots) were against Arminianism, intervened to prevent French delegates from attending the Synod. But James sent four delegates. Three were royal chaplains; one was Bishop of Llandaff. All had instructions from George Abbott, Archbishop of Canterbury, a Calvinist, who believed that Dutch Arminians,

> . . . deny the true properties of God's election and the true manner of his grace, making that to be a cause of his forechoosing which is indeed a consequent, and placing our perseverance not in God's hands but our own, and so added unto it that a man who is truly faithful, or regenerate and sanctified (for it cometh to the same head), may fall from grace both "finally" and "totally". The King is marvelously inflamed against these graceless positions, and I acknowledge to you that so am I.

During the Dort Synod of 1619, the Remonstrants, or Arminians, were emphatically rejected. The English clergymen voted, together with the majority, to uphold Calvinist principles in their entirety, including the irresistible Grace of God and man's inability to determine God's Judgment.

The Dutch Arminians refused, however, to accept this verdict, and after the death of Oldbarnevelt, violence between the two groups continued for a number of years.

ॐ

Behind the scenes in England, however, Arminianism found an increasingly warm reception, especially inside the Church of England. "Dissenters from Calvinism came increasingly to be identified as a group, and they in turn felt obliged to seek out allies in defense of a common cause. Indeed the Synod of Dort was, to an extent, responsible for the creation of an Arminian party in England."[19]

---

19. Tyacke, *op. cit.*, p. 87.

The English Arminians found tacit allies among Humanists, especially at Oxford and Cambridge, and even among Catholics, who found
their Sacramental and sacerdotal approach congenial. One of the first
English Arminians was Lancelot Andrewes, Master of Pembroke College, Oxford, who became a popular preacher at James' Court, and his
Cambridge contemporary John Overall, Regius Professor of Divinity.
Andrewes later became Bishop of Winchester, and was joined in
eminence by his fellow Arminian Richard Niele, Bishop of Durham,
another favorite of King James.

The real turn in Arminian fortunes in England came, however, after
James began to seriously negotiate the marriage of his son Charles,
Prince of Wales, to the Infanta. During the peak of negotiations in
1623, James actually forbade all preaching on predestination except by
bishops or deans or in the universities. That was extraordinary; and as
unpopular as his courtship of deeply hated Catholic Spain.

There was a brief interruption in this trend when Buckingham and
the Prince returned from Spain in early October, 1623, breathing anti-
Spanish sentiments. They had promised the Spaniards everything (with
no intention of keeping their promises) but had grown to hate them.
Buckingham, angry at having made an international fool of himself,
harangued both King James and Parliament in favor of war with Spain.

While spurring the failing James to war, Buckingham, who now acted
as a virtual monarch, turned toward Catholic France and arranged a
betrothal between the Prince of Wales and Henrietta Maria, the
youngest daughter of Henry IV, sister of Louis XIII.

꩜

With King James failing and the new partnership of Prince Charles
and Buckingham creating policy, men's thoughts inevitably turned to
the shape of the future. Thus it was that sometime in November 1623,
while visiting London, Matthew Wren received an early morning
summons from his patron, Richard Niele, the Bishop of Winchester.
Upon arriving at the palace Wren was shown a room where Niele and
the Bishops Andrewes and Laud were waiting. The doors were locked,
and Niele, the influential leader of the Arminian faction inside the
Church of England,[20] told Wren the bishops "had been considering

---

20. And a personal favorite of King James.

'those things which we foresee and conceive will e're long come to pass'
. . . on how the Prince's heart stands to the Church of England, that
when God brings him to the crown we may know what to hope for.'"[21]

Wren was able to speak with more than passing knowledge of that,
because he was the Prince's chaplain, and had been in Spain with him.
More than that, he had been present when Prince Charles had to clarify
and defend his faith to the Spanish Catholic priests who sought to
convert him.

While the bishops listened closely, Wren told them that "for the
upholding of the doctrine and discipline, and the right estate of the
Church, I have more confidence in him than of his father. . . ."[22]

The importance of that small, private meeting, described by Wren
years later, is that it provided the Arminian leaders with a useful insight
into the thinking of the future King. Balked from control of the Church
under James, they "could anticipate such an event following the
accession of a new monarch more committed to their views, and prepare
to exploit the new situation to the full ."[23]

༨

Meanwhile the intellectual atmosphere had grown poisonous. In
1624 the Crown actually forbade the printing or importation of any
book dealing with religion, church government or affairs of State
without previous approval of the authorities.

In the midst of this repression, an immensely important book
appeared titled *A New Gagg for an Old Goose.* Issued with the King's
approval, it was authored by Richard Montague, a former Cambridge
scholar and one of the King's chaplains. Ostensibly written in answer to
a Catholic tract, *A New Gagg* "denied the creedal Calvinism of the
English Church, absolute predestination and unconditional persever-
ance" and said that such beliefs were only "private opinions."[24]

Montague's *Gagg* was a masterpiece of propaganda, for it linked
Calvinists and Puritans together, in what was to become a nearly

---

21. Tyacke: *op. cit.,* p. 113.
22. Ibid., p. 114.
23. Ibid.
24. Tyacke, *op. cit.,* p. 47.

indissoluble confusion. He then went on to describe "Puritanism and Popery as Scylla and Charybdis and said that the Church of England stood in the gap between them, which was also Laud's view."[25]

This created a furor. Calvinists charged Montague with Arminianism, which was certainly true. They were especially outraged by the identification of orthodox Calvinism as dissent, when it had been accepted as the official Protestant doctrine since the Synod of Dort, and had been the official doctrine of the Church of England since the time of Elizabeth.

That King James, who had sent the English delegates to Dort who had voted for the Calvinist position, should have approved of Montague's *Gagg* added to Calvinist fury. Calvinists, who were in the majority in Parliament and the gentry and who counted at least a third of the nobility in their ranks, were outraged to be told that they were no more than the small, despised Puritan faction. They were genuinely enraged to be termed "dissenters" in the Church in which they were the majority and whose creed they believed.

But Montague's argument and the King's approval were not mysterious to their contemporaries. Even average men understood that the victory of Free Will Arminianism would "establish a coercive and despotic government, a sacramental and priestly religion; while Predestination implied privilege of Parliament, liberty of person, Protestant ascendancy and the . . . doctrine of exclusive salvation."[26]

Many were deeply alarmed. Montague had raised specters that Dort had, presumably, buried.

ஒ

James, however, was too enfeebled to be confronted. Those who might do so were distracted by Buckingham and Prince Charles. This duo now appeared everywhere together, and made a strange pair. Buckingham did the talking; the Prince nodded agreement. It was, said one observer later, as if they were together one man, with Buckingham

---

25. Prestwich, ed., *International Calvinism, 1541–1715* (Oxford: Clarendon Press, 1986 [paper]), pp. 221, 222.

26. George Macaulay Trevelyan, *England Under the Stuarts* (London, England: Methuen and Co., 1924), p. 154.

being the voice.

They met secretly with the King's Privy Council—without the King's knowledge. When the counselors wanted to know the Spanish terms, Buckingham and Charles rushed out, ran to the King, and obtained an order keeping such details secret.

When Parliament convened in February 1624, James made his last appearance, and—for the first time—asked for cooperation. After the king was carried away Buckingham called for a Parliamentary meeting in the great Hall of the Palace. The new Duke was in charge.

Buckingham urged war, but Parliament only authorized money to repair the fleet, assist the Dutch, defend Ireland and strengthen national defenses. Talk of a Catholic marriage with France did not please the Members; they were against Catholicism on all levels and feared such a marriage would entail concessions to English Catholics. Both James and his heir promised that no concessions would be made; that if more money was needed Parliament would be reconvened.

The issue of Arminianism was not, however, ignored. The two most active Calvinists in the 1624 Parliament were John Pym and Thomas Wentworth. "His report from committee on 13 May 1624 was a conflation of the petition and accompanying doctrinal articles against Montague."[27] (He was to make more of this issue later.)

৵

As soon as Parliament recessed Buckingham bargained feverishly with Richelieu, promised money (the Crown did not have) to the Dutch Republic, to the King of Denmark, and entered into a joint military expedition with France to save the Palatinate for James' daughter Elizabeth and her husband from the forces of Spain.

A joint expedition was entrusted to Count Manfield, an adventurer with a record of military failures whose soldiers "lived off the land"— i.e., from plunder of civilians. France agreed to match English expenditures. Thirteen thousand unlucky Englishmen were forced into service and shipped from Dover to Calais at the end of January, 1625, with neither supplies nor winter clothing. Transshipped to Gertruidenberg

---

27. Tyacke, *op. cit.*, pp. 130, 131.

in Germany in stages, they began to die at a fearful rate; by March 1625 only 3,000 were still alive. When Christian of Brunswick finally arrived, only a few hundred survivors were left.

In the middle of that same March 1625, James' multiple physical ailments began to overwhelm him. He died on the 27th while the fires he had ignited between Calvinists and Arminians soared around him.

He left his realm embroiled in a conflict in Europe against Spain that launched the Thirty Year's War, an heir intent upon marrying a French Catholic Princess, the Crown bankrupt and England universally disgraced.

Chapter Eleven

JAMIE'S SON

———— ॰ ————

The king who fights his people
fights himself.

— Tennyson

When Charles I inherited the throne, Montague, author of the *Gagg* asked the new King to ". . . defend me with the sword and I will defend you with the pen."[1]

The Calvinist George Carleton said, in rebuttal, "defend the truth and faith, whereof God hath made you the defender, and God (who only is able) will not fail to defend you."

Charles' choice, however, was Arminianism. It was a conscious and deliberate one, apparently based not only on his father's political grounds, i.e., Arminians upheld the royal prerogative, but for aesthetic and personal reasons, for Charles had an artistic bent and a new Catholic wife. The elaborate rituals, the replacement of Communion tables with altars, the use of sacraments, the ornate vestments of the Arminian clergy and the absence of preaching all appealed to his emotions.

Such affinities were part of Charles' personality. When Charles was a small boy his popular elder brother Prince Henry[2] called him "the archbishop" because Charles avoided games, and buried himself in books. Shy and self-conscious,[3] his manner throughout life was stiff and distant. But he liked to be surrounded by fine paintings and antique statuary, handsomely dressed, soft-spoken courtiers and ladies. His Court was formal.

---

1. Tyacke, *op. cit.,* p. 181.
2. Who died when Charles was six.
3. He could barely speak intelligibly before he was 10 and had to speak slowly to keep from stammering afterward.

The only male companion he seems to have ever discovered was the unscrupulous Duke of Buckingham, his father's favorite who had, improbably but effectively, managed to switch from the father's bed to the son's perfectly normal affections.

Buckingham's career was as startling as his presence. Tall, slender but muscular, he had an oddly small head and an almost pretty face. Starting as simple George Villiers, gentleman, he had risen through unspeakable means, from a member of the gentry to a Dukedom in only nine years.

In the course of this rise he outgrew a variety of patrons who first assisted and then obeyed him; his only purpose in life appears to have been to obtain the fruits of influence. His arrogance grew as his circumstances improved; Macauley records that he reduced Francis Bacon to kissing his shoes.

His hold on the fading King James became absolute; he was known to order the King about. His hold on King Charles I was even more uncanny; their relationship was that of psychological twins. His physical courage was unquestionable; he was athletic. His relationship with King James was apparently the only homosexual one in his life—indulged through an indomitable will to rise by any means, at whatever cost.

ᘒ

The new King married the 15 year old Princess Henrietta Maria, the sister of Louis XIII of France on June 13, 1625, less than three months after he inherited the throne, and only five days before his first Parliament convened.

This sequence was a forerunner of Charles' inability to understand his realm: all England had been against a Catholic marriage (with its accompanying concessions to Catholicism), but Charles (and Buckingham) had proceeded as though such opinions were beneath notice.

But more than opinions were involved. The last Parliament had recessed with the understanding that when it reconvened it would resolve arrangements for the war in Europe and that the Crown would make no concessions to international Catholicism.

The Members met five days after the King's marriage to review a military disaster undertaken without its permission and a marriage that involved the King's broken promises. When Charles (and Buckingham) asked for money to pursue the war, he was voted an insignificant sum. "For two centuries the English monarchs had been granted, for the duration of their reigns, the right to levy export and import duties ranging from two to three shillings per tun (a large cask) and six to twelve pence per pound; now the Parliament's 'tonnage and poundage' bill allowed Charles this right for one year only."[4]

The immediate significance was clear: Charles had lied, had entered a war without Parliamentary approval, had probably made secret concessions leading to a Catholic marriage, had continued to rely upon Buckingham, whom Parliament despised. The members did not believe they were refusing the King: they were refusing Buckingham.

They also refused Montague, who enlarged his offenses against Calvinism with a new book titled *Appello Caesarem* in 1625.

Montague was one of the most important figures in the Calvinist/ Arminian dispute, but no physical description of him remains. He was a Fellow at Cambridge, and obviously a scholar. In *A New Gagg* he had contended that Rome was a true Church and that the Pope was not Antichrist. This ensured Arminians the support of Catholics; his *bete noir* was Protestantism and all it entailed; he lumped Calvin with the most extreme sectarians. By this tactic he achieved a propaganda triumph that thoroughly confused basic issues.

Christianity had, from its inception, accepted the irresistible nature of God's Grace and the unlimited nature of God's authority. Calvinism, according to Warfield and other learned commentators, had restored— but not altered—the early teachings of the Church. A clear line of explication runs from Augustine to Calvin, including the doctrine of irresistible Grace which Augustine experienced and described in his *Confessions* (and which Calvin also experienced) and which occurred outside the purview of the clergy.

Montague, however, was a most effective propagandist of the argument that it was not by one's conduct but by cooperation with the clergy that salvation can be achieved. That argument was not presented in scholarly terms so much as it was an argument that entered into—and reshaped popular discourse. By lumping Calvin and Knox with the most rabid sectarians, Montague not only unhinged the dialogue of his own

---

4. Durant, *op. cit.*, p. 201.

day, but for all days to come, including today.

In *Appello Caesarem* Montague repeated his crypto-Catholic arguments and again claimed the approval of King James—but James was dead. Parliament, dominated by Calvinists, echoed denunciations of this work, which took sardonic notice of the fact that the conclusions of the Synod of Dort had never been officially ratified, and which poured scorn on the idea that "foreign" bodies could determine the position of the Church of England.

Parliament had asked Archbishop of Canterbury Abbott to discipline Montague in 1624, but the Archbishop had done nothing, because he had privately been informed (probably by Bishop Niele) that Montague had the protection of the new King. Pym called this "remissness . . . by command."

By August 1625 Parliament decided to impeach Montague for contempt. The redoubtable Sir Edward Coke prepared a case arguing that Montague published a defense while Parliament was still considering his case. Plans were laid to have a conference between Commons and Lords on the Arminian issue, and Commons actually prepared and passed a Bill to "embody the canons promulgated by the Synod of Dort in a Parliamentary statute."[5]

These were startling proceedings, for the right of the Crown to head the Church, and settle Church issues, had not been disputed since Henry VIII had displaced the Pope as the final arbiter of the faith.

That point was not lost on the Arminian clergy, who sent a letter to Buckingham on 2 August 1625, signed by Bishops Laud, Buckeridge and Howson. The letter argued that Montague had expressed the "resolved doctrine of the Church of England," and made the point that the King and the Bishops were the final arbiters of all doctrinal issues in the Church.

It went on to protest that the signers "cannot conceive what use there can be of a civil government in the commonwealth or of preaching and external ministry to the Church, if such fatal opinions, as some of which are opposite and contrary to these delivered by Mr. Montague, are and shall be publicly taught and maintained."

It pointed out that the conclusions of Dort were in a foreign country

---

5. Tyacke, *op. cit.,* pp. 151, 152.

and had no bearing on the national Church of any other country. (This repetition of Montague's arguments is tacit evidence of an Arminian party line, previously devised and skillfully spread.) It ended by pleading for Buckingham's protection.[6]

In this letter Arminianism was defined as the official policy of the Church of England, dissent was either "Puritanism" or "Catholicism" — and a challenge to Royalty.

The Bishop's letter was more of a reminder than an innovation, because in December 1624, Bishop Laud had drawn, for Buckingham's benefit, "a tract about 'Doctrinal Puritanism' which apparently defined Calvinist teachings on Predestination as Puritan."[7] This was a continuation of the propaganda launched by Montague. It narrowed all Calvinism down to a single point which was presented as arbitrary and unjust. That the Grace of God, or that God's Will could be so cartooned was a semantic achievement of no small measure, for it has lasted to this day.

That achievement was the result of a coup planned from the time Wren had met Bishops Laud, Niele and Andrewes in late 1623. In the ensuing months these skillful Church politicians had taken advantage of their proximity to Prince Charles to such good results that within ten days of Charles' accession to the throne, Bishop Laud gave Buckingham a list of the leading clergy, "tabulated on the basis of O(rthodox) and P(uritan) for the perusal of the new monarch."[8]

Since Buckingham spoke for the King, and the Arminians were preaching sermons about the duty of Parliament to give the King whatever he wanted while Parliament balked, it was clear that Arminianism had become the religious arm of royal authority.

❧

Charles, schooled as a gentleman rather than a scholar, inherited his political opinions from his father, James I. James, a scholarly manqué, accepted the premise of Machiavelli that the State should rule through experts, not on the ideas of men "uninformed upon complex problems

6. Tyacke, *op. cit.,* Appendix II, pp. 266, 267.
7. Ibid., p. 167.
8. Ibid.

of international policy, military administration, economy and law."[9] James (and, later, Charles) combined that with the Lutheran doctrine of the divine right of kings.

These arguments fit smoothly into each other. The Arminians believed that only an elite clergy, operating within a hierarchical system replete with symbols, ceremonies and sacraments, could usher souls to salvation. That position included obedience in all matters to an absolute King, who was also surrounded by a trained and educated elite who alone could steer the realm.

Both Charles and his captive clergy used the language of the Reformation, claimed that no essential changes were either intended or under way and pointed to the past as justification. After all, the Tudors and King James had ruled over both Church and State. And almost all Europe (with the exception of Switzerland and Holland) lived under seamless Church and State authority.

᠀

Buckingham, no scholar, was unable to stay away from any issue that involved money, influence and power. Learning that his patronage of the Arminian bishops and Montague had led to a charge that he was " 'the principal patron and supporter of the Semi-Pelagians . . . whose tenets are liberty of free will, though somewhat modified,' Buckingham paraphrased this as accusing him of being 'a patron of heresy, the Pelagian heresy, which opinion I never heard of before.' "

The accusation, however, inspired Buckingham to hold a Conference about Montague (who attended) on the 11th and 17th of February, 1626, five days after King Charles had convened Parliament. Buckingham explained his "good opinion" of Montague when the Conference started, and said this was "certified" by "diverse learned prelates." The conference was private; proceedings were not to be published. All but one of the non-clergymen who attended were peers. That was to ensure that Montague's prosecution by Commons could be thwarted in the Lords.

Montague's arguments, according to later accounts, sought to reduce the distance between Protestant and Catholic and to treat Arminianism

---

9. Acton, *op. cit.,* vol. 1, p. 90.

as equal to Calvinism. He was protected by Bishop Buckeridge from heavy pressure, but at one point (under Calvinist questioning) promised to write another book "correcting" his errors.

That promise was never kept, but Calvinists at the York Conference did not talk the Arminian prelates or Montague down; ". . . in retrospect," wrote Dr. Tyacke, "the York House Conference was seen as poised between two worlds. Calvinist England was soon to be transformed into a country of overtly competing sects and churches and Calvinist bishops were about to be overtaken. . . . The conference also marked the approximate point at which the circle of clerics patronized by Bishop Niele of Durham emerged as the effective spokesmen of the English Church."[10]

༅

Charles' second Parliament met February 6, 1626. Charles had, during the recess, appointed his more effective critics Sheriff in their respective counties, to keep them from Parliament. That disposed of Sir Edward Coke, who had been expected to lead the case against Montague. But it opened a seat for Sir John Eliot.

Eliot, once favorable toward Buckingham, came from Devon and had seen England's rotten and elderly naval vessels, starving English sailors and plundering English soldiers. That convinced him that he should bring down the Duke.

Buckingham was, by that time, a near-obsession with Parliament, which held him responsible for the strange behavior of the new King. Arminianism, with which Buckingham was also connected, was an equal concern. Parliament had, by this time, also devised the system of Committees, by which Members could evade the authority of the Speaker (a royal appointee), elect their own chairmen and allow Members to speak as often as they chose.

A Committee of Religion was created to examine Montague and his Arminian propaganda. It did not report until April, 1626, and then only on those portions of his teachings that might "disturb the peace of the Church and the Commonwealth."

---

10. Tyacke, *op. cit.,* p. 180.

The Calvinist Bishop Carleton, Montague's diocesan, said, "The question is whether they that are according to God's purpose predestinated, called and justified, may loose [lose] these graces of their predestination, calling and justification." He then added, "these things are not, as this man [Montague] in scorn calleth them, scholastic speculations. *They are the grounds of our salvation.*"

Commons found Montague guilty on April 29, 1626, and decided to send his case to the Lords.

By that time all chances of agreement on finances were dashed on the rock of the King's protection of Buckingham. Eliot led a move to impeach the Duke before the Lords. But he made it plain that if Buckingham would retire from office, charges would be dropped. Buckingham refused, and King Charles argued that if he allowed Parliament to choose his ministers, he would no longer be King.

That deadlock led Charles to dissolve Parliament. That left Montague and his Arminian works, the king's "Supply" and a looming problem with France suspended in air.

෭෨

Neither King Charles nor Buckingham, however, were men willing to allow events to unravel unattended. The Duke had been made Chancellor of Cambridge University, where debate over Arminianism and Calvinism had gone on long enough; Buckingham and Charles thought that lesser men had dared, far too often, to express themselves. The King issued a Proclamation silencing debate at Cambridge.

But England was changing. Elizabeth's last years had seen dissension arise, and King James contended with a near-rebellious Parliament for almost his entire reign.

The feudal system was fading and something new was taking its place. The old pattern had rested upon landlords and land; fixed prices and wages, permanent loyalties and allegiances. A newer England was developing a national marketplace that included a country gentry who owned lands but not titles and a middle class consisting of manufacturers, lawyers, physicians and bankers unlisted in feudal laws.

New enterprises and deep-level mines had appeared. Textile plants employing from 500 to 1,000 workers opened; weavers and sewers were scattered in towns and villages. Foreign commerce had multiplied. The economics of this situation were incoherent, however, because inflation had soared beyond wages.

Barons and peasants watched this new, urbanized industrial activity with dismay and replied to arguments in favor of unrestricted markets with arguments in favor of controls and stability.

Charles was obsessed with the idea that he had inherited absolute power, but overlooked his inheritance of festering disputes, with Arminianism and Buckingham at their center. The Calvinists in Parliament, the clergy and the country believed that the King was sponsoring religious changes that had torn Holland apart. They saw Arminianism as Catholicism with all its absolutism, wearing a Protestant mask that was purely semantic.

Charles attempted to placate Parliament by breaking his promise to Louis XIII (and to his wife), by reviving anti-Catholic statutes and even sending his wife's priests back to France.[11] But he refused to abandon Buckingham, arguing that it would place his ministers under the control of Parliament. Rather than do that, he dissolved Parliament.

That left Charles with an angry King of France and the reckless Buckingham. While Buckingham tried to enlist allies against Spain (and offered money the Crown did not have as an inducement), Charles created a mock navy by forcing merchant vessels and their crews into service.

Meanwhile, his disagreements with Louis XIII led to war with France.

That meant that large amounts of money were needed. The King first asked for voluntary "loans." When these did not appear, he sent his agents out to collect forced "loans," bypassing Parliament. Poor men who refused (or could not) pay were sent as soldiers into foreign service. Rich men were sent to prison until they paid. In midsummer 1627 these efforts led to a siege of the fortress of St. Martin's on the Isle of Rhe, led by Buckingham himself. It failed miserably, at a cost of nearly 4,000 more English lives.

---

11. That was a treaty violation, which completely alienated Louis.

Money was forced from Ireland under a system, devised under James I, of levies, penalties and confiscations of land. These property transfers from the Irish to English and Scots Protestants shifted nearly all the arable lands of the six counties of Ulster, and the estates of hundreds who had committed no offense.[12]

Additional properties were given to London companies or trades-men; the dispossessed Irish were left to shift. A Land Title Commission led to so many confiscations that every Irish landowner lived in uncertainty.

Charles I inherited this system, and reaped a rich harvest. Both Catholic and Protestant residents in Ireland had to pay for concessions, or "Graces." These included relaxations of penal laws against Catholics, security of title, and payments to the military.

২৯

Meanwhile an increasing number of men were sent to prison for refusing to hand money over to the Crown. Even Charles and Buckingham began to realize that men torn from their families and sent abroad (leaving the wives and children to become beggars) were not the men to win wars.

Charles could either lose or summon a third Parliament, which alone could finance a war. Swallowing hard, he chose Parliament.

It met in March, 1628; its Members were determined to rein in both the King and Buckingham. Arbitrary imprisonment, permitted by the Tudors and even James I under charges of treason, had been notoriously abused. Men had been deprived of their property without even the color of law; everyone's rights were in jeopardy.

The Members were well aware that their proceedings were protected only as long as Parliament sat; Charles could dissolve Parliament at any time, as he had in 1625 and 1626, and every man who spoke could then be sent to prison.

One member well aware of these perils was Oliver Cromwell, 29, a Member from Huntington. Cromwell was married, moderately rich

---

12. These lands were divided into lots of 2,000, 1,500, and 1,000 acres. Two thousand acres went to the English and Scots, who were to parcel them to English and Protestant tenants—but to no Irish.

and a member of "an immense and ramifying family of squires. When he was first elected in 1628, nine of his cousins were MPs; 17 of his cousins and nine other relatives served, at one time or another, in the Long Parliament. He was one of the few people, even then, who could trace their origins to pre-Conquest times. His family were active in the fight for liberty. Six cousins were imprisoned for refusing the forced loan of 1627; Hampden was his cousin, and so was the man who undertook his defense over ship-money. Cromwell was an integrated Englishman."[13]

Born toward the end of Elizabeth's reign, Cromwell ached over England's decline from those days. It was no accident that his mother, his wife and his favorite daughter were all named Elizabeth; he constantly referred to "Elizabeth of famous memory."

To Cromwell and his relatives, Charles was a King who behaved in a manner alien to the English people; a King who had trampled on the English rights to property and protection from illegal confiscations and imprisonments.

≈⋗

Commons put aside lesser matters to deal with these central issues. The leaders in Commons were Sir John Eliot, a Calvinist, and Sir Thomas Wentworth.

Eliot, a man of immense eloquence, believed that Commons represented the collective wisdom of the realm and was the only body capable of saving it.

Sir Thomas Wentworth did not agree. "Sprung from a wealthy and ancient house in Yorkshire, he was inspired by a lofty consciousness of his own consummate abilities as a speaker and statesman. In every point he was the very opposite of Eliot. He disbelieved entirely in the wisdom of the House of Commons, and thought it very unlikely that a large and heterogeneous body could ever undertake the government of a great kingdom with advantage."

For the moment, the two leaders were able to work together, for both hated the ascendancy of Buckingham. They also agreed that it was important for the peace of the realm for the King to acknowledge the

---

13. Johnson, *op. cit.,* pp. 206–207.

rights of Parliament. (A step James had refused, saying Parliament had no rights, merely privileges granted by the Crown.)

A Petition of Rights was prepared, demanding an end to forced loans, to quartering soldiers in the homes of the people, to martial law in a time of peace and to imprisoning men without charges. Charles was agreeable to everything except the end to his sending men to prison without a charge. A charge, after all, meant a trial. And that would leave decisions in the hands of a judge. Charles preferred to judge everyone himself.

In the end, however, his needs overcame his desires. After the Lords endorsed the Petition, Charles had only one way left to obtain money from Parliament. He hesitated for a week, but finally assented. The Petition of Rights became a Statute of the Realm on July 7, 1628.

"London and all England broke into rejoicing. . . . Few men believed that the King's heart was softened or his reason convinced; on the night of the bonfire it was believed that he had sent the Duke to the Tower. But that heart was never softened, that reason was never convinced. . . ."[14]

Nevertheless the moment is worth review. Although the Star Chamber and the High Commission remained in power, the Petition of Rights marked the first check to arbitrary power since the accession of Henry VIII. News that the King had capitulated was greeted with Parliamentary cheers. Money for the war was voted, and Charles prorogued[15] Parliament.

In August, 1628, Buckingham was at Portsmouth, preparing to lead the Navy in the siege of La Rochelle.

Instead he found his last enemy. John Felton was a Captain who had served in Holland, was denied promotion, was ruined by the war and unpaid. He blamed Buckingham for all these misfortunes, though the two men had never met. When Buckingham walked out of a room after breakfast, Felton struck him with a dagger, saying, "God have mercy upon thy soul." Buckingham, the only uncrowned King in the history of England, fell dead.

---

14. Trevelyan, *op. cit.*, p. 145.
15. Ended the session.

All England rejoiced. "Men drank to the murderer's health in the London streets. Popular songs were composed and sung in his honor. To avoid outrage from the mob, the Duke's body received secret interment in the Abbey; at the false funeral the next day the city train-bands, who protected the hearse, shouldered arms and beat up their drums as if they were marching to a Coronation."[16]

Only King Charles and Buckingham's wife mourned, but his grief was the deeper—for he never again had a close friend.

ᘉ

A little later the English lost La Rochelle. That led to general gloom; Catholic power seemed triumphant nearly everywhere. First, the Palatinate had been lost in 1622, then in 1626 Danish resistance was broken at Lutter; all North Germany lay at the feet of Wallenstein and Tilly and La Rochelle had fallen to Richelieu.

That was not the only dark cloud. In late 1628 the King, who had earlier silenced religious discussion in Cambridge in favor of Arminianism, undertook to do the same for all England. His Declaration prefaced a reissue of the Thirty-Nine Articles of the Church of England in the Common Prayer Book, where it was to remain for centuries.

Asserting that it was his duty not to suffer "unnecessary questions" to be raised, which might "nourish faction in both the Church and commonwealth," the declaration abandoned neutrality "in favor of the Arminians and their doctrine of universal grace."[17]

He also elevated Montague to the high post of Bishop, which enraged all Calvinist intellectuals and clergymen, and set the stage for Bishop Laud's later assumption of ecclesiastical supremacy and his implementation of Charles' policy in the years to come.

One commentator said later that "the final rupture of Charles with Parliamentary institutions, which took place when the House reassembled after the murder of Buckingham, was largely due to religious issues."[18] Another said, "the Arminians and their patron King Charles

---

16. Ibid., p. 146.
17. Tyacke, *op. cit.*, p. 50.
18. Trevelyan, *op. cit.*, p. 148.

were undoubtedly the religious revolutionaries in the first instance."[19]

๛

On January 26, 1629, Francis Rous rose to appeal to "memories of the Armada and Gunpowder Plot, [to] describe Arminianism as 'this Trojan Horse' which threatened to overthrow both religion and liberty."

The following day Sir Walter Earle rose to say that religion should take precedence over all other matters, and spoke of "Popery and Arminianism, joining hand in hand." Other speakers followed, but in the meantime the Arminians were busy inside the Church. And while protests mounted in Parliament, the King kept elevating Arminian clergymen.

"The Commons claimed that the Arminians had gained a monopoly of ecclesiastical preferment, and asked that for the future bishops be chosen on the advise of the Privy Council. Some members suggested taking a religious covenant, which should be defended if necessary to the death, and the House as a whole attempted to place on record a Calvinist statement of faith."[20]

Meanwhile the King and Parliament remained deadlocked over money.

๛

Because Parliament refused to grant Charles' supply, he had—between Parliamentary sessions—continued to collect his "tonnage and poundage" taxes. Parliament, when it reconvened, said this was a violation of the Petition of Right which the King had signed only weeks earlier. But the King's men said this was not a tax, but an "indirect imposition" and therefore not a violation.

The dispute actually ran deeper. The King does not seem to have considered himself bound by any promise. He seems to have believed he was above that necessity; that inferiors did not have rights equal to his own. Such an attitude was nearly unimaginable to Calvinists who

---

19. cf. Patrick Collinson, "England 1558–1640" in *International Calvinism, op. cit.,* p. 220.

20. Ibid., p. 162.

believed in a post Adamic Covenant between God and man. It was equally invalid on political grounds. After all, if the King would not keep agreements, Parliament and the Crown had no grounds for negotiation. But it was to be years before that became clear to all England.

৪৬

Although the King had made Arminianism official in the Church, Parliament (while in session) was free to examine his ruling—and the men behind it. A number of Arminian clergymen were summoned to explain the changes in the Church. (By that step Parliament was actually contending for control of the clergy.)

Cromwell, a Member on the Committee for Religion, rose to complain that a certain Manwaring continued to preach, despite having been censured for his Papist sermons by Parliament. Manwaring had, in fact, been a King's Chaplain and in 1627 had declared that the King's rights came not from consent, or grace, or in law or even custom, but from an immediate investment by God.

By March 1629 the impasse between Crown and Parliament was complete. The King sent word that Parliament was dissolved, but the members refused to accept the order until a Resolution by Sir John Eliot was considered.

The Speaker, Sir John Finch, was actually held in his chair by Denzil Holles and Benjamin Valentine while the Resolution was read. "God's Wounds!" Holles bellowed, "You shall sit till we please to rise."

There were actually three points in Eliot's Resolution, which was read behind locked doors. They said that "Whoever brought in innovations in religion, or introduced opinions disagreeing from those of the true and orthodox Church; whoever voluntarily paid those duties; was to be counted an enemy to the kingdom and a betrayer of its liberties."[21]

No statement could have more clearly shown the seamless nature of religion and politics.

The Resolution was read while the King and an armed escort marched to Parliament to end its deliberations. Ayes erupted, the Motion passed, the King pounded upon the door, the doors were unlocked, the

---

21. Samuel Rawson Gardiner, *The First Two Stuarts and the Puritan Revolution 1602–1660* (New York, N.Y.: Thomas Y. Crowell, 1970), p. 71.

Members poured out, and Parliament was dissolved.

ॐ

A furious King exacted vengeance. Chambers, a merchant who had refused to pay the illegal tax, was summoned to the Star Chamber, fined 2,000 pounds (an immense sum at the time) and thrown into prison for years. Sir John Eliot and his followers were thrown into prison and brought before the King's Bench. A charge was made, which met the provisions of the *Petition,* but the charge was riot and sedition. Eliot argued the proceedings of Parliament could not be so described, but the judges, fearful of the King, overruled him. Fines and imprisonments were ordered. All Eliot's followers, as time passed, tacitly agreed to the judgments, but Eliot refused.

His argument was that Parliamentary members were free to act and speak; to submit to royal control over Proceedings was to lose the meaning of a Parliament, as in Europe.

For refusing to abandon that position, Eliot remained in prison for the rest of his life. When he died in the Tower in December, 1632, Charles refused to allow the body to be buried in Eliot's Cornish home. "Let the body of Sir John Eliot," he replied to the widow, "be buried in the place where he died."

ॐ

The specialists around Charles argued that the King had the law on his side. Parliament was, in theory, only the Grand Council of the Crown. The King was the center of Government.

Commons, they said, had made it clear that it wanted to use its power of the purse to control his ministers and the monarch himself. Charles, therefore, could rule without Parliament.

ॐ

His advisors told Charles that his prerogative gave him the authority to "provide for the safety of the nation." They argued that meant he could do anything that was not expressly forbidden. And since he appointed and dismissed judges at will, and through the Courts of High Commission and the Star Chamber could imprison or fine resisters in either speech, print or action, the King could rule both legally and absolutely when Parliament was not in session.

With these prerogatives constantly in mind, Charles used his power in all directions. The Lord Treasurer Weston, searching the statutes, discovered an antique rule that every man who owned land worth £40 a year should have appeared to be knighted (if not a knight already), and owed a penalty for being absent. Hundreds were, accordingly, fined. Other, similar expedients—all legal, all onerous—raised large sums.

ﻉﻭ

Laud, raised to the post of Bishop of London, became the King's religious advisor and was assured that he would, when the post became vacant, become the next Archbishop of Canterbury.

He at once began to make his mark in London. This began with the alteration of Church interiors and centered primarily on changing Communion tables into altars. He also banned the publication of Calvinist sermons, collected since the time of Elizabeth, Edward VI and James I, from sale in the city. Other Arminian prelates began to imitate these measures in their dioceses.

But Laud did not stop there: at his instigation Calvinist minister Alexander Leighton was indicted before the Star Chamber as an admired author of a book that called the institution of Bishops anti-Christian and satanic. He was put in irons and was kept in solitary confinement for fifteen weeks in an unheated cell full of rats and mice and open to snow and rain. His hair fell out, his skin peeled off. He was tied to a stake and received thirty-six stripes with a heavy cord on his naked back, and was placed in the pillory for two hours in November's frost and snow; he was branded in the face, had his nose slit and his ears cut off, and was condemned to life imprisonment.[22]

This is the treatment that Laud and other Arminian prelates found suitable for dissent, and provides a remarkable paradox. For Arminians accused Calvinists of being cruel in believing that God's salvation is selective. They claimed to be more merciful in arguing that salvation is available for all willing to accept it with the help of the Church and the Arminian clergy.

---

22. Durant, *op. cit.,* p. 190.

The Arminians also accused the Calvinists with being in favor of a theocracy in which the Church ruled the State and all the people. They claimed to be less ambitious, but in practice ruled the people *through* the State.

The Arminians meanwhile used beauty, much as did the Counter-Reformation in the Catholic Church, to beguile. They began to introduce paintings and ornate altars and a variety of Sacraments and soft answers. They offered an easy Salvation based on obedience to forms, and Laud—in later years—said this had been his intention.

When he was called to Parliamentary judgment, Laud's defense was that, "I labored [for] nothing more than the *external worship* of God— too much slighted in most parts of this kingdom might be preserved, and that with as much decency and conformity as might be; being still of the opinion that unity cannot long continue in the Church, when uniformity is shut out at the church door. . . ."[23]

"External discipline, the authority of existing law and of existing governors, were the texts to which he appealed. . . . Men were to obey for their own good, and hold their tongues."[24]

There was no understanding in such a man for the experience of conversion. He could not understand the travail or the joy Augustine related in his *Confessions;* the transformations of Calvin and Knox—all accomplished without the intercession of the clergy—were beyond his ken. He respected "decency and conformity" to the prevailing power of this world, and prevailing power in his world was Charles I and an Arminian Church.

Francis Rous, a Calvinist Member of Parliament, described Arminianism as "an error that maketh the Grace of God lackey after the will of men; that maketh the sheep to keep the shepherd, that maketh mortal seed of an immortal God."[25]

᠄

Sir Thomas Wentworth, another man of unbounded ambition, deserted the Parliamentary and Calvinist cause for that of the King and

23. Gardiner, *op. cit.,* p. 78.
24. Ibid.
25. Tyacke, *op. cit.,* Dedication.

Arminianism. This was a notable triumph for the king, who elevated Sir Thomas to Lord Wentworth, made him a member of the Privy Council and President of the Council of the North. (Later Lord Wentworth would become Earl of Strafford.) English historians use all three of his names at different stages; he is known to history as Strafford.

Wentworth/Strafford is worth a stare. Rich and brilliant, he held the intelligence of others in low esteem. He believed "authority must be based upon intellect, not opinion, and of all living intellects he held his own the first. . . . Justice without the respect of persons might have been the motto of his life."[26]

Wentworth was a type more familiar to the twentieth century than to his own. He disdained Parliament as "the rule of the landowner and the lawyer at the expense of the poor." And he made serious efforts to help those in need. Justices of the Peace were ordered to report on the execution of the Poor Law, *"but everything was done for the people, nothing by them.* They must learn to take everything which the government chose to send them, as they took rain from Heaven."[27]

All this was a sort of shifting about, in the shadow of the throne, for sweeping controls over everyone and everything in England. There was even a name for it: *Thoroughness*—a forerunner of the word "efficiency" today.

It was Thoroughness that impelled John Winthrop and his Cambridge colleagues to gather a thousand Separatists together and to take ship to distant Massachusetts, to lift that tiny community into thriving life.

۲۹

In 1633 Laud became Archbishop of Canterbury and Niele became Archbishop of York. Arminianism thus assumed full control of the Church of England.

"From his Lambeth Palace the new Primate of All England set himself to remolding English ritual and morals. He made a hundred new enemies by levying, through the Court of High Commission, severe fines for persons convicted of adultery; and the victims found little

---

26. Gardiner, *op. cit.,* p. 79.
27. Ibid., p. 80.

comfort in his devoted use of fines to repair the decaying St. Paul's Cathedral and to drive lawyers, hucksters and gossipers from its naves."[28] Calvinists who refused to conform were deprived of their benefices; writers and speakers who dissented were to be excommunicated, put in the stocks—and even lose their ears. Ludowye Bowyer, who charged Laud with being a Catholic at heart, was fined, branded, mutilated and sentenced to prison for life.

᠊

By 1633 Wentworth/Strafford became Lord Deputy of Ireland. His purpose was to raise as much money for Charles as possible and to make the King's rule unquestionable. In pursuit of these goals he trampled on everyone, Catholic and Protestant alike.

The "Graces" for which men had paid were ignored; land titles were broken by intimidation of judges, fines, imprisonments and brutal use of authority. His crimes against Irish property rights were virtually unlimited. "He confiscated nearly all Connaught, and a large part of Munster and nothing prevented a wholesale clearance of these vast districts but the want of settlers. . . . He crushed and ruined, without adequate cause, many of the highest people in the land."[29]

He injured the flourishing Irish wool trade, lest it compete with England, but he encouraged the linen trade, because it did not. In the course of these activities, he raised huge sums for his master Charles I, who smiled on all he did.

᠊

In the hands of Laud and Charles, the Arminian position spread to cover "a coherent body of anti-Calvinist religious thought," in which Calvinism was "attacked as being unreasonable."

"English Arminians vilified their Calvinist opponents as theocrats and in consequence disloyal subjects to the crown. In contrast, Arminians stressed the hierarchical nature of both church and state in which the office and not the holder was what counted. . . . But the Arminian mode, as it emerged during the 1630s, was that of a communal and ritualized

___

28. Durant, *op. cit.,* p. 189.
29. *Social England,* 6 vols. (New York, N.Y.: G. P. Putmans, 1897), vol. 4, p. 197.

worship rather than an individualized response to preaching or Bible worship."[30] It had the effect of leeching the relationship of man and God, and returning man to the priests.

Laud did not, however, operate in a vacuum: a chorus of voices were raised against him. One such voice belonged to William Prynne, a learned lawyer. Between 1626 and 1629 Prynne published three books against Arminianism: *The Perpetuitie of a Regenerate Man's Estate, God no Imposter or Deluder, The Church of England's Old Antithesis to New Arminianism.*

Prynne also criticized "the profanation of the Sabbath and the moving of communion tables to an altarwise position."[31] He also spent several years gathering material against the stage.

During this entire period, from Elizabeth I through James I to Charles I, the stage had grown from broad and bawdy to (many times) filthy, had continued, with rare exceptions, to mock Puritans and other Reform groups. Playwrights only occasionally wrote dramas that satirized vice instead of virtue; John Ford wrote two in 1633. ("The Broken Heart" and "Tis a Pity She's a Whore.")

In 1632 John Prynne published *Histriomastix, the Player's Scourge,* a thousand pages long, in which the author tried "to cram the entire argument of his book into every sentence."[32] This gargantuan tome scourged every form of theatrics from ancient days onward, and held players responsible for virtually all sin. He also criticized the government that allowed such abuses, and termed any woman who took part in theatricals a whore.

This encyclopedic diatribe was scorned even by Prynne's legal colleagues in The Inns of Court, who mounted a gorgeous Masque costing thousands of pounds, which they presented to the King.[33] But it aroused indignation in Whitehall, where the Queen was rehearsing to take part in a play. The Queen made her displeasure known, and Archbishop Laud had Prynne hauled before the Star Chamber for seditious libel.

---

30. Ibid., pp. 245, 246.

31. Tyacke, *op. cit.,* p. 225.

32. Jonas Barish, *The AntiTheatrical Prejudice* (Berkeley, CA: University of California Press, 1981).

33. Gardiner, *op. cit.,* p. 91.

The author apologized for his intemperance, saying he had not had the Queen in mind, but to no avail. He was found guilty, barred from the further practice of law, had his university degrees rescinded, was fined an impossible £5,000 (5 million dollars?), placed in the pillory, had his ears cut off and was sent to prison for life.

Laud, meanwhile, sent men into every church diocese. Communion tables were removed, altars and railings installed "in an elaborate scenic apparatus in which the sacrament of holy communion had a key role. The altar . . . often set on a dais, became the focal point of worship. Theorists of the [Arminian] movement both glossed away Calvinist expositions of the Prayer Book and provided a new liturgical dimension. . . . Laud said, 'in all ages of the Church the touchstone of religion was not to hear the word preached but to communicate.' "[34]

This may have sounded plausible when couched in the abstract to the unlearned, but in practice it meant that liturgical rites and mechanical prayers replaced sermons and individual responses, and that every clergyman who demurred at Laud's innovations was officially questioned, suspended, deprived of his livelihood, or fined and imprisoned.

"Unity of outward worship was the idol of Laud. As he told Wentworth, he was all for 'thorough,' the system of complete discipline in which his heart was set. The clergy were to be drilled as a sergeant drills his soldiers. Human nature rebelled against the yoke. Moderate men began to suspect that all this was but part of a design to bring England again under the papal domination. It was known that an emissary from Rome attached to the Queen's court was frequently admitted to Charles' presence. . . ."[35]

❧

Charles' specialists tried to conquer inflation by fixing wages, prices and administering poor relief, but such efforts were enfeebled by the lack of a true national bureaucracy. Meanwhile the Crown held monopolies in soap, salt, starch, beer, wine, hides and coal.

Under such increasingly oppressive economic, religious and political

34. Tyacke, *op. cit.*, p. 246.
35. Gardiner, *op. cit.*, p. 93.

skies, it was no wonder that Puritans began to stream toward Massachusetts in an exodus that would soon reach 20,000.

In 1634 Charles tried a new "ship tax." Originally limited to coastal cities for protection against marauders, it was extended to all England. That was legally protested by John Hampden, who lost the case before Charles' judges, but won in the court of public opinion.

Charles believed his programs were successful. The Crown was living without Parliament; large sums flowed from Ireland and from domestic exactions; the Church was being transformed. Encouraged by what he regarded as a triumph and deceived by the relative silence of the people, he turned his attention toward Scotland.

ᔕ

In 1625, shortly after becoming King, Charles had revoked the grants of all Church or Crown lands made to Scots families since the accession of his grandmother Mary Stuart. Then he named to the Privy Council of Scotland five bishops and an archbishop (John Spottiswoode) and made the leading prelate Chancellor—the first churchman appointed to that office since the Reformation.[36]

Charles had displeased the Scots by marrying a Catholic Princess. In 1633 he created more shock when he came to Scotland to be crowned, and allowed his bishops to surround that event by virtually every Catholic ritual: vestments, candles, altar, crucifixes and incense.

Laud, with his usual indifference to public opinion, approved of a new set of liturgical rules for the Church of Scotland. These gave the king jurisdiction over the Church of Scotland, forbade assemblies of the clergy except at the King's command, forbade anyone to teach without the approval of the Bishops, and limited ordination to candidates obedient to the new rules.

When these new regulations were proclaimed in the Scots churches, the ministers protested that the Reformation was being annulled. When an attempt was made to apply them in St. Giles' Cathedral in Edinburgh,

---

36. Bishops who had shared in the English Reformation were retained; Bishops who had not shared in the Scots Reformation had been removed by the Presbyterian Church. James I restored such bishops in Scotland with the help of some of the Scots nobility, which wanted to see the Church restrained.

a riot erupted.

Petitions rained upon Charles from the Scots asking him to have the new canons revoked; he responded by saying that petitions were treasonable.

ᴈᴥ

But Scotland was not England. The Scots nobles began to combine with the Scots clergy in combinations that had not been seen for many decades.

In 1636 the earless Prynne published two more anti-Arminian books from prison. One—*A Looking Glass for all Lordly Prelates* blamed all the recent liturgical changes upon the egotism of bishops. The second *The Unbishoping of Timothy and Titus* came close to a demand that bishops be abolished.

This led to new charges and another conviction against Prynne, together with Bastwick, a physician, and Burton, a clergyman. The Star Chamber ordered that all three lose their ears, fined each £5,000 and sentenced each to life in prison.

Unlike the first such sentence, passed on Prynne in 1633, the new penalties created huge opposition. When the trio was escorted from prison to the pillory, they passed a dense crowd who "strewed herbs and flowers in their path. They all . . . talked to the people. Bastwick . . . was pleasant and witty. Prynne protested his innocence. . . . Mr. Burton said it was the happiest pulpit he ever preached in."[37]

When the hangman began to cut off ears the crowd began to roar. The hangman also chopped away at the stumps of Prynne's ears, causing excruciating pain. The general compassion toward the men was so great—and so vocal—that the authorities sent each to remote prisons.

Meanwhile Laud and Charles determined to make the Scots obedient to a new Prayer Book, which radically differed from Knox's *Book of Common Order*. Knox, for instance, did not believe that baptism was necessary for salvation, nor, he said, should one believe,

> virtue or power to be included in the visible water, or outward action, for many have been baptized and yet never inwardly purged, but that our

---

37. Gardiner, *op. cit.*, pp. 98, 99.

saviour Christ, who commanded baptism to be ministered, will, by the power of his Holy Spirit, effectually work in the hearts of his elect, in time convenient, all that is meant and signified by the same. *And this the Scripture calleth our regeneration.*

In contrast the new Scottish Prayer Book called all baptized infants "regenerate."

The purpose of the new Prayer Book was, of course, to "unify" the Churches of England, Scotland and Ireland. The Irish had been subjugated by fire and sword; much of their lands dispossessed, their rights overridden. But the occupation of Ireland was old; Scotland was never occupied. The Scottish resistance to what constituted a new, anti-Calvinist faith was immense, and included virtually all the people.

༄

In February 1638, four Scots Committees, known as the Tables, practically assumed control of Scotland. A party, in other words, had come into existence, linking the Tables. Standing committees represented the nobles, barons, burgesses and ministers and linked the capitol with the localities.

This combination of Church, nobility and gentry was new to Scotland and it combined the ideas of Knox and Calvin with the revolutionary arguments of George Buchanan. "Ministers who rode to war with the armies of the Covenant had, it was said, the Geneva Bible in one saddlebag and Buchanan's *History* in the other. It completed the process which had been going on since the 1590s of a merging identity in the form of a covenanted nation of church and state."[38]

This Scot's National Covenant reaffirmed Presbyterian Calvinism; rejected Arminian canons, and the people pledged themselves to defend the true religion. They did not, however, reject the King, but declared themselves still loyal. Nearly all Scotland signed, and Spottiswoode and all but four of his bishops fled to England.

Charles, privately indignant, was advised to temporize. So he sent the Marquis of Hamilton, from a famous Scots family, to win time. Hamilton was told to promise the Scots a General Assembly of the

---

38. Lynch, "Scotland 1559–1638," cf. Prestwich, *op. cit.,* p. 254.

Church, to revoke the Prayer Book and the various innovations to which the Scots objected, and to promise to limit the power of bishops. At the same time, Hamilton was to introduce a new Covenant, drawn up at Charles' Court, to substitute for the one drawn in Edinburgh.

The promised Assembly met at Glasglow in late November, 1638. Most of its members were clergymen, but nearly a hundred elected laymen were included, who represented the people and the secular nobility.

The King's bishops protested at being excluded, appealed to Hamilton, and found him in agreement. Only the King, he told the Assembly, could make ecclesiastical or civil rulings. When the General Assembly ignored his protests he walked out.

The General Assembly then proceeded to abolish all bishops, annulled all the forms and ordinances of the Arminianized Episcopal Church of England, reestablished Presbyterian Calvinism and declared the Church of Scotland was independent of the State.

This extraordinary step, the first known to Christian history, deserves far more attention and credit than it has received.

෨෮

Such defiance of royal authority could not be allowed to stand, and Charles sent orders to the General Assembly to disband or be charged with treason. It remained in session as though he did not exist.

That placed the King in an awkward position. He hesitated to summon Parliament, because of the questions its Members would raise about his means of raising money on his own, the changes he had mandated in the English Church, and issues similar to those that had enraged Scotland. He decided to raise an army and fight a war without Parliament.

The clergy was asked to contribute (and could hardly refuse), the nobility and the people gave little, and that grudgingly. The Scots, however, were well prepared. Their realm swarmed with old soldiers who had served in Germany during the Thirty Year's War and they did not lack for volunteers.

Charles scratched together about 22,000 men; the Scots had 26,000. The two forces met not far from Berwick on the road to Edinburgh. His leaders warned Charles that his men were in no mood to fight, while both realms knew that the Scots were aflame with religious fervor.

The King, therefore, had to abandon thoughts of fighting. He not only signed a truce in July 1639, but agreed to place all issues before a free Scots Parliament and an unhindered Assembly of the Kirk.

The following month the new Scots Assembly met at Edinburgh and ratified the proceedings of the Glasglow Conference with all their defiance and independence, as did the Scots Parliament. Both realms now knew that Scotland had broken loose from Charles I and Archbishop Laud, and that the next move was up to the King.

꙾

He sent for Wentworth, now known as the Earl of Strafford, who returned from Ireland. Strafford had been away for years, and seems not to have realized what the "Thorough" system he so ardently supported had done to the King's popularity. His advice to Charles, therefore, was logical but ruinous. He suggested that Parliament be summoned, after eleven years—the longest period without Parliament in English history.

꙾

Charles' experts had discovered some letters between some Scots and the French Government. They hoped that the revelation of these would arouse patriotic sentiment. But Parliament had a mountain of its own grievances. Their consensus was that these had to be addressed before they would look at the King's problems.

Charles reacted like a man slamming down a lid on a box he discovered to be full of snakes. He called Parliament "traitorous" and dissolved it on May 5, 1640, after a session of only 23 days.

Riots erupted. The popular opinion was that the King was being misled by Strafford and Laud. A mob attacked Lambeth Palace, seeking Laud. Not finding him, it killed a Catholic who had refused to join a Protestant worship.

Strafford and the King then moved toward Scotland at the head of an improvised army. The Scots moved more swiftly. In August they crossed the Tyne and drove the English before them in panic. Strafford and Charles were forced to agree to pay the Scots £850 a day until a treaty could be agreed. Since Charles didn't have the money, the Scots army settled down to wait at Newcastle. There it constituted a stern, tacit ally of English Calvinists.

Charles, who had never anticipated being helpless (one can hear him crying that he had the law on his side), called a Council of Peers to come and meet him at York. As usual, his advisors had found an obsolete precedent for this.

The peers advised the King to call Parliament, and—unable to defy both the nobility and the country—Charles, at long last, issued the call.

The result was the Long Parliament; the most fateful and protracted in English history.

Chapter Twelve

PARLIAMENT

———— 🙊 ————

*Rebellion to tyrants is obedi-
ence to God.*

— Unknown

The Long Parliament was the first great revolutionary governmental
assembly in modern history, of which the French National Assembly of 1789, the Russian Duma of 1917 and the German Reichstag of
1933 were repetitions.

It did not, of course, arrive upon the English scene without a
forerunner. The Short Parliament had been summoned April 13, 1640,
to provide Charles with money to fight the Scots and had, instead,
immediately started talking about the crimes of Charles' government;
the efforts of Laud to change the Prayer Book, rituals, clergy and religion
of the realm, the illegal taxation of the people, the excesses of the High
Commission and the Star Chamber together with long descriptions of
other abuses.

That Session, only 23 days long, was a geyser of protest that spurted
as soon as Laud's tight lid on speech, print and action was lifted. The
King clapped down again on May 5, 1640, but the glimpse of the mood
of the Calvinists among the gentry and nobility was enough to awaken
a great many.

Events after that made the hollowness of Charles' government even
more evident. The non-fighting army he assembled against the Scots
provided dramatic evidence of the decline, and his "Truce," which was
tied to an agreement to pay the Scots occupying army, created a national
sense of anger and humiliation.

The Long Parliament met, therefore, in a mood new to England. Not
that rebellions had not before occurred, and not that the Kings of
England had not before been overthrown, but in 1640 there was no

alternative would-be King on the horizon; there was no peasant revolt. The English were confronted with a government that was proud of itself, that believed it was "Thorough"—and that was actually in a state of advanced decay.

Turkish pirates were raiding the Irish and Cornish coasts and carrying subjects off to slavery. Finally, Charles had been unable to protect northern England from the feared and hated Scots. "That the English should live to see 'such beggarly snakes put out their horns,' should be at the mercy of 'such giddy-headed gawks' and 'brutish bedlamites' seemed intolerable."[1]

Such a combination of calamities seemed more than fortuitous. Men began to believe that a great conspiracy was underway: an effort to destroy English liberties and the Calvinist religion, and to install an absolutist Catholic monarchy.

That fear was not unrealistic; not unthinkable. Ancient rules of rights and laws were being overthrown all over Europe: "[T]he Cortes in Castille and Aragon was gone, Richelieu had set aside the Estates Generale in France, Gustavus Adolphus had killed the Riksdag in Sweden."[2] Strafford, the rumors ran, would bring in an army from Ireland, or make a deal with the Scots, or even obtain troops from Europe through the Catholic internationale. All England felt the knife at its throat, and identified Strafford and Laud as the dark powers misleading the throne.

᠁

Neither Charles, Laud or Strafford appear to have had a real appreciation of this national anger until the Short Parliament. For eleven years the people had been bereft of newspapers and knowledge of what others thought or did. The secret circulation of pamphlets, rhymes posted at night on trees or doorways (like modern newsletters or the Soviet samizdat[3]) gave hints but no true picture of the strength of opinion.

Neither Charles nor Strafford nor Laud realized the extent to which they had alienated the people until the Short Parliament spoke. The

---

1. Johnson, *op. cit.,* p. 191.
2. Ibid., p. 192.
3. USSR underground, unlicensed, and illegal press.

King moved quickly to stop its outburst, but not quickly enough to stop its effect.

The Members were sent home, but riots—unknown for years—broke out in various places. In London mobs surged through the streets calling for the death of Archbishop Laud. The authorities moved in; punishments were drastic, the people were driven underground again. But the first manifestations had appeared.

By November, when the Long Parliament appeared, there were—for the first time ever—crowds of people gathered on Westminster walks. Parliament was seen, though not defined, as the center of the opposition to the King, Strafford and Laud.

Inside Parliament Laud's dread power vanished: men could speak as they chose. Nor, in November 1640, did they have to fear that the King would abruptly dissolve their session and send them to prison because of what they said, for the King was in a trap.

England had no standing army. The King had only a few hundred guards. In order to raise an army he was reduced to waiting upon Parliament's pleasure—while a Scots Army, invigorated with a new religious vision of itself as the New Israel,[4] sat in England's North. Both the King and the country knew that if Charles did not pay the Presbyterian demands, the Scots would march all the way to London without opposition, and no man knew what changes that would introduce. King Charles was cornered at last.

The Calvinists in Parliament were intent upon reducing the King's authority, his "Prerogative." They did not think of this as "revolutionary," because the word did not then carry the freight it has since acquired. They believed they were dedicated to the restoration of a past whose glory made their present situation dismal by contrast. If possible, they would have resurrected Elizabeth, and her period, which seemed to them a Golden Age.

They wanted, as in John Milton's essay *Of Reformation Touching Church Discipline,* to restore not only the Church in which true

---

4. Lynch, *op. cit.,* p. 254.

Calvinists believed, but to revive England's national sense of destiny. Sir Edward Coke had revived a partly mythical sense of their Common Law and their rights: they wanted to realize and live these half-dreams.

They met, however, well aware that brute power was in high office. Paramount among those brutes was the Earl of Strafford. He had started as simple Sir Thomas Wentworth; he had abandoned Commons and its causes to join the King—and he was dictator of Ireland. He had an army there that was half-Catholic. What was to prevent him from bringing it into England, to enforce the English Catholic style of Laud and Charles?

Strafford, therefore, was the first target. He knew it, and was not afraid. "I am tomorrow for London," he told a neighbor, "with more danger beset, I believe, than any man ever went out of Yorkshire."

Strafford was brave, but it was not courage alone that sustained him. He and his advisors were aware of no laws that he had broken; his record in high office was one he was eager to defend. He was in the city when John Pym, wearing the small pointed, peaked beard and curled mustache of the period, rose to launch the case against him.

Nearing 60, Pym was an overbearing orator and the leader of the 500-man Commons. He had, at the opening of Parliament, called on the people to protect the Members—and crowds appeared carrying clubs and broadswords. For English governmental officials to issue such a call against their King was something new in England, and in the West.

This was not a spur of the moment decision: Pym, John Hampden, St. John, Lord Mandeville and a few others had been meeting "far from London in deer parks and on garden terraces to create was what one of the earliest parties, in the modern political sense. They had decided before coming to Parliament to call the people; those they called roamed the capital to hoot at the King's half-pay captains in the Palace Yard or to knock down Papists at street corners."[5]

In the House on November 11, 1640, John Pym denounced Strafford as a secret Papist plotting to bring in an army from Ireland and to alter law and religion. Members voted his impeachment; Strafford was halted as he was en route to his seat in Lords—and hustled to the Tower to await trial.

---

5. Trevelyan, *op. cit.*, p. 197.

A few weeks later on December 16, 1640, the Calvinist majority in Commons voted that the Arminian changes in the canons of the Church were illegal, and impeached Laud, the Archbishop of Canterbury, of Popery and treason. He landed in the Tower to which he had consigned so many others.

The King, bewildered, sat in the Palace as though frozen while his ministers fled for their lives—for the air was heavy with the smell of blood.

የ፦

Commons raged over Arminianism. A "Root and Branch" faction, which included Cromwell and Milton among others, petitioned Parliament to abolish episcopacy and to restore the Calvinist government of the Church. It branded as "abominable the opinion of some bishops that the Pope is not Antichrist . . . and that salvation is attainable in the Catholic religion."[6]

Commons rejected that Petition, but voted—under Pym's skillful direction—to bar the clergy from all legislative and judicial functions. The Lords agreed, with the proviso that Bishops should retain their seat in the upper house. That was precisely what Commons was against and a war of pamphlets appeared.

Nothing could have more clearly shown the towering nature of the changes underway: London had become "a free republic of political thought and writing," the workshop of change. The episcopal censors had vanished. "Pamphlets on religion and government were daily piled on the stalls, and daily disappeared down streets and through doorways, each on its mysterious mission, making creeds, wars, systems, men."[7]

Men were giving speeches in the streets, in courtyards, in chambers— and in pulpits. The people in nearly every church carried the Communion table back to the nave and tore out the altars and Trevelyan records that "a score of sects seemed to spring in as many days out of the earth, and numbered many thousand Londoners. They scorned the 'steeple house' and met in the largest rooms they could find, no longer as thieves in the night."

---

6. Durant, *op. cit.*, pp. 208, 209.
7. Trevelyan, *op. cit.*, p. 200.

Such scenes were to remain etched in men's memories for centuries, inspiring Paris in 1789 and countless other cities into imitations.

Laud was in the Tower, and all his once-terrible High Commission Arminian prelates and the torturers of the Star Chamber remained sequestered and silent: they feared the people uncaged.

Cromwell, among others, proposed that Bishops be driven out of Parliament altogether, and many outside voices raised the same chant. The Arminian Bishop John Hall, flaring in defense of the Lords of the Church, claimed a divine right for all bishops based on their Apostolic Succession from the time of Jesus. That was answered by five Presbyterians in a famous pamphlet titled *Smectymnuus* from their initials, as well as later responses composed by Milton.

Crowds jeered the Bishops as they sought to enter Lords; it is noteworthy that no crowds appeared to protect them. It is equally noteworthy that the London crowds spoke of religion, Church government and individual conscience. Unlike their French, Russian and German imitators in the centuries to come, they did not come to kill, rob and plunder.

In part this is because they were composed of prosperous shopkeepers, owners of properties too small for pretension; citizens with trades and families, genuine Calvinists who did not pursue the wealthy, but the Bishops who had trampled on their sacred beliefs.

？

In March 1641 Strafford went on trial in the house of Lords. The main piece of evidence against him, filched from the desk of Sir Henry Vane by his son, was a note. In it Strafford had told the King that he was "absolved and loose from all rule of government."

"Your Majesty," he said, "having tried all ways and been refused, shall be acquitted before God and man; and you have an army in Ireland that you may employ to reduce this kingdom to obedience, for I am confident the Scots cannot hold out three months."

It seemed fairly clear that Strafford had advised the King to use the army in Ireland against the Scots. But the phrases indicating the King's unlimited power made it equally clear that such an army could also be used in England. The discussion swayed, and Strafford—by all accounts—handled himself brilliantly.

He had, of course, friends in Lords, mainly (but not entirely) among the Arminian Lord Bishops, who constituted half of the Upper House. There was also the traditional loyalty of the nobility to their highest member, the King.

Seeing that Strafford was likely to be acquitted in points of law, which was what "Thorough" expected, the Commons under Pym changed tactics. They dropped their impeachment charges and substituted a Bill of Attainder (a Bill against a single individual) on May 8, 1641, that simply condemned Strafford to death as a public enemy.

That was passed by both Houses while crowds howled outside. That carried Parliament across a significant psychological barrier, for to depart from law in order to convict an enemy is to enter into revolution.

King Charles had promised Strafford when he came to London that "not a hair of his head" would be harmed. "Upon the word of a King," Charles wrote Strafford two days before the sentence, "you shall not suffer in life, honor or fortune."

After the sentence, a distraught Charles went to the House of Lords to plead for his servant. He was willing, he said, to dismiss Strafford from office, but he could not consent to seeing him condemned for treason. That attempt must have cost the monarch a great deal, for he had to speak slowly to be sure of not stammering; and to appear as a supplicant was something he had never expected to do.

As usual when great pride appears to beg for mercy, it was denied. Pym rose in the Commons to denounce the King's visit, saying it violated the rights of Parliament and was a threat to its members.

That might have been true once, but "great multitudes" ringed the King's palace of Whitehall shouting, "Justice! Justice!" Despite his largesse with government money, the man who held crowds in contempt had made few friends among them.

The King's Privy Councillors, frightened as never before, pleaded with him to give way, but he refused. Niele, the Archbishop of York, one of the Arminian architects of disaster, begged the King to sign Strafford's sentence, and he refused. The courtiers—nobles all—crowded around to tell him that his life and the lives of the Queen and their children were in danger, and he refused.

An immense mob surrounded Whitehall. "The voice of wrath terrible in numbers, heard there once before in distant unregarded warning round the pillory of Prynne, now shook the frail walls of the old timbered Palace. The courtiers confessed themselves to the Queen's priests, and marked on stair cases and passage turnings where men could make a stand."

It was an unorganized siege without leaders, spontaneous and terrifying, that lasted around the clock all day and all night. Congregations rushed from churches to join as others went home to rest. Charles agonized, consulted, heard conflicting advice, was told that he, the Queen and all their children would be massacred unless he signed.

Finally he signed and knew as he did that he was signing an official record of his cowardice.

Strafford was led to his execution three days later on May 12, 1641. An estimated 200,000 people went to Tower Hill to watch. When the doomed Earl passed one of the Tower buildings he saw the Archbishop Laud watching from one of the prison cells. He looked up; the old prelate raised his hands and fainted. The immense throng, however, exulted as "Black Tom the Tyrant" died.

ᔛ

Strafford's death carried all England into a new territory, never before traversed. The future had arrived in England, and the world would never again be the same.

The King's government collapsed and the King's ministers fled the country.

Parliament had, earlier, enacted a Bill making elections mandatory at least every three years. With Strafford gone, that measure was stiffened by another forbidding the king to dissolve the sitting Parliament without its consent. A shaken Charles agreed to that, making Parliament independent of the Crown for the first time since its creation. One wonders if it occurred to him that such a vote would enable it to sit for the rest of his reign.

ᔛ

"One by one," wrote Samuel Rawson Gardiner, the most famous of all the Civil War historians, "the instruments by which the king had been enabled to defy the nation were snatched from his hands. Ship-money was declared to be illegal, and tonnage and poundage were no more to be levied without parliamentary consent." An end was put to the Star Chamber where torture had been conducted only a year earlier. That extinguished the dread powers of the Privy Council, the body that had maintained Kings in power for long decades. The Court of High Commission, the instrument of Laud and other prelates before him, the means by which Bishops strangled freedom of thought and expression, was abolished. These measures not only left the King financially dependent on Parliament, but struck from his hands the two great instruments of authority wielded by the Tudors, James I and Charles I.

Nevertheless Charles was still the King, and there was still a King's army in Ireland, and King's officers and loyal subjects in England. Henry Hyde, the future Earl of Clarendon and the Viscount Falkland had grown fearful of too much change; of mobs and threats to property and stability. They did not see traditional ways returning; they saw them receding. A King's Party began, carefully at first, to form.

The King, meanwhile, engaged in mindless intrigues. He corresponded with the Pope's agents, signed everything put before him, and talked to army officers about quelling resistance. He lived in a swirl of rumors, broken pledges, secret talks, wild plans.

As news of these stupidities reached Commons, the Members decided it might be well to maintain ties to the Scots Presbyterians. In August 1641 the Scots army was paid £25,000 a month for an indefinite period. The Presbyterians dispersed, having saved England, and the English and Scots Calvinists began to move toward an entente.

In August, 1641, Charles decided to go to Edinburgh, to rally support in what he considered his most loyal realm. This was a lifelong illusion, sustained even after the Scots had officially rejected all his efforts to change their religion and their government, had sent an army into England and had kept it there until they collected an immense ransom. He seems, without Strafford or Laud, to have lost his sense of reality—if he ever had any.

The capital was shocked. His supporters in the Palace and among the Arminians pleaded with him not to go, crowding around his coach, but he was adamant. And with his usual carelessness, he had allowed his intentions to be so widely known that he left an alarmed Parliament behind.

৵

The general antipathy and Calvinist fervor against Arminianism wound like a purple thread through all the upheavals and innovations of the revolution. The crowds hooting at the bishops and the people replacing the Communion tables wanted no more lawn sleeves and gilded vestments, no more compulsory Sacraments and lofty clergymen: they wanted preaching and Biblical explication, not ceremonies from the Lords of Heaven.

In September 1641 when Parliament reconvened, Pym, Cromwell and other Calvinists reintroduced their Root and Branch Bill, designed to abolish episcopacy and to restore Calvinist doctrine, preaching and services to the Church. The immediate reason was the refusal of Lords to exclude High prelates from Parliament, but the larger reason was the need to take the clergy out of the control of the King and his "divine right" absolutist, pro-Catholic policy. Beyond all these semi-political reasons, however, was the reasoning of Calvin who did not want the State to intervene inside the Church, and the impact of Knox, who taught that Christians should not obey anti-Christian rulers.

The religious issue overshadowed all else. The Calvinist leaders of Commons proposed that the Church should be ruled by a committee of nine laymen nominated by Parliament. No cleric was to be on the committee. This was popular, especially among men who respected doctrine more than clerics.

But the Calvinists had no intention of stopping there. More ordinances were proposed, which involved moving Communion tables back to the nave and changes in the Service. These included changes in the Prayer Book, which had been altered by the Arminian clergy during its time of power under Charles. These measures were not resolved when Parliament took a short adjournment on September 9, 1641, but remained to fester in the minds of the Members.

The Arminians took advantage of the interval to feverishly canvas and organize their ranks. They did not object to Parliamentary control so much as to the changes in the Prayer Book. The Arminian doctrine that Man could earn his way into Heaven by works and form, with its easy escapes from the higher purposes of God, was simply too seductive to be easily abandoned.

In effect, two parties began to coalesce inside Parliament. The Arminians (later called Royalists and after that, Cavaliers) began to draw upon writers, nobles, professional military men, poets and musicians, and landowners; the Calvinists (later called Puritans) began to appeal to all those who had endured intellectual frustration and abuse from the Bishops and their High Commission.

(In this context its worth mentioning that English historians have always shied from any close examination of the High Commission: it embarrasses them. They choose to discuss their revolution in terms of money and power, not religion and intellect.)

When Parliament resumed in September, 1641, Pym was alarmed to discover that a split appeared. Men rose to warmly defend the Arminian Prayer Book and debates began to grow acrimonious. Asked what he wanted to have replace Episcopacy, Cromwell honestly, if undiplomatically, replied, "I can tell you, sirs, what I would not have; though I cannot, what I would."

The debate was interrupted by terrible news from Ireland. The men Strafford had left in control lacked his pitiless efficiency, and a major rebellion had erupted. All England knew (and still knows) that the Irish people were abominably mistreated not only by one English King or for brief periods, but for the entire centuries-long span of English invasion and occupation. Strafford had been only the latest of a long stream of unconscionable and thieving English overlords. With Parliament preoccupied, the Irish struck.

Each bulletin sounded worse; truthfully heavy casualties were described in horrifying tones; torture and rapine were alleged. That the news arrived on Guy Fawkes Day made its Catholic nature seem especially ominous.

Parliament realized that a new army was needed at once, and set aside (in a typically arrogant seizure of even more from the Irish) two and half million acres in Ireland to pay Governmental creditors and suppliers.

Who would compose, and who would lead, a new army? Pym wanted Parliament (meaning Commons) to select its officers, but the Arminian royalists "saw with alarm how easily their opponents could create praying regiments." Before they could devise some way to avoid that, Pym decided to appeal to the nation.

His means were adroit. Still controlling a Commons majority, he had a *Grand Remonstrance* drawn, listing all the wrongs of Charles' reign, and including all the Calvinist suggestions for reform. The Remonstrance stressed the need to reform the Church; to strip it of its Arminian/Catholic extravagances and to restore it to the Calvinist/ Augustinian basics revived by Geneva.

The Remonstrance was discussed, clause by clause, and when debate over its contents and significance took place, voices were raised and men put their hands on the hilts of their swords. In essence the measure was a vote to continue or to abandon resistance to the King, and contained a provision, redolent with the distrust of the Calvinists, that the King should employ "only such advisors as were approved by Parliament."

That brought the Arminians to their feet. No King, they stormed, had ever been so treated; so circumscribed. The Calvinists were equally determined: they knew what Charles would do to them if he had an army under his control.

In the end, amid flushed faces and angry gestures, the Remonstrance passed by the narrow margin of eleven votes. Cromwell, who had been fervent for passage, said that if it had been rejected, he would have sold all his belongings and "never seen England more; and he knew there were many honest men of the same resolution."

That was only half of Pym's purpose; the other half appeared when a Member rose to propose that the Remonstrance be published. That created another uproar, so passionate that discussion had to be shut off.

෨෮

Three days later Charles returned to London, after enduring a fiasco in Edinburgh. Although the Remonstrance was already in print, the King issued his own appeal to the people (probably drafted by the skilful Hyde) promising that he would reform the Church, would investigate the bishops, but insisted on his right to call his Council and would retain his "natural liberty" of selecting his own ministers, and (as always) asked for funds for his government.

Pym & Co. proposed a Militia Bill, which would give Commons control of the army.

There had been so many changes in so brief a time that many were ready to drop discussion and welcome the King back. He was cheered as his coach trundled to a banquet with the Lord Mayor. If he had surrendered the right to dissolve Parliament, he might—at that brief moment—have restored his position. He had, after all, the letter of the law and half the Lords, as well as a minority in Parliament, on his side.

Instead he decided to appoint some of the officers of Strafford's tyrannical regiments, recently disbanded in Yorkshire and awaiting new commissions, to serve as Palace and Tower guards. These "vultures of the upper class" began to sow terror throughout the City, as though London were no different from Ireland. They undertook to clear the crowds from around Westminster Hall at sword point, and did not neglect to draw blood.

The people's reaction alarmed all factions; they reappeared, armed, in huge and threatening crowds, and Charles had to disband his protectors. As usual, he learned too late; Londoner shopkeepers closed their doors, men sought arms in self-defense and an informal (and illegal) militia appeared.

On January 3, 1642, Charles, going by the rules as usual, decided that the Calvinist leaders had conspired with the Scots Presbyterians. At his instruction his appointed Attorney General rose in the House of Lords to request, in the name of the King, the impeachment of Pym, Hampden, Hazelrigg, Holles and Strode, on charges of treason.

The King's advisors should have known that an impeachment brought by the King was unconstitutional, but the Lords were horrified for other equally large reasons. A bloody proscription was what they feared. The upper House had perfected the art of doing nothing in the crisis. Faced with a new one, they stalled and asked to have the law checked.

That night the King sat late in the Palace among his advisors and courtiers while the Queen urged—as usual—drastic action. The next morning, scenting action, Strafford's "Cavaliers" gathered in the Palace Yard. At three in the afternoon, after long conversations, the king came down his staircase amid a throng of 400 gentlemen in arms. A little later his coach, surrounded by red coats, moved slowly toward Parliament, "outstripped by flying rumor."

Commons, which had watched all these cumbersome preparations from afar, sent Pym and his companions down the river to Coleman Street, where every house was Calvinist. The King's arrival was noisy; the clank of swords and feet was heard, the doors of Parliament were thrown open and the King ordered his followers to wait outside. His young men amused themselves in the open doorway by pointing their muskets at various Members. War was in the air.

The King walked between the rows of the silent Members to the Speaker's Chair, surveyed the House and satisfied himself that his "birds had flown." He departed as he entered, to cries of "Privilege! Privilege!" In the space of twenty-four hours he had undone all that his defenders had accomplished.

૨૭

The need of Commons to be defended against the King was now evident. Calvinist preachers, back in the people's pulpits, chose the text "To your tents, O Israel!"

A Committee of the Commons sat in the City for safety and the Arminian royalists were, for several days, afraid to speak. Even a majority of the Lords voted for nineteen propositions, or ordinances, to present to the King, demanding that he turn over to Parliament all control over the army and fortified places, revise the liturgy and government of the Church, dismiss all ministers of the Crown, and give Parliament control over the creation of all new peers.

Meanwhile the "train-bands" of London were called out and put on a war footing; 4,000 armed squires and freeholders from the Thames valley and the hills of Buckinghamshire arrived to protect the five Commoners wanted by the King. Mariners from the Royal Navy marched to the Guildhall, where Commons sat; all the elements of an armed insurrection appeared.

On January 10, 1642, Charles and his courtiers fled from the capital; the Queen took the Crown jewels to France, to raise men, ships and arms; the following day Commons returned to Whitehall to deliberate its next moves.

૨૭

Over the next eight months Parliament slowly prepared a civilian nation for a showdown with its King. The Arminians in Lords and Commons began to slip silently away to York, where Hyde was composing persuasive appeals in the King's name.

The King, angry and bewildered at the turn of events, talked about summoning a Grand Council, "of a type already obsolete in the twelfth century, but nobody came."[8]

"His only decisive act," Paul Johnson wrote, "in a desperate attempt to curry favor and prove his suspect allegiance to the State, was to seize and hang two Catholic priests, one a harmless old man of 90; to my mind this cruel and meaningless murder absolves the English, then and now, of any moral duty to pity this doomed sovereign."

If the King was doomed, what of Parliament? The Arminian Bishops and their supporters in Lords and Commons had silently departed; the Calvinists were reduced to 300 in Commons and thirty Peers.

All their lives were forfeit; they sent a message to Charles to come to a discussion about the management of the country—and the King, not accustomed to being summoned, refused. By 1642 Commons had created a Committee of Public Safety[9] and on the 12th of August instructed it to "raise an army."

Cromwell and others went home to their Counties to rally their forces; in July Parliament appointed the Earl of Essex its commander in chief; in August it issued a proclamation declaring that the nation was in peril.

That was accurate, for if Charles and his Arminians defeated the forces of Parliament, there was no doubt that they would have turned England into a European-style despotism. Tens of thousands of Calvinists would have poured toward America, where 20,000 had already settled, and England would have become a small branch of Europe.

Charles declared that Essex and his officers were traitors and raised his standard at Nottingham on August 22, 1642.

Johnson has commented on the oddity of these proceedings: "Such an act usually figured in formal charges of treason" (which may have been why Parliament outwaited the king). "Hence the strict logic of Parliament's indictment that Charles Stuart was in rebellion not merely against the nation but against the Crown itself."

That is logic after the event. At the time, the English Parliament was setting an example that America, France and Russia would later imitate.

---

8. Johnson, *op. cit.,* p. 193.
9. A title which the French would repeat in the 1790s.

A revolutionary-minded legislature declared that a legally installed hereditary monarch was a rebel against it, and raised an army to punish him.

Nothing like this had ever before occurred. The Netherlands had rebelled against a foreign despot. The Republic of Venice had a different history. The Swiss examples had more peacefully evolved.

The English were on their own, and were not repeating, but making history; their revolution was the first of its kind.[10]

---

10. English historians, including Johnson, came to similar conclusions.

Chapter Thirteen

WAR

— 〰 —

Kings will be tyrants from
policy, when subjects are rebels
from principle.

— Burke

At a time when most English cities had barely 10,000 people, London loomed. It was not only the largest seaport facing Europe, but held cathedrals and palaces, schools and slums. It was the capital where King and Parliament confronted one another, it was the scientific and intellectual center—and it harbored England's only slums.

Situated outside its walls and known as "liberties," its denizens included not only workingmen "but the broken population that collects around a great capital . . . herded in conditions of squalor, misery and disease that made London famous for its plagues, and terrible in riot and revolution."[1] London was modern when the rest of England was mired in medievalism, and London was the center of the revolution.

England in the 1640s was a hierarchical society with a tiny tip and a small ruling circle. There were only 122 noble houses,[2] 26 bishops and slightly over 300 Scots and Irish peers. There were less than 2,000 knights, about 9,000 squires and perhaps 14,000 "gentlemen." These included men whose money came not from land but from the professions, from commerce, or governmental office.

This tiny elite governed a population of about 4 million. Most people had no vote and no official voice; their opinions were worthless.

The Calvinist revolution changed that. Religion both levels and joins people; everyone can live and work for God. This opinion seeped slowly

---

1. Trevelyan, *op. cit.*, p. 51.
2. Under Elizabeth I only 50.

through the land from the time of Henry VIII, and warmed even the cool English.

꿍

When the revolution actually began, Parliament held London and, through its Members, extended tentacles into the Counties. The Members in the 500-man Commons were mostly gentry; 48 were younger sons of peers, 50 were merchants; all were landowners.

The revolutionaries held the prosperous east and southeast. The Navy was on their side, with its bases and custom duties, its control of goods and supplies.

The Royalists had Wales and the west, and a useful cavalry from the outdoor staffs of the nobility and the gentry. But Parliament occupied the commercial center of the realm; it could raise money from ongoing activities, while Charles had to rely upon the wealthy Catholic/Arminian nobility.

The capital resources of this group were initially immense. The Earl of Derby owned more than either Parliament or the King; the Earl of Worcester was able to save Charles from bankruptcy in June. They and some others maintained an almost feudal state in their great country houses and were deeply alarmed at the rise of the people.

The conventional military forces of the time consisted of noble officers and drafted men forced into service, miserably paid and poorly supplied—if supplied at all. There were no quartermaster corps; troops in Europe lived by robbing farms and towns for food and money. That was the horror of the Thirty Year's War, which had beggared the German States. That was the European pattern that Charles' "Cavaliers" fell into as though by rote.

Parliament, or rather Oliver Cromwell and assorted Calvinists, were to change that.

꿍

The King's forces seemed, at first, to have a great advantage. Their officers were experienced at fencing, hard riding, outdoor sports that required quick reflexes and decision; unspoken teamwork. Cavalry was then considered the decisive weapon of an army, and Charles' cavalry was superb.

In the first serious battle at Edgehill on October 23, 1642, the King's forces, led by Prince Rupert,[3] descended upon the Parliamentary infantry so effectively that it was almost a massacre. But after it thundered its bloody way through Essex's men, the horsemen stopped to plunder baggage. That gave the Parliamentary infantry time to successfully counterattack.

Captain Cromwell arrived with his hundred or so handpicked horsemen (all volunteers known to him) in time to take part in the counterattack.

In the end the battle was important because it had halted a Royalist effort to get to London, and because of what Cromwell grasped, and later put into motion.

He was deeply impressed by the speed and force of Rupert's cavalry, but saw that "it could only sting once." The Prince was unable to control them after that first strike. Cromwell told his cousin John Hampden afterwards that, "At my first going into this engagement, I saw our men beaten at every hand."

Then he added, "Your troopers are most of them old decayed servingmen and tapsters and such kind of fellows; their troopers are gentlemen's sons, younger sons and persons of quality; do you think that the spirits of such base and mean fellows will ever be able to encounter gentlemen that have honor and courage and resolution in them?"

This was not prejudice: it was recognition that men from the lowest levels forced into service were unequally matched against men accustomed to independent decisions.

"You must get men of spirit," Cromwell urged, "and not take ill what I say—I know you will not—of a spirit that is likely to go as far as gentlemen will go, or else you will be beaten still." Hampden shook his head: Cromwell seemed to be dwelling on the abstract.

&

Defeated in his first drive for London, Charles settled at Oxford, less than 60 miles away. It had theaters, actors, courtiers and their ladies, Jesuits and Bishops, all the comforts of court. It was difficult, sur-

---

3. The son of Charles' sister Elizabeth and the Elector of the Palatinate.

rounded with so many signs of Kingship, served on bended knee, to believe in the possibility of royal defeat. Charles accordingly spurned negotiations with Parliament, and Oxford teemed with his Cavaliers, Catholics and Arminians.

In November 1642 enough engagements took place to reveal that the Parliamentary commander Essex was a conventional soldier with little originality and, even worse, no killer instinct.

As the year 1643 yawned and stretched Cromwell began to collect more men, and distinguished himself enough to be promoted to Colonel. The men he chose were mostly freeholders or their sons, who joined "as a matter of conscience."

What was more unusual was that Cromwell made officers out of men "not such as were soldiers or men of estate, but such as were common men, poor and of mean parentage, only he would give them the title of Godly, precious men. . . ."

That was revolutionary, and it was to change the world. It was not introduced by French Jacobins or Russian Marxists, but by an English Calvinist. It was Cromwell who saw value in tradesmen, artisans, farmers and even laborers; "men of estates so small they were not even entitled to vote at elections."[4]

Richard Baxter said that from the start Cromwell "'had a special care to get religious men into his troops' because these were the sort of men he esteemed and loved; and . . . from this happy choice flowed 'the avoidings of those disorders, mutinies, plunderings and grievances of the country which debased men in armies are commonly guilty of.'"

But Cromwell disciplined. In April 1643 two of his troopers who tried to desert were whipped in the marketplace at Huntington. By May the Parliamentarian newspaper *Special Passages* said that "Cromwell had 2,000 brave men, all disciplined; no man swears but he pays twelve pence; if he be drunk he is set in stocks or worse, if one calls the other 'Roundhead' he is cashiered; in so much that the countries where they come leap for joy of them, and come in and join them."[5]

In May 1643 Cromwell, badly outnumbered, attacked a Royalist

4. Johnson, *op. cit.*, p. 198.

5. Antonia Fraser, *Cromwell, The Lord Protector* (New York, N. Y.: Alfred A. Knopf, 1973), p. 101.

force at Belton and killed over a hundred at a cost of two men. His report said, "God hath given us, this evening, a glorious victory over our enemies." And later, in a private letter, ". . . it pleased God to cast the scale."[6] He was to see the Hand of God in every outcome, and to look for it in every event. (That basic Christian habit continues to startle and puzzle non-Christian historians.)

꙳

He enlarged his methods with experience. It remains puzzling that his use of Biblical principles in military recruitment has never been imitated. Cromwell's men became steadily more famous for being religious, obedient, fearless, disciplined. They represented the previously submerged, ignored, despised people of England.

But the end of the first year of war found the Parliamentary forces foundering. The Queen had returned from France to herald the arrival of arms and ammunition, and joined the King's forces at Oxford. Essex dallied while his forces dwindled from disease and desertion; Parliament was defeated at Adalton Moor and again at Roundway Down, Bristol; Hampden was mortally wounded.

In this extremity Parliament turned toward Scotland. The Scots, however, would not intervene unless England became Presbyterian. The name springs from *Presbuteros* or elder. The Scots, who had come to the conclusion that their divine mission was to reform the world, wanted their Presbyteries and governing Synod to serve as an example for the English. Unless Parliament agreed, the Scots would stay home.

Pym was agreeable: if England was not Episcopal, it might be Presbyterian. The only snag was that the Scots Presbyterians did not accept governmental authority over their Church, and the English Parliament wanted to govern the Church of England.

On the other hand, Scotland was a foreign country; the English had never ratified James I's attempt at Union, but Parliament needed its help.

The revolution, however, was against Arminianism more than against Charles. On July 1, 1643, 121 English divines, 30 English

6. Ibid.

laymen and (later) eight Scots delegates met at Westminster Hall to define a new doctrine for the Church of England. As ever when theological issues are involved, divergent opinions appeared. Some Independents withdrew because they believed that churches should be as free of Presbyteries or Synods as of bishops. Nor was the Westminster Assembly free of political strings: Parliament itself abolished the Arminian Episcopacy and laid the groundwork for a return to traditional Calvinism. The resulting deliberations, word by word and clause by clause, were not to be completed for another five years, but they were begun.

That beginning led to an agreement between Parliament and Edinburgh, concluded in September 1643, in a Solemn League and Covenant to maintain the Church in Scotland as established, and to reform religion in England "according to the Word of God." Despite this vague wording, it was clear that English Calvinists had made a moral commitment to Presbyterianism.

In the same month Charles made peace with the rebels in Ireland and sent for some to help him in England. This verification of what English Calvinists had, all along, predicted, intensified opposition against him—and expanded the revolution to involve three countries.

෧

In October 1643 Cromwell shared the credit for a victory at Winceby with Lord Fairfax. It was by then clear that the Earls Essex and Manchester, military chiefs of the revolution, were not equal to their task. Cromwell began to complain, with clumsy obliquity, about noble incompetents. His opinion of "plain men" was rising; of the aristocracy, falling. The revolution was moving.

That motion was clouded by propaganda. The Arminian clergy then (and later) charged that Cromwell was an iconoclast, and left a trail of smashed churches and cathedrals in his wake. But G. F. Nuttall[7] proved that, "Damage attributed to Cromwell was, as a rule, committed during the Reformation. There is no proven instance of him or his men deliberately despoiling churches; though he systematically 'slighted' royalist castles."

---

7. "Was Cromwell an Iconoclast?" *Transactions of the Congregational Historical Society, XII.*

A contemporary, Anthony Wood, angrily said, "To give a further character of the court, though they were neat and gay in their apparel, yet they were very nasty and beastly, leaving their excrements in every corner, in chimneys, studies, coal-houses and cellars. Rude, rough, whoremongers; vaine, empty, careless."[8]

ᘏᕼ

The revolution took another turn when John Pym, the masterly diplomat and Calvinist leader in Parliament, died in December 1643. "He was buried," said Macaulay, "among the Plantagenets," after an elaborate funeral. His departure meant that Parliamentary splits and fissures increased.

In January 1644 the Scots army entered Northumberland. In March it besieged York, but was unable to gain entry. Prince Rupert led the King's forces to the rescue in July; en route he paused to massacre the people of Bolton, a Calvinist clothing town. Arriving at York, Rupert relieved the city, and the besiegers withdrew.

The Prince, 23 years old, pursued and found the Calvinists at Marston Moor, eight miles west of York. The Calvinists had three armies: one from Scotland and two English. Rupert and the Earl of Newcastle had less foot soldiers but the same amount of cavalry—and Rupert's cavalry had never been defeated. Together the armies were the largest yet fielded; it was clear the engagement would be important.

Rupert was confident. Looking toward the opposition, he asked, "Is Cromwell there?"

Late in the day, when Rupert was at supper, the combined Calvinists struck. Battles were then finally hand to hand, as in primitive times; the Border Whitecoats fought to the last man. Rupert's cavalry was driven from the field by Cromwell's. Rupert escaped with 6,000 horsemen; the rest of his 21,000 force had dissolved; Marston Moor became the largest burial ground in the nation, and Cromwell became the military hero of the revolution.

ᘏᕼ

---

8. cf. Johnson, *op. cit,* p. 211.

Ordinarily that would have ended the war, but the Earl of Essex chose to lead an expedition into Cornwall, the heart of the King's region. He was encircled, his men were cut off; the Earl had to escape by ship.

Sir William Waller was appointed to save Essex, but despite all his efforts was unable to raise a sufficient force. Men pressed into service on his behalf ran off. "Hundreds of soldiers wandered about from shire to shire, from regiment to regiment (from army to army, from King to Parliament) in search of more regular pay or greater license to plunder." Waller told Commons "We cannot win until we have an Army of our own."

Cromwell, who had come to similar conclusions, rose in Parliament in December 1644 to propose a "Self-Denying Ordinance," in which all Members should resign their military commands. He managed, by this suggestion, to avoid the quagmire of recriminations and to open the way for a new military command. He had learned; the revolution was learning.

ൟ

One of its lessons was that the past has a way of lingering. The Lords were offended at the criticisms of the Earl of Manchester. Months were to pass before they gave way.

Another was one that all protracted wars produce: a Peace Party, willing to forget all divisions, no matter how deep. Charles was sending feelers to the Scots. These resulted in the Treaty of Uxbridge, designed to pull the Scots out of the struggle. It only lasted a month; the Scots emerged more knowledgeable about the "eel-like Charles," who twisted out of all agreements on all occasions.

Cromwell, meanwhile, toiled with ways of putting the Army on a sound financial basis. Parliament, the traditional collector of taxes in the land and master of its commercial core, was well equipped, by experience and inclination, to deal with such a problem.

ൟ

In January 1645 Parliament recalled the Archbishop of Canterbury, sequestered in the Tower and almost forgotten. In retrospect he seems to have been tried to remind people of why the revolution was launched.

His trial in Lords elicited his explanation that he had been more concerned with forms than substance in religion. That echoed an earlier time, when such religious coolness reflected majority opinion.

But the admission that he had men mutilated, imprisoned and executed for violating "forms" was enough to destroy sympathy for him. He went to the block on January 10, 1645. Afterward much mawkish sentiment was written by Arminians about this pitiless prelate. But few remarked that Laud was forgiven his debts, as the Lord's Prayer says, as he forgave the debts of others.

৯৬

Through the winter and into the spring of 1645, Parliament and the Calvinist camps (for they had by then marvelously multiplied) argued over a New Model army.

The crucial issue was not its needs, but whether or not the men to be recruited would be from all varieties of Protestantism. Christianity had always, from its first centuries onward, denied this practice. The early Church had pursued the Paulists with fire and sword—and not only the Paulists, but all forms of heresies. Had it not, Christianity would have remained only one of dozens of contending sects; its message would have drowned in a cacophony of confusion. There would then have been no Christendom; no international civilization marked by diversity and innovation amid unity; no Europe as we know it.

An indissoluble combination of Church and State had created Christendom. Its riches and power and emerging position as world leader seemed unanswerable verification of the value of that combination. Yet that combination allowed the State to impose a form of Christianity over the beliefs of the people, and no tyranny is worse than one based upon the denial of the individual's unique relationship to God.

The Government of Charles I had attempted to force Arminianism upon the English and the Scots and provoked the people into revolution. Parliament, therefore, confronted the possibility of losing its war with the King if it forced traditional Calvinism upon all its own supporters.

Cromwell saw this from a military viewpoint—and he was a twice-born Calvinist. It is one of the great surprises of history that Cromwell

should have emerged as a military genius so late in life; he himself
ascribed it to The Hand of the Lord. From a strictly military viewpoint
he needed dedicated troops. But his observations of men led, indirectly,
to an opinion that their beliefs did not have to mirror his own.

After the siege of Bristol he wrote to the Speaker,

> Presbyterians, Independents, all here had the same spirit of faith and
> prayer. . . . They agree here, know no names of difference; pity it should
> be otherwise anywhere. All that believe have the real unity, which is most
> glorious because inward and spiritual. . . . As for being united in forms,
> commonly called uniformity, every Christian will for peace sake study
> and do as far as conscience will permit; and from brethren, in things of
> the mind, we look for no compulsion but that of light and reason.[9]

ॐ

There was also a social element in the impasse over the New Model
Army during the winter and spring of 1645. Peers smarted over
Cromwell's repeated elevation of "common men" over those of prouder
lineage. He was accused, by the Earl of Manchester himself, of having
told the Earl that he would be a better man "if he were plain Mr.
Montague."

This was part of the Earl's rationalizations of why he had military
defeats; accusations flew. Cromwell was accused of building his own
reputation by talking to the special correspondents of the newspapers of
the day, and of having a claque of supporters. Cromwell responded that
his "Self-Denying Ordinance" would remove him—as well as Manchester—from command.

The two central issues for the Lords were whether the traditional
insistence of the Government on one faith was being flouted by
Cromwell and his group—and whether the ancient principles of
aristocracy were being downgraded.

Cromwell argued that unless the army was restructured, the war
would be lost. He made some sharp observations. He said the "profane-
ness and impiety and the absence of all religion, the drinking and
gaming, and all manner of license and laziness" in the army led to its

---

9. cf. Johnson, *op. cit.*, p. 212.

poor performance. He argued that "till the whole army was *new modelled* and governed under a stricter discipline, they must not expect any notable success in anything they were about."

His Parliamentary opponents cited history. The leaders of Greece and Rome served in both Senate and the military. But Cromwell had the heaviest of all arguments: that defeat would mean the execution as traitors of everyone in Parliament and everyone who had taken arms against the King. Painful restructuring was better than that.

≈

After the Lords agreed, Manchester lost his command, Lord Fairfax was appointed commander in chief with Cromwell second in command—and both left Parliament.

The New Model Army took to the field. It constituted only 22,000 of the 88,000 Parliamentary troops in existence, some of which were present when Fairfax and Cromwell, after complicated maneuvers, met King Charles and Prince Rupert and their army at Naseby. Once again Cromwell and his cavalry saved the day, mainly because Cromwell could control his cavalry after their initial charge. He hurled them against Rupert's foot troops, who gave way, *while Rupert was two miles away, plundering the Parliamentary baggage.*

Rupert returned to find his infantry in chaos. Despite his frantic exhortations and the presence of the King, his army fled. Even at this moment Cromwell's iron discipline kept his men from looting the abandoned wagons of the enemy, but the Parliamentary troops were not so inhibited. They rushed at the wagons, and massacred 100 Irish female camp followers, and slashed the faces of the English ones.[10]

≈

London rejoiced. Had the battle gone the other way King Charles would have returned in triumph. On June 21, 1645, 3,000 royalist prisoners were paraded through its streets. The mass of Charles' army had been destroyed. Though large pockets remained, victory was—for the first time—foreseeable.

---

10. Fraser, *op. cit.,* p. 161.

Cromwell was raised to Lieutenant General. The Royalists' cavalry took refuge in Cornwall. In six months their looting alienated even loyalists in that region. The New Model Army then began to besiege and topple the various castles and strongholds in which Charles, dedicated to the past, had stationed garrisons.

Prince Rupert surrendered at Bristol in August, Winchester toward the end of September. Basing House, a complex Catholic stronghold maintained by the Marquess of Winchester, resisted to the end; a quarter of the defenders died before it was overcome. The Marquess was physically taken; Inigo Jones was carried out naked, wrapped in a blanket; six Catholic priests died.

༄

By mid-November 1645, the Scots Commissioners sent terms to King Charles. The Independents, who had become an important minority inside Parliament and the New Model Army, were against this: they wanted to fight to the end. But the Scots were upset because Parliament had not yet declared all England Presbyterian, as it had promised.

Charles negotiated with the Scots at the same time that he promised the Irish Catholics that he would create a Catholic England.

Parliament, not to be outdone, drew its own terms for the King. These included a dukedom for the Earls of Essex and Warwick, a marquisate for Manchester, earldoms for Lord Fairfax and a viscountcy for Holles; Thomas Fairfax and Oliver Cromwell were to be barons. Old forms die hard.

The Scots asked Charles to agree to a Church settlement produced by Parliament and the Assemblies of both nations—according to the Presbyterian system.

Even the Independents had a plan. They offered to emigrate as a body to Ireland, leaving the New Model Army and the fallen fortresses to the King. (That brings to mind the image of a New Ireland, similar to the New England being created by Congregationalists and others in America.)

Such a welter of plans and possibilities, never before witnessed, was not to be repeated until the French excitement of the 1790s, over 135 years in the future.

In retrospect it is remarkable that Charles could not find enough elements of cooperation amid these various proposals. They seem, instead, to have increased his ridiculous conceit. He believed that he was the one man all others had to have, and that this gave him some sort of power, when the truth was that he had lost all power; he was wanted only as a figurehead.

⁊●

Parliament, however, saw itself as the victor in the struggle for power over the King. A new struggle began over the spoils.

These ranged, as had the war, across religious and political lines. The hated Arminian Prayer Book was outlawed and the pro-Catholic Arminian service was forbidden by law. In keeping with the times, 2,000 Arminian clergymen were ousted from their benefices (with, however, pensions) and replaced by Calvinists. Parliament also loaded the costs of war upon the vanquished by levying huge fines upon the adherents of the King. These ranged from a half to a sixth of the value of their estates, continuing a process that began during the war.

"Many old and honorable families disappeared," said Macaulay, "and many new men rose rapidly to affluence." For "months and years after the last shot was fired," said Trevelyan, "Royalist gentry were still cutting down their trees, mortgaging and selling their estates in a fallen market, and sending their wives to soften . . . Committeemen in London, with need of bribes and tears for the lords of the hour." But, unlike the French and the Russians later, there were no massacres; no wholesale confiscations; no "purge."

⁊●

Cromwell was told, in January 1646, that he had been voted a handsome £2,500 a year, to come from the properties of the Marquess of Worcester in Wales, and other "delinquent" Catholic properties.

But there were still military holdouts. The King was still at Oxford, though he heard daily of continuing losses. He fled, finally, on April 17, 1646, to the Scots army at Newark. (He was to always believe, despite all evidence, that he was loved by the Scots.)

His remaining men in the university town surrendered on June 20,

1646, and England—for the first time in four years—relaxed in peace.

ॐ

In 1646 Parliament finally kept its pledge to the Scots—with reservations. It made Presbyterianism official in terms of organization and creed, but kept a veto power over all ecclesiastical decisions and appointments. This was, of course, a violation of the Scots system, which held the Kirk separate from the State.

Nor did Parliament stop there. Having established the Church of England as Presbyterian, orders went out to persecute all dissenters; Baptists and Seekers and "Nonconformists" of every stripe. Unitarians were to be put to death; Baptists and others imprisoned for life. No laymen were to be allowed to preach or expound on Scriptures.

In December, 1646, Parliament also agreed to pay £400,000 to the Scots, who in turn agreed to leave northern England—and to hand over King Charles.[11]

That arrangement was not universally admired. At Newcastle the people taunted the departing Scots, called them Jews for having sold their King and their honor, and threatened to stone them.[12] Parliament made arrangements to sequester the monarch in Holdenby Hall in Northamptonshire in February, 1647.

ॐ

By 1647 the Westminster Abbey finally ended its labors, and issued the Westminster Confession of Faith, Larger Catechism and Smaller Catechism, reaffirming the Calvinist doctrines of predestination, election and reprobation. (These have, ever since, undergirded all Presbyterian churches.)

The Presbyterian core in Parliament then voted to disband the Independents and the New Model Army. The official reason was to form a new army to suppress the rebellion in Ireland. Unofficially, it was a prelude to the persecution of all dissenters.

That unofficial reason appeared between the lines when Parliamen-

---

11. The Queen and the Prince of Wales were both in France.
12. Fraser, *op. cit.*, p. 184.

tary Presbyterians announced that the officers of the new army would have to swear to uphold the Covenant. Further, only half the men would be accepted. When the New Model men asked for their pay, Parliament voted half in cash, half in promises.

The New Model Army then created a crisis by refusing to disband. Cromwell attempted to mediate, but he had enemies in Parliament who now considered him an unimportant war hero whose time had passed. Parliament meanwhile negotiated with the King, who was in state at the vast, turreted palace built by Queen Elizabeth's favorite Christopher Hatton.

Charles, a man who would demand silver shoes for a gift horse, said among other demands that he would honor Presbyterianism for only three years. The Independents, learning that Parliament was joining the King, knew that such a combination meant their deaths.

෨

Under army orders the Cornet Joyce, a former tailor who had served in Cromwell's regiment, went to Holdenby with 500 men and secured the King. Charles asked what commission he had, and Joyce—at a loss for words—pointed to his armed men.

Charles, with a flash of the Stuart charm, said, "It is as fair a commission and as well written a commission as I have seen a commission written in my life."

When Parliament learned that the Independents had seized the King, it voted to arrest Cromwell and send him to the Tower when he next appeared. He fled in the early morning hours for the army headquarters in Newmarket.

Parliament, deeply frightened, immediately voted to pay the New Model Army arrears—but the whirlwind had arrived.

Chapter Fourteen

THE PEOPLE ACT

——————— ❧ ———————

Let the end try the men.
— Shakespeare

Parliament in 1647, greatly reduced by the attrition of Arminian/ Royalists from its membership since 1641, was dominated by Presbyterians. These were convinced that the King's forces had been defeated by the intervention of the Scots Presbyterians. The Westminster Confession, recently formulated, provided them with a solid Calvinist framework for the realm. The Presbyterian majority in Commons believed it was only fulfilling promises made to the Scots when it mandated a Presbyterian faith and voted that the King should become head of a Presbyterian national Church of England.

The rest of Parliament, however, did not want to replace Arminian absolutism with a Presbyterian version. The Independents no longer believed in a National church, but wanted all varieties of religious worship, except Catholicism, to be free of governmental limits. That was especially true of the members of the New Model Army and Cromwell. Independent religious beliefs inescapably intertwined with new opinions about the limits of Parliament, much as they had earlier led to opinions about the limits of the King.

The Presbyterian majority decided to settle this problem by dissolv-ing the New Model Army, but it refused to disband. Instead, it restructured itself, as though Parliament had, silently, lost all authority over it.

The restructuring was surprisingly innovative. It created an Army Council of generals and senior officers, which included two commis-sioned officers and two agents (or Agitators) from each regiment. That was not only advanced for its time: it has yet to be equalled by any armed force in the world.

The Army Council, which Cromwell joined, sent a message to Parliament denying that the Army intended to overthrow Presbyterianism; it merely wanted liberty of conscience for its members. "He that ventures his life for the liberty of his country," Cromwell wrote, "I wish he trust God for the liberty of his conscience, and you for the liberty he fights for."

An army that allowed enlisted men to debate policy with generals—and that sent messages as if from an equal body to Parliament—seemed to many to contradict the principles of established order.

❧

Meanwhile the Army held a trump card in the person of the King. Cromwell, Fairfax and the other senior officers met with Charles, and found him surprisingly affable. "Sir," he told Fairfax, "I have as good an interest in the Army as you."

But Cromwell and Fairfax also found the King as elusive as quicksilver. He reserved the right, he said, to change course at any time in the interest of the Crown. But he could also charm when he chose. The sight of the King with the royal children brought tears to Cromwell's eyes; he decided that Charles was an upright man. Charles did not have the same opinion of Cromwell: he told his aide Sir John Berkeley that "the fact that none of the Army officers asked anything for themselves made it hard for him to trust them."[1] Principles were alien to Charles.

The Parliamentary Presbyterians sent secret word to the King that the Scots army would come to his rescue, while agitators in the New Model Army wanted to march on the capital and settle matters by force. The Army Council called a large meeting to discuss this, attended by between fifty and a hundred officers, to which Agitators were admitted.

After debate it was agreed that the Council would draw up a program to be ratified by a special committee of a dozen officers and as many Agitators. Then it would be forwarded to Parliament. (This reminds one of the Soviet councils of 1917, 270 years in the future.)

The Army plan initially called for biennial sessions of Parliament, a

1. Fraser, *op. cit.*, p. 201.

Council of State, free elections and an enlarged franchise, the right to dissent with both King and Lords, no bishops and no compulsory Prayer Book, repeal of disabilities against Catholics and no compulsory obedience to Presbyterianism. Berkeley told King Charles that "never was a Crown so near lost, so cheaply recovered"—if the King agreed.

❧

All this led King Charles to conclude that, with his opponents quarreling, the tides had turned in his favor. Flanked by the Earl of Maitland from Scotland and others from the City, the King openly exulted. He swept the Army Council's proposals for peace off the table contemptuously and said loudly, "You cannot do this without me! You fall to ruin if I do not sustain you!"

Colonel Rainsborough, whose sister was married to Governor Winthrop of Massachusetts, lost no time telling the troops about Charles' transformation. Cromwell was to never forget it; it was an insight that ultimately led to the King's death. It also led to the Army's march on Parliament.

On August 6, 1647 the Army, 18,000 strong with the King in their midst, entered London. The Speakers and sixty Independent MPs were with them; eleven Presbyterian leaders, "symbols of counterrevolution," discreetly vanished. Parliament hastily saluted irresistible power.

Charles was not wrong in assuming that this meant a great change in the revolution; nor was he far off the mark in expecting it to collapse in internal disarray. His great error was in overlooking Cromwell.

❧

Cromwell's task was to unite the Army, Parliament and the sectarians. The Army came first. For two weeks beginning on the 28 October 1647, about 40 men of the Army met informally in the Church of St. Mary in Putney[2] and in Johnson's words, "proceeded to invent modern politics—to invent, in fact, the public framework of the world in which nearly 3,000 million people now live."[3]

---

2. C. H. Firth, ed., *The Clark Papers*, vol. 1 (The Camden Society, 1891).
3. Johnson, *op. cit.*, p. 171.

That assessment narrows the significance of the 1640s to politics, but the men who met at Putney Church were less concerned with politics than with man's relationship to God, and what that meant to the relationship of men with one another. The revolution, in other words, was *religious;* its political significance was a side issue, a result.

Much has been made, for instance, of the flowering of English drama, poetry and literature in the late Elizabethan and early Stuart periods, ranging from Shakespeare and Johnson to John Donne, Herbert and others.[4] But Sir Herbert Grierson has written that by the time the Long Parliament met, plays and poems were "merely a sparkling side-stream beside the huge river of religious treatises, volumes of sermons, and political and sectarian tracts that poured from the presses. Afterward the river became a torrent. . . ."[5]

All the factions in England in late 1647, therefore, were Christians first and politicians second. The Presbyterians wanted a Church as well-defined as that which Knox established, with a limited monarchy and a stronger Parliament. The Independents believed that all believers are important in the sight of God, and that led to the idea of individual freedom and independence.

John Lilburne and John Wildman, leaders of the "Levellers," asserted that "every man in England hath as clear a right to elect his representatives as the greatest person in England." But what men such as Cromwell, John Milton, Ireton and others really wanted was "rule by the virtuous, selected by men of standing."

Maurice Ashton, a distinguished English specialist in the period, has observed that "historians of many nationalities from Americans to Russians have seized upon . . . pamphleteers and bloated them into veritable Platos, Rousseaus and Marxes. But a sense of proportion may be used. What these men had in common was not a premature bent for Marxism, but a . . . faith in the value of Christian revelation to inspired individuals, in the virtues of . . . Christianity, and in the immediacy of the Second Coming of Christ."

ॐ

---

4. Both Donne and Herbert were Arminian clergymen.
5. Maurice Ashley, *England in the Seventeenth Century* (Penguin Books, 1967), p. 109.

The men at the Putney Church meeting represented every level of English society[6] and their religious ardor was shown in their frequent breaks for prayer. Three Levellers were present.

Despite the illusions of the Presbyterians in Parliament, the Army knew it alone had defeated the King. It also knew that it included officers and men who had, previously, been excluded from the religious and political consensus. These men knew that Parliament intended to send them back to that oblivion—and they were determined not to go.

That led to a series of problems. What was their alternative to the patterns of the past? They had fought for a revolution that transferred power from the King to Parliament. Now they disputed the power of Parliament.

The Fifth Monarchy men, basing their arguments on the Book of Revelation, wanted a Government of saints. But, like saints, they were few in number. Another group, known as Diggers because they set about digging in the earth of common land, called for an end to private property and all social distinctions; if nobody owned anything there could be no theft, no crime, no distinctions.

These views were politely heard by Cromwell and the Independents at the Putney Church meeting, and not without sympathy—for Cromwell was a leader of the Independents, who favored the freedom of all groups to form and maintain their own churches (except Catholics, who were regarded as representatives of absolutism and, therefore, enemies of everyone's religious rights.)

The Levellers proposed to change Parliament's opinions by changing its composition—and by setting limits on its powers. (This anticipated what was accomplished at Philadelphia 142 years later.)

The Levellers were misnamed by their enemies, for they had no argument with the social structure of society, nor did they believe in levelling people's property.[7]

The Levellers wanted to expand the right to vote to all except women, children, servants, paupers and criminals. They also wanted to abolish

---

6. Thanks to the Reformation and the English Bible, most of the men were better grounded in the faith than much of the modern clergy.

7. Edmund S. Morgan, *Inventing the People: The Rise of Popular Sovereignty in England and America* (New York, N.Y.: W. W. Norton & Company, 1988), p. 68.

the erratic distribution of seats (established by the Crown), to represent people by population, and to eliminate the House of Lords (but not to forbid Lords from sitting in Commons, if elected).

The Levellers had also thought about the powers of Parliament. Richard Overton, one of their Leaders, argued that a group of men could not do to people at large what individuals could not do to one another. A year later Overton told Parliament that "neither you, nor none else can have any Power at all to conclude the People in matters that concern the Worship of God. . . ."

Cromwell was repelled by the sweeping nature of Leveller proposals. It would overturn, he observed, virtually the entire pattern of government. If it were approved, what would prevent another group from making further drastic changes? England would become another Switzerland; it would produce "an absolute desolation to the nation."

He, Ireton and others believed that a man without any more fixed property than what "he may carry about with him," a man who is "here today and gone tomorrow," would be enabled, by numbers, to enact confiscatory laws.

Voices rose to question the assumption that most men are evil; others wondered aloud why a 40 shilling freehold should be a barrier to a man with less property. Ireton said he wasn't defending the existing provision; he merely maintained there should be one.[8]

The radicals argued that free men should not be hindered by property qualifications and questioned the inequality of property. This led to division over the laws of "Nature," or Natural Rights and property rights. Edward Sexby, another Leveller, observed that men without property had risked their lives, only to be told that they had no rights without property.

This carried matters almost to the brink; it is remarkable that Cromwell was able to moderate the debate. Someone said a half loaf is better than none; Cromwell and Ireton agreed that men who had fought should have the vote. Whether that right should be expanded might be left for another day to decide.

To expand the vote to all, he mordantly observed, might be to lose all: the people might vote the King back in power. In early November, after

---

8. Johnson, *op. cit.*, p. 202.

two weeks of a most remarkable debate, the men returned to their regiments and the Army proposal was presented to the King.

It would have spared the estates of the royalists, allowed the Episcopacy to be retained shorn of coercive power, permitted the use of the Prayer Book by all who chose it (these clauses alone would have reconciled half the realm), and enabled Parliament to limit royal power. "The scheme," wrote Trevelyan, "was wrecked by its very merits. It was drawn up to conciliate all parties, but it came too late; all parties were now inflamed, and it displeased all alike." No group liked the concessions to others.

Finally, the proposal was wrecked by the traditional symbol of unity: the King. He escaped from Hampden Court, where he had been living luxuriously, to Carisbrooke Castle on the Isle of Wight on November 15, 1647.

৵

Charles negotiated with the Scots, and agreed to accept Presbyterianism in England for three years and to suppress all the sects, if he regained his throne. The Scots, who had launched the revolution against Charles in the first place, then decided that it was God's Will that Presbyterianism should be established as the ruling faith everywhere. Their Parliament, convinced that Charles had been persuaded to their cause, ratified plans to invade England. On May 3, 1648, the Scots issued a Manifesto calling on all England to take the Covenant, suppress all religious dissent from Presbyterianism and to disband the New Model Army.

Despite objections by the Marquess of Argyll and some others, the Duke of Hamilton led a Scots army across the border to restore Charles I as absolute King. Royalist Cavaliers both in and out of England hurried to join the new conflict.

The men of the New Model Army were outraged. The King had played with them, had pretended to negotiate, and then treacherously fled to incite a new war. Calling him "the man of blood," they swore to call him to account. For the first time, the war took a personal turn against Charles.

৵

Royalist insurrections blazed on every side. Cornwall rose; Devonshire rose; London rioted. A cry of "God Save The King" arose, and the long affinity between the Stuarts and the theater, the poets and the ballad-singers began to make itself felt. "One of the great motifs of popular English history—the captivity of the King—was beginning to play on men's emotions."[9] Cavaliers were to benefit by this then and later.

Meanwhile Presbyterians made common cause with Arminians against the Independents and the New Model Army. How these theological absolutists expected to settle their differences with one another if they defeated the New Model Army was a conundrum their leaders dared not mention, let alone answer.

The Arminian Cavaliers and Presbyterians, however, represented minorities. The majority of the English people were war-weary and refused to volunteer; Cavaliers riding to war were not interrupted by any except Cromwell's New Model men.

On May 3, 1648 Cromwell led part of the Army to Wales where he laid siege to Pembroke Castle. This stronghold, nearly impregnable, took an agonizing and difficult six weeks to reduce.

Those who surrendered were treated with relative leniency excepting the three leaders: Poyer, Laugharne and Powell were sent to London and the Tower. There they received the death sentence, but General Fairfax intervened to reduce this to a single man. In accordance with custom a child drew the lots, Laugharne and Powell drew papers reading "Life Given by God." But Poyer's paper was blank and he was duly shot in public at Covenant Square.[10]

While Fairfax suppressed revolts in Kent, a Scots army crossed the Tweed on July 8, 1648 and moved to within 40 miles of Liverpool. Cromwell had barely time to reach a point to intersect them by early August, after a forced march all the way from Wales.

The ensuing three day battle was one of the most gruelling of the time; the Scots troops were green but fought ferociously. Milton wrote later of "Darwin's stream with blood of Scots imbued." In the end, despite what Cromwell called "their great resolution," they were defeated. Cromwell divided his Scots prisoners into two groups: pressed men,

---

9. Trevelyan, *op. cit.,* p. 286.
10. Fraser, *op. cit.,* p. 241.

whom he sent home and volunteers, whom he had shipped to Barbados, where they worked as slaves on plantations. That set a precedent England would follow until 1715.

The news of that victory diminished the enthusiasm of the King's forces in other places. Cavaliers at Cochester surrendered to Fairfax, who, with an unusual severity, had two of the three Cavalier commanders shot for what he believed to be wanton shedding of blood by engaging in a new war. That reflected the new, hardened attitude of the New Model Army, which was infuriated at both the Presbyterian Parliament and the King for pretending to negotiate while planning war.

But while Cromwell continued North, Parliament once again resumed negotiations with Charles.

Inside Scotland the moderate faction, which had opposed Hamilton's invasion, was strengthened by his defeat. Chief among these was Archibald Campbell, Marquess of Argyll, owner of vast western domains and chief of a notably fierce clan. Argyll, a Calvinist who rose at five and prayed till eight, had much in common with Cromwell, who prayed often and fervently—and encouraged others to do the same.

Cromwell and Argyll parted as allies though records are vague as to the details of what they agreed. All that seems definite is that no further incursions were to be expected from Scotland.

> ?◆

En route to the South, Cromwell paused to besiege the Castle of Pontefact. That was as complex and difficult as a battle, while Arminian royalists launched guerrilla efforts. In one such raid Colonel Rainsborough was kidnapped and, in a scuffle, killed. That created a sensation in Parliament, for Rainsborough was known to have called for a trial of King Charles.

Meanwhile the King on the Isle of Wight seemed unperturbed. He paused in his reading to copy the verses of Claudian at the court of the Emperor Honorius saying that it was an error to call service to a distinguished Prince slavery, "since there was no sweeter liberty than under a worthy King."[11]

---

11. Fraser, *op. cit.*, p. 263.

The New Model Army thought differently. On November 7, 1648, they sent a *Remonstrance* to Parliament saying that Charles had betrayed his trust, calling for his trial—and the trial of other major instigators of the recent war.

That *Remonstrance* did not please Fairfax, who was against a change in Government, and was drawn and delivered without Cromwell. John Lilburne, the hypnotic leader of the Levellers visited Cromwell at the siege of Pontefact and found him anxious for peaceful settlements among all factions.

In a letter to his cousin Robin Hammond, who was guarding the King on the Isle of Wight, Cromwell wrote, on November 6, 1648, "I profess to thee I desire from my heart, I have prayed for it, I have waited for the day to see the union and right understanding between the godly people (Scots, English, Jews, Gentiles, Presbyterians, Independents, Anabaptists and All)."

Meanwhile, as was his habit, he watched for signs of God's Will. That habit, dating from his conversion, was to stay with him all his life, and was the reason that he was never the first to suggest a cause of action. He waited to see the trend of events not out of caution, but because he believed that was how God made His Will evident.

But later in November 1647, Cromwell began to move closer to the New Model Army demands. In several letters to Hammond, he began to feel his way, step by step, toward the idea that the Army might be an instrument of God's Justice against the King.

੨➤

Parliament decided to wait a week before answering the Army's demand that it step down and allow new elections. That was a risky delay, because the Army's patience was exhausted. Its General Council met November 26, 1647 at Windsor, prayed, and considered its "great business." Should Parliament be dissolved or merely purged? If purged, that would leave a minority that had been constitutionally elected.

Having decided to purge, the Army began to move toward London. That began on December 1, 1647, at the same time that the Army ordered the King shifted from the Isle of Wight to Hurst Castle on the mainland, in the care of Colonel Ewer, the former serving man.

Meanwhile Parliament, by a vote of 125 to 58, refused to pay the Army the £40,000 owed to it, and rejected the *Remonstrance.* The Army by then had reached Hyde Park, and was camped under heavy rains. Cromwell, en route from the North, did not arrive in London until December 6th.

That morning Members arrived to find Colonel Pride, the former brewer's drayman and Lord Grey of Groby ("that grinning dwarf"), at the door checking names. Those known to favor negotiations with the King were turned away. Some simply shrugged, but some resisted. These were locked up together in a chamber; 39 were forced to spend the night in a tavern known as Hell.

When Cromwell entered Parliament the next morning, there were only 80 Members left of the Long Parliament that had launched the revolution.

₂❧

Inside Hurst Castle the King seemed, as always, serene. His position was that a King could not be tried because a law permitting such a trial had never been passed. Charles clung, always, to the literal law. Even when he ruled without Parliament for eleven years and enacted his own taxes, he believed the advisors who told him that was his legal prerogative.

He hinted that the City magnates would not permit such trial; that Europe might intervene. He seemed to have forgotten that the English had cut off his grandmother's head.

Colonel Harrison, the son of a butcher, sent an escort to convey the King to Windsor on December 10, 1647. Crowds along the highway cheered him; a King was, after all, a rare sight.

He arrived at Windsor to find the Duke of Hamilton, another prisoner, kneeling in the courtyard mud in humble welcome. A few days later a tailor arrived with a trunk of new clothes for the King: these had been ordered when it seemed negotiations would bring Charles back to power. They were in time for Christmas—and for his trial.

December 28, 1647, Parliament read an ordinance setting up a special court to try the King. The House of Lords, now reduced to twelve, had the courage to reject it at once. The Earl of Northumberland said the charge was that the King had unlawfully levied war against

Parliament and the kingdom. But if he had, there was no law making it treason. How could the sovereign commit treason when treason was only committable against the sovereign? Even the trial of Mary Stuart, Queen of the Scots, did not present such a dilemma, since she had been Queen of a foreign country. William Prynne, who had thundered against the theater and had been released from a distant dungeon by the revolution, ushered in the new year 1648 with an interminable pamphlet ironically titled *Brief Memento to the Present Unparliamentary Junto* denouncing the Army. A more succinct reply was titled *Rectifying Principles*. Drafted by Milton's friend Samuel Hartlib, it said, "the State at large is King, and the King so-called is but its steward or Highest Officer."

More problems arose when the Chief Justices Rolle and St. John, and Chief Baron Wilde were unwilling to serve. On January 3, 1648, a new ordinance defined the High Court of Justice as consisting of 135 commissioners who were to act as judges and jury. The next day three resolutions were added: "That the people are, under God, the original of all just power," that the Commons of England "in Parliament assembled" had the supreme power in the nation; and that anything enacted by the Commons had the force of law, to be obeyed by the people—"although the consent and concurrence of King or House of Peers be not had thereunto." These echoed the Putney arguments of the Levellers that a House of Lords and a King were unnecessary.

৵

When the names of the 135 men nominated to the High Court of Justice were published they were greeted by Arminian Royalists and Presbyterians as "the dregs of the people, shoemakers, brewers" and "other mechanic persons."[12] This was untrue. Men of obscure lineage were a minority; the majority represented the most respectable elements in the country. The list was headed by Lord Fairfax (whose title was Scots); Lord Mounson (an Irish title) was included, as were the two eldest sons of English peers Lord Grey of Groby and Lord Lisle. One Knight of the Bath and eleven baronets were also named.

---

12. C. V. Wedgewood, *A Coffin for King Charles* (New York, N.Y.: Time, Inc. [paper] 1966), p. 86.

The rest included Mayors, or former Mayors, of York, Newcastle, Hull, Liverpool, Cambridge and Dorchester and other officials of equally impressive towns. The list was, to an extent, padded: Army officers and Members of Parliament were not expected to appear. But no fewer than 46 appeared each day, and the verdict was signed by 59.

One man, Colonel Algernon Sidney, the younger son of the Earl of Leicester, attended only to criticize the proceedings. He told Cromwell that no one could be tried by such a Court. Cromwell said grimly, "We will cut off his head with the crown upon it."

The trial started on Monday, January 8, 1648, in the exceptionally large Painted Chamber in ancient Westminster palace. Originally built in the time of William Rufus just after the Conquest, almost 300 feet long, its roof was hammer-beamed by Richard II and rose to almost a hundred feet. Edward II had abdicated in this chamber; Richard II had been deposed. It was where Sir Thomas More and Guy Fawkes had been tried—as well as the Earl of Strafford.[13]

It had once been the bedchamber of the "cultured, aesthetic and politically incompetent Henry III." Its walls were, at his direction, decorated with scenes from the Bible, the lives of the saints and English history. Once brilliant, these had grown dingy after 400 years; the windows had been bricked up and a fireplace knocked out of one wall.

Tables and chairs were set for the commissioners; the room was lit by the fireplace and candles. Special arrangements were made to keep the King from the spectators. Proceedings began the afternoon of January 20, 1648.[14] The King was brought by a complex route under heavy security. While he was being conveyed the roll of judges was called, during which a masked lady in the gallery protested and was removed.

The King appeared dressed in black, wearing the blue ribbon and bejeweled George and the great irradiating silver star of the Garter on his black cloak. He kept on his tall black hat, a mark of disrespect; the hair falling to his shoulders was seen to be grey-white. His face was impassive.

He sat in an armchair covered with red velvet; a small table beside it held paper, pen and ink so he could take notes for his defense.

---

13. Gladstone and Winston Churchill are interred here.
14. The dates are from the Old Calendar.

Despite efforts by the King to interrupt, the indictment was read aloud. It was fairly succinct; its essence was that Charles "had been trusted with a limited power to govern by, and according to the laws of the land, and not otherwise." He had, however, conceived "a wicked design to erect and uphold in himself an unlimited and tyrannical power to rule according to his Will and to overthrow the Rights and Liberties of the People." In pursuit of this aim he had "traitorously and maliciously levied war against the present Parliament and the people therein represented." The places where he had appeared with troops were listed, and the fact that he had renewed the war was adduced. He was therefore responsible for all the evils of those wars. Finally, it concluded that "the said Charles Stuart [be impeached] as a Tyrant, Traitor and Murderer, and a public and implacable Enemy to the Commonwealth of England."[15]

While this was being read the King looked at the galleries and the judges, and turned around in his chair to look at the onlookers. "He laughed when the words [Tyrant, Traitor and Murderer] were read. Reactions to his attitude varied with the sympathies of the observer. Arminians and Cavaliers admired his poise and courage; Colonel Ludlow was indignant. . . ."[16]

Called to reply, Charles' emotion blocked his stammer and he spoke clearly and fluently. "I would know by what authority, I mean *lawful,*" he stressed, "There are many unlawful authorities in the world, thieves and robbers by the highway . . . remember, I am your King . . ." and continued to make the point in several more phrases.

John Bradshaw, one of the prosecutors, told him testily to "answer in the name of the people of England, of which you are *elected King.*"

Charles responded that England had been "an hereditary kingdom for near these three thousand years." In this exchange both men were being disingenuous; Kings had never been directly elected in England, and the several changes of dynasty in the period Charles named were certainly not marked by any great respect for heredity.

As Charles continued to argue, Bradshaw ordered him removed and while the King kept talking, the Court adjourned. As Charles was led out

---

15. Wedgewood, *op. cit.,* p. 119.
16. Ibid., p. 121.

between lines of soldiers, the troops called out "Justice!" which was echoed by some spectators, while others cried "God Save the King!"

ॐ

Charles returned to his room so excited he refused to undress or go to bed that night. He spent the next day, Sunday, in prayer and meditation with his chaplain.

He had created a problem for the commissioners by refusing to acknowledge their authority. He had hit their most vulnerable point by stressing their break with English Common Law. They would have done better to have openly asserted their break with tradition.

On the other hand, a prisoner who would not plead was, in Common Law, treated as guilty. If the prisoner stood mute, a demonstration of guilt was unnecessary—but that omission would undermine the purpose of the trial.

Remarkably, the prosecutors decided not to proceed with witnesses and testimony to make their case, but to simply tell the prisoner that his refusal to plea meant that he stood convicted in law.

They may have hoped that this would persuade him to defend himself, to reconsider his refusal to plead. They sent him a copy of the charge to study, and decided to allow proceedings to continue for two more days, on Monday and Tuesday. If Charles did not plead by then, he would be treated as guilty, sentenced on Wednesday and executed on Friday or Saturday. That would end matters quickly, and it is impossible not to see that they found the entire experience excruciating, and wanted to be done with it as soon as possible.

ॐ

Charles slept well Sunday night despite the presence of soldiers and appeared in Court Monday afternoon. Seventy commissioners were present. John Cook, one of the two prosecutors, told the commissioners and the spectators that if the prisoner refused to plead he was, by law, considered to have confessed to being guilty and that justice would proceed on that basis.

The King, in a deadly statement, said in part, ". . . if power without law may make laws, may alter the fundamental laws of the Kingdom, I do not know what subject he is in England, that can be sure of his life, or anything that he calls his own."

This was an incredibly arrogant statement from a man who had illegally taxed the realm, who had men imprisoned, mutilated, tortured and killed because they dared to differ with him, and who had trampled on the Common Law of England for decades. But by a single legal point Charles had diverted the commissioners from proving their case against him.

When Charles once again challenged the right of the commissioners to judge him, Bradshaw said, "They sit here by the authority of the Commons of England, and all your predecessors and you are responsible to them."

With bureaucratic alacrity Charles immediately said, "Show me one precedent." And he added, "The Commons of England was never a Court of Judicature; I would know how they came to be so."

Of course he was right; there was no English legal precedent for his trial, but not because Charles was not guilty of crime. What was lacking in his trial was a John Knox, able to illustrate from the foundations of Christianity the basis of laws that place a King under—and not above— the law.

The court adjourned but Charles refused to rise. "Well Sir," he said, "remember that the King is not suffered to give his reasons for the liberty and freedom of all his subjects."

Bradshaw, outraged, said quickly, "How great a friend you have been to the laws and liberties of the people, let all England and the world judge!"

The King was shaken, and as the guards closed in to escort him away, he stammered, for the first time, and said, "Sir, under favour, it was the liberty, freedom and laws of the subject that ever I took—defended myself with arms—I never took up arms against the people, but for the laws." But his tone was defensive.

That night he asked about the commissioners, saying that he only recognized about eight of them. Most of them were unknown to him, though the English elite was small. These were men who had previously played "no noticeable part in the affairs of the nation."[17] That was the

---

17. Ibid., p. 131.

most significant element in the King's trial—and the one least mentioned later.

On Tuesday, January 23, 1648, the commissioners and the King met again with the same results. Charles filibustered about the illegality of the proceedings[18] and kept talking even while the verdict of guilty was read aloud.

ॐ

Calvinists were appalled; the trial had been clumsily conducted and the King had behaved better and more effectively than they had expected. Lord Fairfax remained aloof; the Presbyterian clergy thundered protests against the trial and the commissioners belatedly decided to hear witnesses against the King.

Thirty-three of them appeared to testify. Their depositions were taken and distributed in an attempt to recall waverers, whose numbers had increased. Meanwhile, suggestions began to trickle in regarding the fate of the King.

Major Francis White of the New Model Army, no lover of the King, suggested prison. "Because once he was dead, his son would claim the Crown and be infinitely more dangerous, being young and free, than his imprisoned father."

Matters were further clouded when one of the commissioners, John Downes, accused another, John Fry, of having denied the Trinity and the Divinity of Christ. That was a capital offense, and the argument did not enhance the dignity of the commissioners.

Arminians and Cavaliers assiduously papered the realm and Europe with pamphlets against the legality of the trial; Scotland (which had hoped to enlist Charles in a Presbyterian regime in England) sent an official protest to Commons amid rumors of interventions by European powers.

Finally 46 commissioners (the smallest number recorded) met on January 25th, 1648, to sentence the King. A subcommittee was appointed to draw up the sentence. Cromwell was not a member of this

---

18. The defense of the Romanian dictator Ceausescu when tried by the Romanian army in late 1989.

body; it consisted of only seven.[19] The commissioners reviewed and ratified this, and at ten o'clock on January 27, the King was brought in to hear his fate.

One glance was enough to tell him what awaited, for prosecutor Bradshaw, for the first time, was dressed in red. The King immediately asked permission to speak: he had a proposition to make and he wanted to be heard by the Lords and Commons.

While Bradshaw tried to head him off, Charles, heavily ironic, complained he was being sentenced before he was heard—though he had refused to defend himself three times in a row, on as many days.

At this point John Downes, who had already embarrassed the commissioners by bringing blasphemy charges against commissioner John Fry, began to struggle in his seat. "Have we hearts of stone?" he demanded loudly, "Are we men?" His companions tried to silence him but he struggled to rise. "If I die for it, I must do it," he shouted.

Cromwell, seated directly in front of him, turned around. "What ails thee? Art thou mad? Canst thou not sit still and be quiet?"

Downes got out something like, "Sir, no, I cannot be quiet," rose and in his loudest voice declared that he was not satisfied.

This unexpected disruption started a flurry among other commissioners and Bradshaw hastily called a recess. The commissioners went into another room and Cromwell confronted Downes, who pleaded that the King might have an offer that would bring peace to the nation. Cromwell in response called Charles "the hardest hearted man on earth," and stiffened the rest of the commissioners. They filed back to the Painted Chamber firm in their resolve, leaving Downes to weep in the Speaker's room. But he had wrecked the high point of the trial.

Charles rose. "If you will hear me," he pleaded, "if you will but give me this delay, I doubt not but I shall give some satisfaction to you all here, and to my people after that; and therefore I so require you, as you will answer it at the dreadful Day of Judgment, that you will consider it once more. . . ."

When the man of many propositions stopped, Bradshaw proceeded with his summation. It took forty minutes and was well prepared; the

---

19. Alderman Scot, Henry Marten, Ireton, Harrison and three lawyers, William Say, John Lisle and Nicholas Love.

King was subject to the law.

In answer to charges that the trial was unprecedented, he called on the oldest traditions of Christendom.

> There is a contract and a bargain made between the King and his people, and your oath is taken; and certainly, Sir, the bond is reciprocal, for as you are the lord, they are your liege subjects . . . the Bond of Protection . . . is due from the sovereign; the other is the Bond of Subjection that is due from the subject. Sir, if this bond is ever broken, farewell sovereignty!"

It was in this area that Charles failed. "The authority of a ruler is valid only so long as he can provide protection in return."[20] His supporters may have argued that the King was within his rights, *but he had made war on his own subjects.*

Charles tried to reply, but the prosecutor reminded him that he could not both reject the Court and also claim a right to speak to it. He repeated the sentence that Charles be put to death by "severing his head from his body."

Even then Charles rose to speak. "You are not to be heard after sentence," he was told, but even as the guards pulled him away he continued to protest, "By your favor, hold! The sentence, Sir,—I say, Sir, I do—"

As he was being pulled from the hall he managed a last full protest, "I am not suffered to speak; expect what justice other people will have. . . ." Some of the soldiers, among whom he was bitterly hated, blew smoke in his face as he was hustled along the corridor.

ะ๏

The King was to die outside the Banqueting Hall of Whitehall, built for him by Inigo Jones twenty years before. *The Moderate* newspaper said the site was appropriate because it was the very place where Charles had first drawn his sword against the people. But it had actually been chosen because it was easier to guard than Tower Hill or Tyburn.

Tuesday, January 30, 1648, Charles put on two shirts so he would not

---

20. Ibid., p. 150.

shiver from the cold and give the impression of fear. Summoned by Colonel Tomlinson between 9 and 10 A.M., he walked with his servant Thomas Herbert and Bishop Juxon from St. James to Whitehall.

He waited in a room there for his final summons. It did not arrive until two in the afternoon, because Commons was busy passing an ordinance that forbade the Proclamation of a new King.

Finally summoned, Charles stepped through a Whitehall Banqueting room window (enlarged for the purpose) with Bishop Juxon (Herbert had begged not to be forced to watch), to find Colonels Tomlinson and Hacker already on the scaffold. The official executioner, Young Gregory,[21] wearing a mask, a heavy coat and even a false beard, flanked by a similarly disguised assistant, was waiting, ax in hand.

The spectators behind rows of soldiers could see that the King had greatly aged; his hair was silver and his beard was grey. His voice could not be heard, but he spoke facing them, reading from a small paper he drew from his pocket. Then he removed his George (the insignia of the Garter) and gave it to the Bishop saying, "Remember."

He took off his doublet, put his cloak back on, and observed, for the second time, that the block was too low. The executioner said, "It can be no higher, Sir."

The King raised his hands in prayer, slipped off his cloak and lay down with his head on the block. The executioner bent down to make sure the King's hair did not hide his neck, and Charles, thinking he was preparing to strike, said, "Stay for the sign."

"I will, an' it please your Majesty," Brandon assured him.

The watchers held their breaths, the King stretched out his hands, the executioner swung the ax, the head fell off. A 17 year old boy among the spectators said later the people let out "such a groan as I never heard before, and desire I may never hear again."

---

21. His real name was Richard Brandon; he had succeeded his father Gregory Brandon in the job.

Chapter Fifteen

THE ENGLISH REPUBLIC

———— ?❧ ————

*On such a full sea we are now
afloat.*

— Shakespeare

On the day of King Charles' execution a book appeared titled *Eikon Basilike*, subtitled "His Majesty in his Solitude and Suffering." Widely believed to have been written by the King himself, it was actually the work of John Gauden, an Arminian Bishop.

Written in popular style, it combined a persuasive Arminian argument with an apologia for Charles, portraying his death as a martyrdom for his faith. It swept the realm. Within a year it went through 30 editions with more to follow. It provided the inspiration for a torrent of legends about Charles' nobility, his grace under pressure, his religiosity and the injustice of his trial and execution.

The revolutionaries, who until then had represented liberty against oppression, suddenly found the balladeers, poets and literati fervently hailing the late King as a saint and the Archbishop Laud as a martyr.

?❧

The revolution, however, was not to be stopped by a single book or a forest of pamphlets, by songs or sermons. More immediate enemies appeared to assay that task. The Arminian Earl of Ormonde in Ireland added to the new government's enemies by combining with Irish Catholics; in Edinburgh the Scots Presbyterians hoped that Charles II would accomplish what they thought they had gained in Parliament, and recognized him as King of Scotland.

The balladeers (then and now) linked this allegiance of the Scots to the House of Stuart as a romantic dedication, linked by descent and culture to a noble house, but in reality it was a continuation of the Kirk's belief that the Scots had been the new Chosen People. That belief flamed into life when the English Parliament signed the National Covenant after the Scots invaded England to thwart the Arminian Charles I.

That "signing was hailed as 'the marriage day of the kingdom with God.' Scotland was acclaimed as the New Israel, they being 'the only two sworn nations of the Lord.' The renewal of Scotland's covenant with God was also for the head of the Kirk 'the gloriousest day that ever Scotland saw since the Reformation.'

"The intervening years had been characterized by the church's 'gadding about after strange lovers,' but the revolt against Charles I took place during the 'honeymoon betuix the Lord and his runaway spouse.' As often before, the Scottish Calvinist insularity shaded . . . into a sense of the Calvinist internationale: the Scottish church in its rediscovered perfection would be 'a pattern to other nations' to imitate . . . Scottish Calvinism had from its beginnings been a missionary faith. . . . It sought new fields in England and Ireland. . . ."[1]

That was why the Scots were willing to spend tens of thousands of men fighting for Charles I after first helping to thwart his Arminianism— and why Scotland was willing to send more tens of thousands to fight Cromwell and the English Independents for Charles II. The Scots believed that they had a Covenant with God to convert the world to Presbyterianism.

〜

What was left of Parliament, after "the winnowing and sifting" of Arminian Royalists and Presbyterians, proclaimed itself supreme, abolished the House of Lords, and nominated a Council of State consisting of three generals, three peers, three judges and thirty members of Commons.

The Council renamed the various executive branches of the Government, changed judges (and renamed the Courts), ordered a new Seal and new coins; removed the King's arms and used the arms of England and Ireland as rapidly as practicable.

In early March the new High Court condemned the Duke of

1. Lynch: *op. cit.,* pp. 254, 255.

Hamilton, Lord Capel, Earl of Holland, Lord Norwich and Sir John Owen to death for their roles in starting the second war. Shortly afterward the Council asked Cromwell to become Lord General of a new army to subdue Ireland.

He accepted this as an inescapable necessity, but warned that the Levellers were an internal menace that would have to be halted. He also listed, in ascending order, the other enemies confronting the new Commonwealth. "I had rather," he said, "be overrun with a Cavalierish interest than with a Scotch interest, I had rather be overrun with a Scotch interest than an Irish interest, and I think of all this is the most dangerous . . . all the world has known their barbarism."

In this list the Levellers came first. They not only had orators who influenced the troops; they had writers and leaders who influenced the people. They were incensed against Cromwell and the Council, because their entire program had not been immediately installed. One of their pamphlets, titled *England's New Chains,* described the army leaders as Grandees. Another, satirically titled *The Hunting of the Foxes from Newmarket and Triploe Heath by Five Small Beagles,* called Cromwell the "new King" and mocked his piety.

Chains was condemned as seditious by Parliament and Colonels Lilburne and Overton were hauled before the Council of State. Lilburne, author of over a hundred inflammatory pamphlets was, as always, defiant under questioning. Afterward, while waiting outside the Council chamber, he put his ear to the keyhole, and heard Cromwell pounding the table and saying,

> I tell you Sirs, you have no other way to deal with these men but to break them or they will break you; yea, and bring all the guilt of blood and treasure shed and spent in this kingdom upon your head and shoulders, and frustrate and make void all the work that, with so many year's industry, toil and pains, you have done, and so render you to all rational men in the world as the most contemptible generation of silly, low-spirited men in the earth to be broken and routed by such a silly, contemptible generation of men as they are. . . . I tell you again, you are necessitated to break them.

Even after this peroration, the Council was so reluctant to halt the expression of opinion that it voted to imprison the Levellers by only one vote. The revolution had difficulty in understanding that it was now the government.

ॐ

Governments need money; armies eat money. To pay the army arrears and raise another 12,000 men to go to Ireland, the Rump Parliament (as it was now called) proposed to confiscate property from those who had fought for King Charles. In most instances it was satisfied with a fine equal to shares of estates. Many younger sons, facing poverty in England, chose to emigrate to America, where they founded new families.

After the Leveller leaders were imprisoned a mutiny erupted in a London regiment. The leader of that effort had fought all through the two revolutionary wars; he was shot. In May 1649 there were four more mutinies in as many regiments, which Parliament declared treasonous. Cromwell descended swiftly on Burford; three leaders were captured and shot at once, a fourth was caught and shot three days later. That was the end of the military effort of the Levellers; their intellectual arguments have lingered to this day.

ॐ

Ireland was England's dark side, the site from which the English always feared continental invasions. These had been tried on numerous occasions. The Commonwealth, whose leaders may have executed Charles I so speedily because they feared a new one, now that the Thirty Year's War had ended (1648), had no time to waste.

Only in Ireland did an undefeated Royalist/Arminian army exist, and Prince Rupert lurked off the Irish coast with eight ships. Parliament had only one army, under General George Monck, barely holding its own around Dublin. The Marquis of Ormonde headed an army of Arminian settlers. The Irish Catholics consisted of English descendents, mildly royalist, and Ulstermen under Owen O'Neill, hostile to all English.[2]

Ormonde hoped to unite the English, Scots and Irish against the Commonwealth. O'Neill, cooperating with the Vatican, hoped to unite

---

2. Christopher Hill, *God's Englishman* (Harper & Row, 1970), p. 111.

all the Catholics. The Levellers argued that all common people should unite, regardless of their faiths.

That was ideal, but hardly realistic in 1649, for the English hated and feared both the Irish and the Scots. Their hatred of the Irish came close to psychopathic; they had treated that people abominably for centuries, knew it, denied it, and sought to extirpate it by repeated atrocities.

Cromwell, a man of his time in this as in so many other respects,[3] was determined to subdue the Irish as quickly and finally as possible. He spent six months between his appointment and departure planning, and made sure he had sufficient financing before embarking in early August, 1649.

"Cromwell's first action on reaching Ireland was to forbid any plunder or pillage—an order which could not have been enforced with an unpaid army, and which introduced something quite new into Irish warfare."[4]

Two men were hanged for disobeying that order, and men began to desert Ormonde's army for the Parliamentary force. On September 10, 1649 Cromwell besieged 2,000 of Ormonde's forces inside the city of Drogheda. The defenders were under the command of Sir Arthur Aston, an English Catholic. Although badly outnumbered (Cromwell had 8,000 foot and 4,000 horse), Aston was confident, for the city was well-situated and buttressed.

Cromwell offered peace and a white flag; when it was refused a red flag was run up. When his guns began to hammer the city, its walls began to sag—and Aston was in trouble. The rules of siege at the time were well-known: if a town did not surrender, all its lives were at stake, for all were de facto combatants. Once the walls were breached it was too late for mercy.[5]

The assault, when it came, was successful; the overrun defenders, reduced to a remnant, made a last desperate stand. Cromwell, sword in hand, took part in the fighting. He personally ordered that all resistors be put to death. Aston was clubbed to death with his own wooden leg which the soldiers, for some mad reason, thought was filled with gold pieces.

---

3. All men are men of their time.
4. Hill, *op. cit.,* p. 116. He meant "English warfare in Ireland."
5. This was still the rule in Wellington's time.

Blood lust swept through Cromwell's army; one thousand people died in the streets. Orders were given that all who bore arms should be killed, so civilians were, officially, spared—but there is little doubt many were put to the sword. Even worse, all priests and friars were murdered. The defenders of another church, St. Peter's, who, (perhaps out of fear), refused to surrender, were immolated when the structure was set on fire.

By nightfall there were still stray resistors on the walls; some of them were snipers. Cromwell ordered the deaths of their officers and every tenth man captured. Some deaths were especially dramatic. Colonel Boyle was dining with Lord More the next day when one of Cromwell's soldiers whispered to him that his time had come. As Boyle rose from the table Lady More asked him in surprise where he was going. With perfect *savoir faire* Boyle turned and replied, "Madame, to die."[6]

۽

The official verdict is that 3,000 people died at Drogheda. Nothing comparable had occurred during the two revolutionary wars in England, rules of war notwithstanding. Cromwell held fiercely to the view that it was God's Work; the English military viewpoint thought it the sort of terror that assists a conquest.

It was followed, as if to prove that it was not an impulse, by "another massacre under Cromwell at Wexford, a town long a thorn in the side of English traders as a privateering center. Again the town refused to surrender, and after an eight day's siege it was sacked. Anything from 1,500 to 2,000 troops, priests and civilians were butchered."[7]

A week after Drogheda the Council of State wrote Cromwell instructing him to let all forfeited estates in Ireland at the highest possible rents, and to use the proceeds to pay for his army. The war would not finance itself unless it was finished soon.

۽

News of Cromwell's victories reached London just after the Council of State and Parliament had the humiliation of seeing John Lilburne

---

6. Fraser, *op. cit.,* p. 338.
7. Hill, *op. cit,* p. 117.

acquitted of treason by a jury.

The trial had been sensational; thousands attended. Lilburne orated and held the court spellbound. When he was acquitted "such a loud and unanimous shout as is believed was never heard in Guildhall, which lasted for about half an hour without intermission, which made the judges for fear turn pale." This made Lilburne the hero of the army, and a worry to the government.

In Ireland deliberate terror did not create fear, but defiance. The towns of Duncannon and Waterford did not surrender when Cromwell appeared; Clonmel was taken only after a loss of 2,000 men.

Due to sickness, battle losses and the need to leave staffed garrisons behind as he marched, Cromwell's army shrank from 12,000 to 5,000.

Nevertheless, his name demoralized Ormonde's forces; England sent the supplies Cromwell demanded. He campaigned until December, longer than was then conventional, and Charles II (or the Young Pretender, as the Commonwealth called him) began to abandon his plan to come to Ireland.

In January 1650, after only six weeks in quarters, Cromwell's troops marched again. He issued statements promising land to new settlers; forgave all Protestant settlers and in May, 1650, allowed the Irish people of Kilkenny to peacefully emigrate if they surrendered.

It was by then clear that Cromwell had subjugated the major resistance in Ireland. English settlers were flocking; Ireland was, said one commentator later, England's first colony.

The Government in London, aware of its unpopularity, took to printing and displaying Cromwell's field reports; a tactic that elevated his reputation rather than its own. In May, 1650, learning that Charles II had landed in Scotland, Cromwell left Ireland, leaving Ireton to complete the victory and occupation.

ꝫ❧

Young Charles II signed the Scots National Covenant and Solemn League and Covenant, and swore to maintain Presbyterianism in his household and all his dominions.

The "Don Juan of Jersey was not permitted in his northern kingdom to 'walk in the fields' on the Sabbath, or to indulge in 'promiscuous dancing.' . . . He was made to bewail the sins of his father, and the idolatries of his mother in solemn and public fasts."[8]

In London, Cromwell spent his time soothing the Levellers. He had dinner with Lilburne and they embraced at its end; he promoted the "formidable ex-agitator Joyce to Lieutenant Colonel" and sent him to a remote post. One complication arose: Lord Fairfax, a Presbyterian, believed England should keep its promises to the Scots Calvinists, and although willing to defend England against their invasion, refused to lead an English army into Scotland.

Cromwell, who proposed such an invasion to Parliament, succeeded Fairfax as supreme commander. Organizing with his usual fearful efficiency, he led 16,000 well equipped, experienced, determined troops into Scotland within a month after Charles II had arrived there—and defeated the Kirk's Army at Dunbar on September 3, 1650.

In this famous victory, he took 10,000 prisoners and soon held Edinburgh and Leith. The campaign was not ended, however, and he tried propaganda. He asked "'our brethren of Scotland,' Are we to be dealt with as enemies because we come not your way?"[9]

"I beseech you in the Bowels of Christ, think it possible that you may be mistaken," he told a church in Dunbar. "We look at ministers as helpers of, not lords over, the faith of God's people," he told the Governor of Edinburgh Castle on 12 September.

Turning to the Presbyterian criticism of Independent lay preaching, he said, "Are you troubled that Christ is preached? Is preaching so inclusive in your function? . . . Your pretended fear lest error should step in is like a man who would keep all wine out of the country lest men should be drunk. It will be found an unjust and unwise jealousy to deny a man the liberty he hath by nature upon a supposition he may abuse it. When he doth abuse it, judge."[10]

He upheld the religious rights of laymen against the clergy on not only that occasion but on others also. "So anti-Christian and dividing a term as clergy and laity," he told some Irish clergy, ". . . was unknown

8. Trevelyan, *op. cit..*, p. 298.
9. Referring to the Presbyterian insistence that no non-Presbyterian services should be allowed.
10. Hill, *op. cit.,* p. 128.

in earlier times. It was your pride that begat this expression, and it is for filthy lucres sake that you keep it up, that by making the people believe that they are not as holy as yourselves, they might for the penny purchase some sanctity from you; and that you might bridle, saddle and ride them at your pleasure." In this, Cromwell reflected the true Reformation spirit.

ॐ

The Scots, however, were not to be "summoned" by Oliver Cromwell. They crowned Charles II at Scone. The English Parliament, assisting Cromwell's passionate religious exhortations, pretended to believe the Scots people had been misled by their nobility and gentry and offered inducements to stop fighting.

But Cromwell's arguments were not entirely lost: some Covenanters in Glasgow and the southwest listened; some even decided to become neutral. One of these was the Governor of Edinburgh Castle. The campaign dragged through the winter and spring of 1651. Finally the Scots army left the security of Stirling Castle, bearing Charles II, to invade England.

Cromwell, who had become a great and canny general, followed discreetly while all England rallied against the invasion. Even Fairfax emerged from retirement to organize the Yorkshire militia.

Cromwell and his army met the Scots at Worcester on November 3, 1651, a year after Dunbar. The Scots were outnumbered two to one. They fought, as ever, bravely but the issue was never in doubt. Charles II fled.

In his flight "he cut off his hair, stained his face and hands, exchanged his clothes with a laborer, began a long march on foot and horse from one hiding place to another; sleeping in attics, barns or woods, once in a 'Royal Oak' tree in Boscobel while Commonwealth soldiers searched for him below. Often recognized, never betrayed, he and his party after forty days of flight, found at Shoreham in Sussex, a vessel whose captain agreed, at the risk of his life, to take them to France on October 15, 1651."[11]

With that defeat of its final army of 30,000 men, Scotland lay virtually defenseless, its great dream of Presbyterian dominance over

---

11. Durant, *op. cit.*, Vol. 8, pp. 188, 189.

England in shards—but only temporarily. The Covenanters were to continue to dream of a Stuart Restoration and a final triumph for years to come.

❧

As the Presbyterians, the Arminians and their Episcopacy regarded their defeat as temporary. So did the Catholics, who had before them the triumphs of the Counter-Reformation and their faith in an eternal, unconquerable Church.

All these groups believed in the tradition of a single faith in a single land, but that ancient politico-religious argument had splintered under English resentment of ecclesiastical absolutism under Archbishop Laud. Parliament only acceded to the Presbyterian Covenant in order to enlist Scots assistance against Charles I. Once that assistance was no longer needed, the pledge to make England Presbyterian was renounced by a "winnowed" Rump Parliament.

In effect, all groups and individuals who developed a distrust of the power of clergymen joined those called Independents. Eventually Independents governed the Rump Parliament, and had Cromwell as their great leader.

The Independent position was an extension of Calvin's argument that worship inside the Church should be free of the State, but went further by arguing that an array of churches should be allowed, each free to worship as it chose. Catholicism was excepted because its adherents had never allowed another church to exist wherever Catholics were dominant; Presbyterianism had been defeated in its attempt to assume such power in England by the battles of Dunbar and Worcester.

Arminianism and its Episcopacy, however, straddled the Catholic and Protestant worlds in terms of service and structure, although its argument that Man could summon salvation from God was heretical to all basic Christian beliefs.

Because of its Episcopal structure and its support of an absolute King, Arminianism in England had the support of both Catholics and Royalists. Although defeated in the field, its adherents regarded that defeat as conditional. Arminianism also had tacit support from Presbyterians (who expected Charles II to keep the promises he had made) and

Catholics, who loathed Calvinism. These were unlikely but real coalitions.

ॐ

Cromwell turned his command over to General Monck and returned to London at the end of 1651. Immense crowds appeared to watch him arrive, and he commented that more would have appeared to see him hanged. The Rump Parliament voted him a 4,000 pound allowance and the once-royal palace of Hampden Court. The Members sincerely hoped the great general would be satisfied with these rewards.

ॐ

During the revolutionary wars, the English Navy had split between King and Commons. A number of vessels joined the Arminian/Royalist forces, found harbor in Dutch ports, and were commanded by Prince Rupert.

Some Parliamentary sailors were unhappy because army officers were put in command of naval vessels, but they proved more capable than the aristocratic sprigs of the past; some were outstanding. One, Admiral Blake, chased Rupert around the Iberian Peninsula, scaring Portugal and teaching Spain that it could not harbor enemies of the Commonwealth with impunity. It was by these operations, which occurred as part of the exigencies of war, that England was drawn to send its fleet into the Mediterranean, which Charles I had barred to the navy.

When Rupert fled across the Atlantic, the Commonwealth fleet became masters of the islands in the English and Irish Channels, crossed the ocean and restored Virginia and the Barbados to England. Rupert was, in the end, reduced to one ship.

With English sea power at a level unknown even to Elizabeth I, Parliament turned toward overseas trade. A Navigation Act, passed in late 1651, established an English monopoly of trade in its three nations, as well as its overseas possessions.

This was a retaliation against the Dutch, who barred English traders and ships. But because the dream of a Protestant Europe had not yet died, the English also offered the Dutch a union. When the Dutch protested that the terms were not much better than those offered to the defeated Scots, the English—on the theory that if they couldn't join them they'd fight them—prepared for war, though a trade war is never popular.

It was a sea war with the usual long delays between engagements. The fleets were fairly evenly matched, but the Dutch had more merchantmen, all loaded with goods. Victory for the English was costly because of the loses of ships. The new war, therefore, led to increased taxes and disruptions of trade. Hopes of peace and prosperity after the victory at Worcester faded.

The English Parliament did believe, however, that its policy in Ireland was successful. Massacres were abandoned in May 1652, and the Articles of Kilkenny substituted. Irish who surrendered were allowed to emigrate. In August an "Act for the Settling of Ireland" was enacted, which confiscated part or all of the property of Irishmen (of whatever faith) who could not prove they had been loyal to the Commonwealth.

By this means 2.5 million acres of Irish land passed into English hands. The Counties of Kildare, Dublin, Carlow, Wicklow and Wexford were formed into a new English Pale, and an attempt was made to exclude first all Irish proprietors, then all Irishmen. Thousands of Irish families were dispossessed, and were given until March, 1655, to find new homes. Hundreds were shipped to Barbados or elsewhere, on charges of vagrancy.[12]

It was estimated that 616,000 Irish perished from war, starvation or plague in the years from 1641 to 1652, out of a population of 1.4 million. That was almost half of all the Irish people. In some counties, said one observer, "a man might travel twenty or thirty miles and not see a living creature, either man or beast or bird."

"The sun," said another, "never shined on a nation so completely miserable." The Catholic religion was outlawed; all Catholic clergymen were ordered to leave Ireland within twenty days; to harbor a priest was made punishable by death; severe penalties were decreed for absence from Protestant services on Sunday; magistrates were authorized to take away the children of Catholics and send them to England for education in the Protestant faith."[13] All this fused the Irish people into a hatred for the English that has yet to die.

---

12. Durant, *op. cit.*, p. 187.
13. Ibid.

۲۹

The war with Holland was resented by the New Model Army, which had not been demobilized. By 1653, the soldiers wanted to know when they would see the reforms for which they fought. Parliament had not yet abolished the tithe, nor disestablished the Church (which would have had the same effect.) Cromwell, aware of these grumblings, privately asked if a new King was possible, or, if not that, what?

The Rump Parliament, now accustomed to power, made the mistake of "refusing to renew the Commission for the Propagation of the Gospel in Wales—the Army's favorite instrument for evangelizing that politically unreliable country."[14]

That created a storm. Parliament began to mutter about a new election, with the proviso that the present Members could retain their seats without having to undergo such a risk. Cromwell wondered how anyone could be sure that a new Parliament would not again be dominated by Presbyterians anxious to clamp an ecclesiastical lid on the nation? "This, we apprehended," he said later, "would have been throwing away the liberties of the nation into the hands of those who never fought for it."

The Members answered smoothly that they would, themselves, screen newcomers. That led to a meeting between the Generals and the Parliamentary leaders which ended in a deadlock. All that was resolved was that they would meet again; in the interim Parliament would hold its plan in abeyance until then.

But the next day, April 20, 1653, word reached Cromwell that Parliament's leaders had broken their word and were presenting their plan to the Members. He gathered some soldiers, emerged in his plain suit and, accompanied by Major General Thomas Harrison, entered Parliament and sat down to listen darkly to the discussion.

When the issue was put to a vote he rose and began to speak while everyone else fell silent. He began moderately but his voice rose with his rage, and he ended by denouncing Parliament as a "self-perpetuating oligarchy unfit to govern England."

"Drunkard," he shouted, indicating one member. "Whoremaster!"

---

14. Hill, *op. cit.*, p. 135.

he shouted at another. "You are no Parliament. I say, you are no Parliament. I will put an end to your sittings." Turning to Harrison he said, "Call them in; call them in." Soldiers appeared and Cromwell told them to clear the room. The members left, some under protest.[15]

Cromwell looked at the Mace and said, "What shall we do with this bauble? Here, take it away." The next day the Hall was locked and a notice was tacked on the door saying, "This house to let, now unfurnished."

Cromwell also went to Council of State while it was in session, and said, "If you are met here as private persons, you shall not be disturbed; but if as a Council of State, this is no place for you. . . . Take notice that the Parliament is dissolved."

So ended the Long Parliament that had dethroned a King, abolished the House of Lords, created a new government and won a revolution—only to be itself abolished by a leader the revolution raised.

ॐ

"When they were dissolved," Cromwell said later, "there was not so much as the barking of a dog. . . ."

As is usual when great changes occur, all sides felt new hope. Fifth Monarchy men thought their day had finally dawned; Royalists whispered that Cromwell would certainly have to call in Charles II, restore the monarchy and the old ways—now that the new had collapsed. Cromwell, they said, would surely accept a Dukedom and wealth; he was, after all, 54 years old and his career was nearing its close.

Cromwell did not agree. He and his fellow generals knew that they would not win an election, so the dream of the Levellers was out of the question. There would be no expansion of the vote; no change in the number of seats. In fact, no elections.

Yet the idea of doing without a Parliament still seemed too outrageous to consider, especially by men who had fought so many battles for so many years for what they believed was a Parliamentary cause.

The solution was a Nominated Parliament, consisting of men chosen by Cromwell "with the advice of my Council of Officers." In other words, by the Independent leaders of the New Model Army.

---

15. Durant, *op. cit.*, p. 190.

Not too many names were chosen: 140.[16] Some of these had been chosen by churches, others by individual Generals, some undoubtedly by Cromwell. Five were from Scotland and six from Ireland. Nearly half had either been or would be members of elected Parliament; gentry predominated, as did Londoners.

Cromwell, who had always believed that the nation would be best governed by the morally superior, exulted in what he expected to be the final answer to the problem of a good government. In an optimistic speech to the new Parliament,[17] he said, "Truly you are called by God to rule with him and for him; I confess I never looked to see such a day as this . . . when Jesus Christ should be so owned as he is at this day and in this work."[18]

He meant every word of it. He really intended to hand over power. The new body, which he expected to call itself a Constituent Assembly (for he asked it to draw up a new Constitution) decided instead to call itself a Parliament.

Although it soon split into traditionalists and innovators, it was a businesslike body. A committee reviewed the Judicial system and voted to abolish the Court of Chancery; the finances of the government were to be unified and rationalized. Tenants were provided protection against arbitrary expulsions; new arrangements were made for the probate of wills, marriages, births and deaths. For the first time in English history marriages were made possible by a civil ceremony. Efforts were made to end inequality in clerical incomes and to eliminate tithes as well as layman's powers to give benefices. They planned to codify the laws, as in Massachusetts.

Proposals not to execute pickpockets and horse thieves for the first offense shocked the lawyers, as did proposals to stop the burning of women as a death penalty and an end to pressing to death. It was also suggested that real bankrupts should be released.

These reforms were constructive but not particularly radical; they did not alter the fundamental structure inherited from monarchy. But many were alienated by the attack on tithes, which—it was charged—was a

---

16. The Long Parliament originally had over 600.

17. Which in time would be satirically named the Barebones Parliament after one of its members, the Fifth Monarchy man Praise-God Barebones.

18. Hill, *op. cit.*, p. 139.

prelude to an attack on all property. Images of the Levellers and rumors of wholesale confiscations if innovators were to have their own way, led to a *rapprochement* between Presbyterians and Independents against too many changes—or changers..

Cromwell was shocked at the attack on tithes; in common with many others, he considered it an attack upon all clergy: all churches.[19] The Generals were shocked at a proposal that they serve a year without pay. The Army made minatory sounds; complaints arose that the Parliament was too long on speeches and too short on practicalities. This was an exaggeration, but the Army—and Cromwell—were the real powers.

On December 12, 1653, traditionalists in Parliament rose early to make denunciatory speeches claiming that all property rights were in danger of being destroyed, and persuaded 80 Members to dissolve Parliament. They then marched to Cromwell, to whom they surrendered their authority.

This was as spontaneous as proposing the diadem to Caesar. Cromwell had, after all, come to think of the Barebones Parliament as "a story of my own weakness and folly."

Miraculously, within three days a Constitution appeared, titled the "Instrument of Government," created behind the scenes by Cromwell and the leaders of the New Model Army in preceding weeks.

On December 16, 1653, Oliver Cromwell was proclaimed Lord Protector of the Commonwealth of England, Scotland and Ireland in an elaborate public ceremony. The revolution had come full circle.

---

19. Most western European nations still tax the population for the support of an Established Church.

Chapter Sixteen

THE FUTURE APPEARS

———— ?♥ ————

Where shall I now begin, or
where conclude, to draw a fame
so truly circular?

— Dryden

England had seen Lord Protectors before: it was a title and an
authority held by Regents who governed during the minority of an
infant monarch. But the post had never before been written into a
Constitution[1] which called itself an Instrument of Government. (That
phrasing echoes Cromwell, who always saw himself as an instrument
rather than a prime mover.)

Because the revolution was now in strange, uncharted waters, attention was focused on the Lord Protector's circumstances and title (it was,
after all, a time when aristocratic principles prevailed). He was to move
into Whitehall, the palace of the King; he was to be called "His Highness
the Protector," but his office was to be elective, and not for life; not
hereditary.[2] The Lord Protector was to be Chief Executive, assisted by
a Council of 15 members (8 civilians and 7 army officers) chosen for life.
Parliament was to retain its ancient power alone to levy taxes and grant
"supply" to the government. But it was to sit only once every three years,
and then only for a mandatory five months. In the interim, the Protector
could apply temporary measures, but Parliament had to agree if they
were continued. On the other hand, the Protector could not dissolve
Parliament when it was in session.

Nine months were to pass before Cromwell had to meet his first

---

1. The Instrument was the first of all the written constitutions which have since
circled the world.

2. This was the model for the U.S. Presidency a century and a half later.

Parliament, giving the new government time to establish itself, and the Lord Protector time to officially head the three nations.

෨෪

Cromwell believed in an established, non-Episcopal, evangelical Church with ample toleration of dissent and separate congregations. In 1654 one ordinance provided for "Triers" to approve public preachers appointed to benefices. Another created a commission to reject "scandalous and insufficient" ministers and schoolmasters.

Cromwell's established Church did not create a national organization; it had no Church courts, assemblies, laws or special ordinances of its own. The new government was silent about rites, ceremonies and sacraments. How to administer the Lord's Supper or Baptism was left to each congregation.

The Commissioners determining the fitness of a minister were to judge on the basis of personal piety and intelligence. If he was found to be worthy, he was installed at once. "The Church buildings were regarded as the property of several parishes, and in one was to be found a Presbyterian, another an Independent and in a third a Baptist. If there were churches that preferred to worship outside the national system, they were at liberty to do so. The Articles of Government declared that such person 'shall not be restrained, but shall be protected in the profession and exercise of their religion, so as they abuse not their liberty to the civil injury of others, and to the actual disturbance of the peace on their part.' This liberty, however, was 'not to extend to Popery or Prelacy, nor to such as, under the profession of Christ, hold forth and practice licentiousness.'"[3]

This system allowed the rise of new groups supported by the governmental tithes, including free congregations and ministers—and sometimes no ministers at all. Provided the Episcopal Prayer Book was not used, any form of Protestant worship was permitted. Cromwell, had, in reality, created a Congregational system, partly endowed; partly unendowed.

The Commissioners or Triers and Ejectors were both honest and tolerant, and "kept up the education and usefulness of the endowed

---

3. *Social England, op. cit.,* pp. 256, 257.

clergy to a level which there is no reason to think inferior to the level reached under Laud."[4]

Open competition enabled the unorthodox to gain. Free "nonconformist" groups increased, especially among the poor and those "too near the primary needs of body and spirit to be interested in theologies and Church systems."[5] George Fox (originally no pacifist) had several cordial meetings with Cromwell and his Society of Friends flourished until its habit of interrupting the services of other religious groups evoked unfriendly reactions from the authorities.[6] They were nick-named "Quakers" from a witty response made by a Magistrate when Fox told the Bench to "tremble" at the name of the Lord.

Despite peculiarities such as using the informal "thee and thou" instead of the formal "you," refusing to take their hats off to anyone and marrying only one another, Fox's Quakers drained other congregations and made hundreds of converts everywhere he traveled.

ॐ

Meanwhile Holland suffered the rigors of a trade war. The bulk of its commerce relied on merchant fleets that passed through the English Channel to Africa and Ceylon, Smyrna and Venice, China and Japan. She could not survive on her own resources while the English navy haunted the Channel. Starvation loomed; mobs of workingmen roamed the streets. Dutch ships sat idle in the Zuyder Zee. The Netherlands could defy Spain or France, whose fleets were inadequate, but not new English sea power.

In 1654, Cromwell agreed to peace on terms that placed Holland below England in terms of overseas trade. In the long run the English nation gained immensely from this victory, as well as others to come. But all that was visible at the time was its immediate cost, raised from the sale of Crown lands, confiscations of Royalist estates and special taxes.

ॐ

---

4. Trevelyan, *op. cit.,* p. 311.

5. Ibid., p. 312.

6. The Inner Light sometimes led them to appear naked, with blackened faces, or swathed in sheets, to make their protests.

The Lord Protector lived in state, with bodyguards, servants and assistants amid luxurious surroundings. Whitehall was redecorated before he and his family moved in April, 1654; Hampton Court, Windsor and other royal residences were at his disposal. He did not choose to use Windsor but soon formed the habit of working during the week in London's Whitehall, and spending his weekends at Hampton Court, much as modern Prime Ministers alternate between 10 Downing Street and Chequers.[7]

He liked elegant tapestries and especially music and musicals, as did most Calvinists of his time. His weekly dinners with his officers were balanced by musical entertainment, which included dancing.

Contrary to seemingly inextinguishable canards, Calvinists had nothing against dancing except when it was lascivious. The English ambassador to Sweden had to convince Queen Christina of this by having his gentlemen in waiting teach her ladies some new steps. It was during the Commonwealth that the violin became popular and that solo singing began to be enjoyed.

The theater was a more sensitive arena because of its ancient, deeply rooted political significance. In the time of Elizabeth I, Shakespeare's *Richard II* had incited the Earl of Essex, and his young men sick of an old Queen, into rash defiance. During the reigns of James I and Charles I the theater had spearheaded a wholesale assault against Puritans that slopped, inevitably, into a subversion of Calvinism in favor of Episcopal and regal pomp and "divine right."

That, and its licentiousness, was the major reason the Presbyterians (not the Puritans, who lacked numbers and political importance) closed the theaters.

These closings were never completely effective; sumptuary laws are always nearly impossible to enforce. Although several theaters were rated, performances continued at the Red Bull Theater, at the mansions of various nobles (especially at Holland House) and continued underground.

One unexpected ruse to overcome anti-theatrical efforts was the rise of play-readings, as opposed to enactments. Many of these, naturally enough, satirized the government. Cromwell allowed them, and their advertisements appeared everywhere.

---

7. Fraser, *op. cit,* p. 460.

In contrast, writers found Cromwell more lenient than his bureaucratic predecessors; literature flourished, and the Calvinist love of poetry appeared everywhere. In fact, under Cromwell, there was a noticeable brightening of the national mood. Women were observed by John Evelyn to be painting their faces again; English translations of French novels appeared; Christmas was once again festive.

The generally favorable treatment of masques and musical entertainments by Cromwell and his government, as opposed to hostility toward prose plays, was not lost on alert theatrical entrepreneurs. A series of efforts blending music and librettos from 1649 throughout the span of the Commonwealth led to the appearance of the first full-length, five act English opera *(The Siege of Rhodes)* in 1656, under the Lord Protector.

Cromwell not only lived like a Prince; he thought as one. In the summer of 1654, a workman placed a "sphere in Whitehall for the use of His Highness." Cromwell studied it; he had a plan for the expansion of the Calvinist world—in opposition to the Vatican and all Catholic powers.

Before these plans appeared, however, the new Parliament, Cromwell's first, met September 3, 1654. With Arminian/Cavaliers and Royalists barred from sitting for twelve years, this Parliament—loaded with Presbyterians and Independents—should theoretically have been cooperative with Cromwell and his Council; but it was not.

Parliament disputed the Instrument of Government not because it wanted to dismiss Cromwell, but because the Members did not like the idea that the Army had drawn up a Constitution.

Behind that objection was one of even longer standing among Englishmen: that there should be no standing army. Europe's despots were maintained by standing armies. Had Charles I had such an army, there could not have been a revolution.

Cromwell knew this as well as the Members; he had been a Member himself, and had discussed this from his youth onward. But he had also enough experience with his countrymen to know that a Parliament in power would institute an ecclesiastical terror similar to the one he had helped overthrow.

He also knew that in another twelve years, when Arminians and Royalists would inevitably become among those elected, some future Parliament might unravel all the revolution had accomplished. The distant future, however, was uncontrollable; Cromwell's problems were immediate.

They were also circular. The Army would not permit him to become King and establish a new dynasty; Parliament would not accept a genuine Republic because it was too foreign to English traditions, customs and society.

Parliament, he reminded the Members, had been elected according to the Instrument. They had sworn when they took office to obey its conditions. In response a hundred Members refused to sign such a document.

Parliament then voted to reduce the Army's pay—and its numbers. The Army came pounding to the Lord Protector for protection, and he spent long hours in fruitless persuasions.

Parliament's intransigence was poorly timed for the Lord Protector, who had decided, during the summer of 1654, to attack Spanish possessions in the West Indies. In August he summoned the Spanish ambassador and told him that Englishmen in Spanish territories should have liberty to worship as they pleased free of the Inquisition, and that English traders should have equal rights in commerce.

The ambassador was astonished. Catholics had no liberty of worship in England, nor did England allow Spanish traders in its territories. "It is to ask," he said, "for my master's two eyes."

Cromwell flared, and sent a fleet to San Domingo in reprisal, he said, for Spanish seizure of English islands in the Caribbean. Just in case Spain saw this as a pretext for war, he also sent feelers toward France for an alliance. France, although Catholic, at least allowed Calvinist Huguenots the right to worship freely.

It was in the middle of these international maneuvers that the Lord Protector found himself forced to mediate between the Army and Parliament, before his new government was a year old. The Instrument he had toiled over, and expected others to obey, mandated that he allow Parliament to sit, unhindered, for five months.

When the Army threatened to rebel, he gave way, and announced that after five *lunar* months, Parliament had done its duty, and ordered it dissolved on January 22, 1555.

❧

The Calvinists were still in charge, though they had split into several factions. The Arminians had been militarily and politically defeated; their clergy had been expelled from their posts, but they had not vaporized: they continued to live. Many Arminian clergymen continued to preach in private homes and in Royalist mansions, for Cromwell's toleration was imperfect; it did not cover Prelacy.

A number of English people, however, longed for the forms and pomp of the Arminian Church; they had grown up with it. The English like forms; they are famous for their attention to manners and nuance, tradition and dress. Most of those who longed for the old Church did not think of English Prelacy in terms of Arminianism versus Calvinism: a grasp of theology is as rare as all forms of higher learning: they simply ached for an end to novelties and new men, to mentions of God in everyday matters; to an end to an established Army that had replaced an Established Church.

Unrest had social reasons. The gentry had increased at the expense of the aristocracy, which increased opportunities, but the manners of the newcomers set teeth on edge. "Extempore prayer offers abundant facilities for the display of folly and profanity as well of piety, and there were thousands who compared the tone and language of the new clergy with the measured devotion of the Book of Common Prayer, altogether to the advantage of the latter. . . ."[8] It should not be forgotten that the new piety unwittingly opened the gates to some odious hypocrites.

All these resentments flared in Salisbury in March, 1655, when a man named Penruddock, with 200 followers, seized the judges who had just arrived for the assizes. The effort was quixotic and foolish, and almost instantly suppressed. But it changed Cromwell's mind about the Instrument of Government, Parliament and, possibly, the English people and God's purposes.

---

8. Gardiner, *op. cit.*, p. 179.

Chapter Seventeen

THE PROTECTOR'S END

———— ?• ————

Broad England harbored not his peer.

— Emerson

In April 1655 Admiral Blake led his naval vessels into the pirate stronghold of Tunis, destroyed the Bey's ships and forced the potentate to release all English prisoners. He wondered if he had exceeded his authority but Cromwell sent his warm congratulations: the two men thought alike.

In the same letter, the Protector urged Blake to proceed to Cadiz, where he might intercept Spanish ships carrying treasure from the New World. The days of Elizabeth I seemed, to both men, to have returned—with the difference that Cromwell's England was becoming a Mediterranean power, able to menace Catholic powers in their strongest area.

Other news reaching Whitehall did not have the same warming effect. The Catholic Duke of Savoy ruled over Huguenots who, by an old treaty, were to remain in the mountainous areas of the Vadois (or Waldenses) where they could practice their religion peacefully. Abruptly the Duke claimed the Huguenots had violated these boundaries and launched a vicious persecution against them. By May 1655 the Commonwealth newspapers reported "a Devilish Crew of Priests and Jesuits"[1] had incited the Duke, and described atrocities.

Cromwell sent an agent to the scene, whose report verified the scandal. The Lord Protector headed a subscription list that raised several hundred thousand pounds for the relief of the victims: the Council of State was deeply concerned; Cromwell entered into closer discussions

———————————

1. Fraser, *op. cit.*, pp. 538, 539.

with France. Pressures were brought to bear on the Duke, and he stopped the campaign. Not only was Calvinism restored in England; it was felt, once again, as a major force in Europe.

Nevertheless the uprising under Penruddock continued to rankle. No group of men are less able to overlook rebellion than former rebels; they know too well the consequences of an inattentive government. Cromwell and his advisors, always wary, imagined that a Royalist/ Leveller cabal was at work against the Protectorate. Local authorities were warned to watch out for strangers who might be sent "to kindle fires."[2]

Finally the Lord Protector transferred his brother-in-law,[3] Major General John Densborough, from the Council of State to Worcester and the six western counties to act as an overlord of the restless area.

The expedition to San Domingo, meanwhile, was a fiasco. English troops, poorly equipped for the tropics, were reduced by dysentery and repulsed with heavy losses. The assault enraged Madrid, which declared war on England everywhere. Cromwell then had to move, whether ready or not, into a French alliance.

The best the Government could do was to trumpet a success in Jamaica, which the expedition had succeeded in conquering. Cromwell dreamed that Calvinists from New England would settle there because of its warmer climate. It became, instead, another Barbados, another place to ship criminals and rebels, and became an island maintained by plantation slaves, both black and white.

In August 1655, in the belief that Densborough and his troops had pacified the West Counties, the Protector installed a new plan to govern his restive countrymen. Beginning in October, 1655, ten (later eleven) Major Generals were given new and more sweeping authority in their respective districts.

They were to control the county horse militia: reserves to be called in a future emergency. By autumn this force was transformed into a permanent cavalry capable of being used anywhere in the country.

---

2. Ibid., p. 555.
3. He had married one of Cromwell's sisters.

This new expense was to be raised by a new 10 percent tax on all Cavaliers and anyone who might be suspected of favoring monarchy. The Major Generals in charge of these districts were, of course, the heroes of the New Model Army; names made famous in the battles of the revolution.

And because fear of revolution was now rampant among those whom the revolution had lifted to power, the Major Generals were encouraged to restrict all gatherings, all crowds of people who might seek to cloak deeper designs beneath benevolent protestations.

Therefore Ale Houses were restricted, cock fights and bear baits halted, racing stopped, actors and Gypsies chased, plays hunted and extirpated, and all other occasions for crowds to gather were treated as potential, even seditious opportunities for the secret, malignant enemies of the Protectorate.

Wandering players whose occupation was not illegal, minstrels, Gypsies, drunken veterans—the entire nondescript part of the population clinging to the rough edges of survival—were subject to being swept up by the military, hauled before officers and forced to justify their existence, or be sent to prison or to forced labor outside the country on charges of vagrancy.

This was, of course, exactly what all the opponents of a standing army had always feared: the imposition of rule by bayonets, by force, in a nation that had always prided itself on being free, unlike Europe. That much of this tradition had been largely illusory was not the point: illusions sustain many in this treacherous world. To strip men of illusions is to darken their lives and narrow their hopes.

Cromwell then increased his error by moral rationalizations of what was, essentially, autocratic fear: ". . .there is a great deal of grudging in the nation," he said in a speech, "that we cannot have our horse races, cockfightings and the like." He was not against these pleasures in principle, he added. "I do not think these unlawful." (He indulged in them himself.) He argued that they had too great a hold on people, who "should be content to make them recreations."

This muddled argument provided a rationale that anti-Calvinists (then and now) seized upon. They used the Protector's own words to argue that Calvinism is against pleasure, against sports, against even joy. "The Puritans hated bear-baiting, not because it gave pain to the bear, but because it gave pleasure to the spectators," said Macaulay. The great historian was usually accurate, but forgot that it was not Puritans, but bemedalled Major Generals who stopped bear-baiting, not because it gave pain to the bear—but collected spectators who frightened the Protectorate.[4]

≈

The division of the nation into army units led to variations in government. Some of the Major Generals were severe; some were lenient. One man described them as "like Turkish Bashaws:" little kings. General Whalley allowed horse racing; General Worsley forbade it.

The disruption of traditional local governments was nearly complete. The ejection of powerful county families from posts of authority shocked the people and was, if not unjust, at least impolitic. County committees created to help the revolution were disbanded, which was ungrateful and shortsighted. "Lord Lieutenants found their roles usurped, and local perquisites fell into the laps of those agents of the central government, as Thomas Kelsey, for example in Kent acquired the governorship of Dover Castle from neighboring families who had previously controlled it. The people as a whole, who were just beginning to bask in the gentle warmth radiated by the stability of the Protectorate, found themselves subjected yet again to the chill wind of change."[5]

Discontent swept through the land and seeped into the sumptuous corridors of the Protectorate's palaces. Cromwell felt it, and commented on "the wretched jealousies that are amongst us, and the spirit of calumny, which turns all into gall and wormwood. . . . Many good men are repining at everything."

≈

Jews had been officially expelled from England in 1290, but the revolution launched a campaign for their return. Fifth Monarchy men, intent upon calculating the Second Coming (despite Christ's warning that no man would know beforehand) believed the conversion of the

4. Whatever the Puritan's reasons for being against bear-baiting, the fact remains that Puritans never governed England.

5. Fraser, *op. cit.,* p. 556.

Jews played a part in the process by which Antichrist would fall. It was observed that Jews were tolerated by the Pope, the Florentines and the Bavarians; why not the English?

They had, of course, secretly returned long before. The expulsion of Jews from Spain and Portugal made England a place of refuge and clusters lived in London, Dover and York. They passed, in most instances, as Spaniards or Portuguese, "and used on occasion to attend the Catholic ambassadorial chapels by way of disguise; certain of their number were also deputed to remain uncircumcised with the same object of concealment in the face of sudden persecution."[6]

Nevertheless, English Jews flourished in a growing atmosphere of philo-Semitism. Puritans and other Calvinist sects began to consider legalizing their presence. In 1650 Menasseh ben Israel saluted England as a new refuge in a book *Spes Israel;* in 1651 John Thurloe met Menasseh ben Israel in Holland and persuaded him to apply to the Council of State.

Cromwell did not theologically approve of Jews or Unitarians, or any other group that denied the Divinity of Jesus, but as Lord Protector thought that the international commercial network maintained by the Jewish Diaspora could bring benefits to the English nation.

Thurloe found Jewish "intelligencers" helpful in keeping track of Royalist efforts in Europe. Some of these were so useful that when one had his property confiscated in Portugal, Cromwell himself intervened. When England went to war against Spain, Jewish observers and agents, bitter against Spain, went out of their way to help England.

In September 1655 Menasseh ben Israel arrived in London by invitation, accompanied, among others, by three Rabbis. He was lodged by the Protector in the Strand close to Whitehall. He met Cromwell and charmed him; became a dinner guest at the Palace and enjoyed a brief social whirl.

Anti-Semites, of course, flared at these proceedings. Prynne the theater hater charged that Cromwell had been bribed. On December 4, 1655, Cromwell made a speech about the Jews (later saying it was his best) and smothered the objections of the Council by saying the matter was his to resolve. He chose to readmit the Jews.

---

6. Ibid., p. 560.

London merchants were not happy; they foresaw fearsome competition by a close-knit network, but the nation benefited.

ॐ

War obsessed the Protector's mind in 1656: it is expensive, and the need to continually raise funds was a tiresome burden. Meanwhile, aware of growing discontent, he sought—whenever he could—to lighten the burdens of the people. When the Quakers got into increasing difficulties, he talked with George Fox, who impressed him—and even invited the Quaker to dinner at the Palace.

But in February 1656, it was necessary to issue a Proclamation making it illegal to disturb "Ministers and other Christians in their Assemblies and Meetings." The early Quakers were spectacularly intolerant.

Meanwhile Cromwell's personal observations became increasingly broad; the necessities of governing made him aware that there are more than a few kinds of people in the world; God's instruments are not all alike.

His health began to fail. The Lady Protectress, as she was known, was also ill; Cromwell had bladder trouble, the stone and the gout. His suffering became both pronounced and public, leading to rumors of insanity spread by his enemies. Many commented on his careworn aspect, though he had good days as well.

Meanwhile there was the ongoing question of paying for the expenses of the war with Spain.

ॐ

In early autumn 1656, the people once again elected a Parliament that did not match the Protector's standards. He had, according to the Instrument of Government, no actual need to call a Parliament at all. But he had to continually raise money to fight Spain (an enemy he considered Satanic in every respect)—and he remembered Charles I and his non-Parliamentary rule.

A hundred elected men were refused their seats, for Cromwell was determined to square the circle: to have a Parliament of his own choosing that was, nevertheless, elected. Centuries later the Soviets, reasoning along similar lines, held elections in which the people could vote only for those whom the Government preselected.

He spoke at length to the New Parliament, using many Biblical citations and was partly successful with it. In January 1657 Parliament voted 400,000 pounds toward the war not so much because it was popular, but because people had begun to wonder about what—or who—would come after Cromwell.

For the first time, a Member rose to suggest that the Protector be made King. Densborough and other Major Generals immediately objected. In discussions later, the most that Densborough would concede was that Cromwell might be allowed to name his successor.[7]

It did not seem to occur to those engaged in such discussions that the principle of hereditary leadership was being dealt a series of heavy blows; the revolution had moved further than even its own leaders recognized. All that was obvious was that the Lord Richard Cromwell was frail compared to his father.

In the midst of these serious contemplations of the future, religious issues—always present—surfaced in a sensational case.

૨৶

A well-known Quaker preacher named James Naylor, whose followers believed resembled Jesus, rode in triumph into Bristol on an ass, to the cries of "Hosanna!" and "Holy, Holy, Holy!"

Naylor's supporters, claiming that he had raised people from the dead (a seventeenth-century term for conversion), wanted Naylor's name changed to Jesus. All this led the authorities to arrest Naylor and bring him to the Capital, to be tried by Parliament for blasphemy. That had traditionally been the prerogative of the House of Lords, but Lords had been abolished. Doubts regarding the validity of the House alone hearing a blasphemy case were aired, but the Members went ahead, tried, convicted and sentenced Naylor to barbaric penalties. (He was sentenced to be whipped through the streets of London, branded, his tongue bored, and the sentence to be repeated at Bristol followed by imprisonment for life.) Cromwell was appalled, sought to alleviate the sentence, and was told he could not.

---

7. Who knows what names went through his mind?

That led, by a subtle concatenation, to a discussion of whether the system of Major General overlords should be continued. Parliament, like the nation, was wary of these military potentates, and clearly wanted to be rid of them. Making Cromwell King was, some decided, the best way. Accordingly on February 23, 1657, an *Humble Petition and Advice* was drawn, calling for the return of the monarchy and the House of Lords, together with a generous settlement upon the Crown.

No step could more clearly show the psychological allegiance of the English to their old forms, their old ways.

ह

Surprisingly, Cromwell was in favor of restoring Lords. He who had once said the Duke of Manchester would be better as plain Mr. Montague now said "unless you have some such thing as balance, we cannot be safe.... By the proceedings of this Parliament," he added, "the case of James Naylor might happen to be your case."

If there were to be a House of Lords, however, questions arose regarding its composition. Cromwell was still against a hereditary nobility: he wanted life peers. (That innovation did not arrive in England again until the twentieth century.) A Bill to this effect was enacted in March, 1657. Seventy future Lords were to be named by Cromwell. After some argument, Commons reluctantly agreed not to have a veto over such nominations; the Protector could refill vacancies as they occurred.

The question of becoming a King took more thought. One factor was expressed by the rebel Penruddock, who said at his trial that he would not have led an uprising if Cromwell had been King, for that would have made it treason. That was important at a time when Thurloe kept uncovering plots to murder the Protector. Forms, again.

While Cromwell waited for a sign from the Lord, Parliament offered him the Crown on March 31, 1657, via the Speaker of the Commons at the Banqueting Hall in Whitehall.[8] It came at the end of a long speech, to which the Protector responded uncertainly.

A public dialogue ensued, in which Cromwell wondered if the powers

---

8. In front of which King Charles I had lost his head.

could be separated from the title, or if they were welded. The response from Commons, assisted by shadowy monarchists, was that the title and the power came together, because "the law knows no Protector" and, above all, "the nation loves a Monarchy." Forms above all.

While this exchange was being conducted, several meetings between Cromwell and the committee had to be suspended because of the Protector's increasingly uncertain health. Meanwhile the turns of the debate leaked throughout the country and abroad, to intrigue people and nations.

The day after he made up his mind to accept, Cromwell took a walk in St. James' Park, and was met by Major Generals Lambert, Fleetwood and Densborough. They had waited for him to tell him that if he became King, they would resign.

To Cromwell that was a sign. On May 8, 1657, in the same Painted Chamber where Charles I heard his fate, Cromwell told the committee that he "cannot undertake this government with the title of King."

Virtually the entire world was astonished, but Calvinists hailed the decision. They respected it; it was proof that Cromwell did not bow down before the honors of the world.

☙

That left the powers of a King to be resolved. A new debate started, and ended when Cromwell agreed to be invested as Lord Protector, (a ceremony held to be greatly significant at the time), able to name his successor, with a Council that would swear to be loyal.

The investiture was as pompous as any Englishman could desire; it included the Coronation Chair, a Cloth of State, elaborate draperies and a Bible gilt and bossed (recalling the coronation of Edward VI), purple robes and an impressive audience of dignitaries on Friday, June 26, 1657. Everything was provided as for a King except the title—and the installation of a family.

☙

Despite this expansion of powers into regality, the Protectorate continued to need money; expenditures continued to outstrip revenues. Cromwell did his best, however, to improve and strengthen the economy and the nation. It was not only Jews whom he welcomed to England, but Protestants of all nations. In his view a good ant was an asset, as was a distinguished Huguenot from France. The Norwich and London colonies of Portuguese immigrants received permission to trade freely in England despite local opposition, and Portugal was made an immensely valuable ally of England.

The University of Oxford received an influx of distinguished foreigners; education in general profited immensely from the Commonwealth and the Calvinists.

ﻌ

The new Parliament began its session on January 20, 1658, and preparations were made for the new House of Lords. Cromwell spoke more briefly than before, because "I have been under some infirmity." Meanwhile members of the old nobility had refused to be renamed, leaving an imbalance in favor of the military among the new Lords.

This time no guards prevented any Member from taking his seat, but old republicans who had protested against a King were in no mood to be peaceful. Wrangles ensued, and Cromwell came back to tell them they were playing "the game of the King of Scots"—a notoriously unstable precedent.

At this juncture Thurloe, the tireless chief of intelligence, uncovered more nests of Royalists, headed by the Marquis of Ormonde, who had slipped into London. It was necessary to adopt a disguise, so he had his blond hair dyed black. The effort was botched; his scalp was scalded and he emerged halfway through the ordeal with a hair of several colors. Thurloe, aware of his presence, sent a warning through intermediaries and Ormonde vanished.

This episode provided Cromwell with a reason to visit Parliament, which was in the process of preparing a monster Petition to deny the Upper House any of the prerogatives of the old House of Lords. This plan to renege on an agreement arduously reached was, to the Lord Protector, a final provocation.

"You granted I should name another House," he told them, "and I named it with integrity. . . . Men of your rank and quality, and men that I approved my heart in God in choosing. . . ." He reminded them of the army of Charles Stuart (Charles II, across the water) "ready to be shipped to England."

Finally he said, "If this, I say, be the effect of your sitting, I think it high time that an end be put to your sitting and I do declare to you here that I dissolve this Parliament." He stopped then, and stared at them, and said slowly, "Let God judge between you and me."

≥●

After that politics declined. England floated like a sailing ship in a near calm, more or less in place while awaiting new breezes from unknown points of the compass.

The alliance with France led 6,000 English soldiers to join the French in assaults against Mardyk, Gravelines and Dunkirk—all in the Spanish Netherlands. The first and last were, after surrender, ceded to England, restoring its footholds in Europe after losses of several generations.

These triumphs arrived in June 1658. A little later in the summer Cromwell's favorite daughter Bettie fell ill and died. Her father spoke of "the Mirror broke, and the dear image gone."

In August 1658 those who saw him were shocked at his appearance. George Fox the Quaker, who came to Hampton Court, said, "I saw and felt the waft of death go against him."

A series of attacks resembling malaria hit him in late summer. When they subsided, he was troubled by a painful infection of kidneys and bladder caused by the stone.

From late August until early September 1658, he lay intermittently ill, passing in and out of delirium, murmuring about the Covenant and how there were once two, but put into a single one before the foundation of the world.[9]

At one point he awoke and turned anxiously to ask, "Tell me, it is possible to fall from Grace?"

The minister said soothingly, "No; it was not possible."

Cromwell fell back, relieved, and said, "I am safe, *for I know I was once in Grace.*"[10] On Friday, September 3, 1658, he assured his wife he was not going to die "at this hour." But, a few hours later, he slipped away forever.

---

9. Fraser, *op. cit.,* p. 674.
10. Every believer knows this fear; it is only the smug who do not.

Chapter Eighteen

THE CROWN'S REVENGE

---- 〰 ----

*The worst of revolutions is a
restoration.... The people of
England, in my opinion, committed a worse offense by the
unconstitutional restoration of
Charles II than even by the
death of Charles I.*
— Charles James Fox

The great temptation of historians is to assume that whatever
happened was inevitable, that all victories were destined from the
start—and that winners have always been superior to losers.

Cromwell proved invincible in life; only his death made it possible for
lesser men to crowd upon the stage of England. The first of these were
the Major Generals, who were so much smaller that only a few of their
names remain in modern books.

They crowded the gentle Richard Cromwell off his father's legacy in
a brief five months, and then fell to quarreling over pieces of power. The
shrewdest of them, Major General George Monck, head of the English
military in Scotland, resolved matters by occupying London and
illegally summoning a new Parliament—in the name of legality.

The new Parliamentary elections resulted in a largely Presbyterian
Parliament whose members were still, apparently, hopeful that Charles
II would keep his vow, made years earlier, to install a Presbyterian
Church of England. But because Cromwellian restrictions were ignored
in the election of the "Convention" Parliament, Presbyterians were
joined by traditional Royalists. Together they invited the third Stuart
back to the throne.

〰

He arrived in London on May 29, 1660. He was 30 years old, predominantly French. His mother was French, his father was the great grandson of Mary of Lorraine; one of his grandmothers was the Italian Marie de Médicis; his Gascon grandfather was Henry of Navarre.

Cromwell had assessed him years before as "feckless, self-indulgent and unworthy: 'he will be the undoing of us all.' All he wanted was 'a shoulder of mutton and a whore.'"[1]

When Charles landed at Dover he accepted an English Bible from the Mayor, saying, "it was the thing that he loved above all the things in the world."

Neither the Mayor nor the cheering crowd had any idea that the new King had been a pensioner of the King of France for years and had become a secret Catholic.[2]

≈

The first large effort of the Convention Parliament after that was to pay and disband the army, despite the war with Spain.[3]

That step, historically attended by misery and crime on the part of discharged veterans, was as phenomenal as the Commonwealth. Fifth Monarchy men, orthodox Calvinists, Anabaptists, Quakers, Independents, Congregationalists, Puritans—all steeled by war and accustomed to discipline—took their pay and faded away.

"In a few months there remained not a trace indicating that the most formidable army in the world had just been absorbed into the mass of the community. The Royalists themselves confessed that, in every department of honest industry, the discarded warriors prospered beyond other men, that none were ever charged with any theft or robbery, that none was heard to ask for alms, and that if a baker, a mason, or a waggoner attracted notice by his diligence and sobriety, he was in all probability one of Oliver's old soldiers."[4]

≈

1. Johnson, *op. cit.*, p. 207.

2. Lord Acton, *The Secret History of Charles II, Essays in the Study and Writing of History, vol. 3* (Indianapolis, IN: Liberty Classics), p. 135.

3. The war was mainly naval.

4. Macaulay, *op. cit.*, p. 179.

Charles II had, before he returned, promised to pardon everyone except those whom Parliament would choose to select for punishment. Once in Whitehall, he said he wanted those who signed the death warrant against his father to be the only ones punished. This was, of course, for public consumption; it was clear from the start that many would pay the price of revolution.

A third of the "regicides," as they are invariably termed, were dead. Another third had presciently fled.[5] Twenty-eight remained to be arrested and tried. Of these fifteen were sent to prison for life; thirteen were—in the grisly custom of the day—hanged, drawn and quartered.

Major General Thomas Harrington was one of these, and his execution was witnessed by Pepys. He said that Harrington spoke bravely from the scaffold, saying that in voting for the death of Charles I, he had followed God's dictates. "He was presently cut down," Pepys said, "and his head and heart shown to the people, at which there were great shouts of joy." (They would have shouted if Pepys had been in Harrington's place; they cheered all such exhibitions.)

On December 8, 1660, the Convention Parliament ordered that the cadavers of Cromwell, Ireton and John Bradshaw should be exhumed from Westminster Abbey to be hanged on January 30, 1661, as a way of commemorating the death of Charles I.

That was ironic, because in his last prayer, Cromwell had said,

> Pardon such as do desire to trample on the dust of a poor worm, for they are thy people too.

The bodies of Cromwell and Ireton were taken from Westminster to the Red Lion Inn at Holborn, were guarded overnight by soldiers and at dawn conveyed through the streets of London the next day from Holborn to Tyburn in open hurdles.

The purpose of the dawn timing was to prevent the crowd from pelting the hurdles with stones, brickbats and offal. "O the stupendous and inscrutable judgment of God," said the Royalist John Evelyn as he watched the swaddled mummies pass.

At about ten o'clock the hurdles reached Tyburn, the traditional

---

5. Pursued by assassins hired by the Stuarts.

hanging site, with the bodies "still in their grave clothes. Cromwell and Ireton were in green sere-cloth, Bradshaw in white but stained with the green of corruption—they were hung up in full gaze of the public, at angles to each other. . . . "[6]

Later in the day they were taken down and the hangman hacked off the heads, a task made difficult by the muffling of the grave clothes. The trunks were buried beneath the gallows at Tyburn; the heads were impaled upon tall poles at Westminster Hall, where they remained, gradually darkened by time and the weather, for years. Cromwell's head finally fell in a gale, and was picked up by a sentinel. It passed through various hands in subsequent centuries, and is today hidden at Sidney Sussex College, Cambridge. The fate of the others is unknown.

≈

England was fortunate in that first Convention Parliament under the "restored" Charles II, for its Presbyterian Members prevented a wholesale bloodletting by returning Cavaliers. They did, it is true, provide scapegoats in the regicides, but they protected a great many more.

On the other hand, they could not prevent the return of Church and Crown lands to their original hands—without compensation. Independents and others who had invested in these properties suffered huge losses; most of them—officers in Cromwell's New Model Army—were thrown back to their former conditions. "The Independent aristocracy was ruined. But in Ireland—on condition of turning Anglican (Arminian)—it became the landlord caste."[7]

The Convention Parliament could not, however, settle the religious issues that had ignited and sustained the revolution. There was some discussion of Bishop Usher's compromise, based on changes in the Book of Common Prayer and a limited Episcopacy by a Council of Presbyters.

Charles II might have accepted this, had it been accompanied by a willingness to tolerate Catholicism. But the new Lord Chancellor Edward Hyde, who had separated from John Pym in the Long Parliament years before, and had shared Charles' exile (and semi-starvation at times), was too bitterly against Calvinists—and Calvinism. He wanted

---

6. Fraser, *op. cit.,* p. 693.
7. Trevelyan, *op. cit.,* p. 335.

no compromises; he wanted the Arminians and their divine right of Kings and "Apostolic Succession" back in power.

                                    ૨ઌ

"The Presbyterians did not foresee that a restoration in religion would follow from a restoration in society and politics. They did not know that in reestablishing squirearchy they were setting up a persecuting Anglicanism (the term now used instead of Arminianism); for the squires they remembered had been haters of parsons and bishops. Nor did they suspect that in realizing at last their cherished ideal of a monarch controlled by a free Parliament, they were laying firmer than Laud the foundations of an Anglican (read: Arminian) State Church, for their recollections of a free Parliament recalled groups of angry gentlemen shouting approval while Pym demanded the suppression of the Arminians, or while Pym declared that Prelacy had been tried and found wanting."[8]

They forgot, in other words, that the men the revolution had overthrown would not forgive the Calvinists, simply because the Calvinists helped overthrow the Major Generals. They did not realize that the eager volunteers of the Forties had dissolved. The Revolution was over; it was time for the Counter-Revolution, not for a coalition government.

                                    ૨ઌ

As if on cue, a number of Fifth Monarchy[9] men inadvertently made that clear to all. Inflamed by various preachers who watched the trend of events with alarm and who predicted God's vengence in the form of earthquakes, plagues and the like, they ran, heavily armed, into the streets on Sunday, January 6, 1661.

They scattered throughout London for about two days until hunted down, were captured, and led to the gallows by the new King's guards. They had expected to ignite a new uprising; they succeeded only in convincing people that the past was as dead as Cromwell.

                                    ૨ઌ

---

8. Ibid., pp. 335, 336.

9. Millenarians who believed they were to prepare the way for the Second Coming.

On April 23, 1661, Charles II was crowned in Westminster Abbey. On May 8, a new "Cavalier" Parliament convened, representing the old order returned. Its Members were from "loyal" families but were, for the most part, young men. Told this, Charles shrugged and said he'd keep them till they grew beards. He did: they lasted 14 years.

The Cavaliers were in charge of a victory they had won only by Cromwell's death; their return was only possible because the Convention Parliament had dissolved the Protector's Army. Because that Army had defeated a King, however, future Kings would be against any more standing armies. That was one of the happier consequences of the Restoration; it was virtually the only one.

~

The Cavalier Parliament, as might be expected, put the pieces of the Old Order back together—but not completely. Some key elements had been removed by the revolution, and would stay removed. The Star Chamber would remain in limbo; so would the High Commission.

The King would be, in effect, under Parliament—because only Parliament could raise royal revenues and dole them out to the Crown. Time would prove they doled in niggardly fashion.

The old House of Lords was reestablished. *And the Arminian Church was reestablished.* It did not have a High Commission, but it had a Code that was just as effective.

This was known as the Great Code, named after its originator and prime mover, Chancellor Hyde—now known as the Earl of Clarendon.

~

The Code forever divided the people of England on religious grounds. Its Corporation Act restricted membership in the municipal bodies that ruled localities to those who received Communion in the Arminian Church of England.

Its Act of Uniformity (1662) threw 2,000 Calvinist clergy out of their posts for refusing to give their "unfeigned consent and assent" to everything in the reestablished Book of Common Prayer.

Its Conventicle Act punished attendance at religious rites other than those of the Established Church by imprisonment for the first and second offense, transportation on the third, and death if the offender returned.

Its Five Mile Act forbade any clergyman or schoolteacher to come within five miles of a city or corporate town, unless he swore "he would not at any time try to change the Government of State or Church." Because Calvinists were mostly in cities, this cut them off from their faith entirely.

The Clarendon Code was rigidly enforced.

ک

Historians have drawn a discreet veil over the persecutions this narrow-minded Code created; Clarendon remains one of the Arminian saints, extolled to this day as a great statesman and author of a literary masterpiece. Arminianism is identified as merciful; Calvinism as harsh. But the Arminians in power proved that this was an inversion of the truth.

Every aspect of anti-Christian tyranny familiar to the twentieth century had its forerunner and pattern in Arminian England during the Restoration under "The Merry Monarch."

To end Quaker "conventicles," Parliament defined these as meetings of five or more persons. The penalties for attendance were £5 the first time or three months in pesthole prisons, £10 or six months for the second, banishment to a penal colony for a third. Offenders unable to pay the costs of their transportation had to serve five years as indentured servants.

After the Quakers, these conditions and penalties were extended to Presbyterians and Independents. By 1662, a year after the Cavalier Parliament sat, there were nearly 5,000 Quakers in prison. "Some were crowded so close that there was not room for them all to sit down . . . they were refused straw to lie upon; they were often denied food."[10]

Between 1660 and 1688 there were 60,000 arrests for religious "nonconformity;" 5,000 were known to die in jail.

But these are relatively minor statistics compared to the overall horror of England under Charles II.

ک

---

10. Durant, *op. cit.*, p. 255.

As if real reasons for terrible actions were not enough, a charlatan named Titus Oates claimed to have discovered a Popish Plot to take over the realm and slaughter all non-Catholics. His fantasies were more plausible than he knew; the King perpetually schemed to reintroduce Catholicism, and his brother the Duke of York was open in his devotion to the Papacy.

Oates created national hysteria; imitators and corroborators appeared; arrests escalated and a reign of terror was launched that lasted for nearly four years. Men were jailed, tortured, executed; informers proliferated, and the climate was poisoned.

Hysteria, religious persecutions; rebellions and the creation of a semipermanent under class were only some of the features of the Restoration.

What amounted to acute psychological torture to Calvinist believers of every variety was the fact that these injustices were promoted at the same time that the most immoral Court in Europe paraded—and inspired a decadent and licentious upper class to imitate—its excesses, and when religion was mocked on every level, at every occasion.

Manners were used to disguise morals; ceremonial grace to gild obscene literature and theatrics, profane speech and behavior. Adultery became fashionable; men swore to be faithful only to their mistresses, preceding Paris by a full century or more.

Clothes became unbelievably elaborate for both sexes: men wore powdered wigs and silk stockings; suits of many colors. The sexes kissed on meeting; velvets and laces, ribbons and frills were worn by both.

Drinking became more than social; with bad water, the excuse was that liquor was safer. Drunkenness was common. Games and sports flourished; nearly everyone smoked. Circuses, puppet shows, cockfighting, bull and bear baits: entertainment masked grim realities.

Chapter Nineteen

EPILOGUE

Yet, although the revolution seemed to have lost almost everything it accomplished, it really remains the most significant in our civilization—so far.

Its surface triumphs seemed to have been swept away by the Restoration, but that is an illusion. It had, under Cromwell and his men, swept away the remains of feudalism, preserved the Common Law, created the world's first global sea power, established Parliament over the King and laid the basis for both the Industrial Revolution and the British Empire.

There were undeniable setbacks accomplished by the Counter-Revolution and the Arminians, of course. Arminianism has remained, thanks to the Restoration, to undergird the televangelists and others who offer illusions of Salvation by maneuvering God; Calvinists have suffered from the propaganda promoted by Arminian scholars and preachers to this day.

It is difficult to unravel, after all these years, the hoary myths and dark legends accumulated through the generations, but the truth keeps welling; Calvinism remains Augustinianism and early Christianity revived. Luther and Knox and Calvin and Cromwell lifted millions from the swamps in which they were placed by elegant men in power.

Charles II sent the Calvinists to the New World as did his father and his grandfather, and in that uncharted wilderness they laid the foundations for the United States of America.

When James, Duke of York, suppressed the liberties of the colonials while Charles II was still on the throne in 1676, he lit a match that resulted in the fires of our War of Independence. And in that war, it was Presbyterian divines who raised men like Cromwell's, who fought like Cromwell's, for the same reasons that Cromwell fought.

The men at Philadelphia echoed the history of the 1640s and 1650s when they wrote the Constitution with its limitations on the power of

Congress, the Presidency and the Courts. That these have since been stretched is another story, whose conclusion is yet to be written.

When they said in the Constitution that this nation would not have an Established Church, they reflected the experience of their forbears with Laud and his successors.

When they spoke about open doors to all, open careers to all, they spoke in the accents of Cromwell and the Calvinists; the Independents and the Congregationalists and the Puritans and the Presbyterians and the Levellers and those who fought under these banners.

All this and more came from the great Christian revolution; all the liberties men know have come from Christianity, from its lessons about the individual and the State; God and His Covenant. The Christian revolution that Cromwell came to lead was the only one of modern times that had for its inspiration not the attractions of power, but the transcendental purpose of life, which is to fulfill God's Will by bringing justice, truth, faith and joy to the world.

Selected Bibliography

Acton, Lord. *The Secret History of Charles II, Essays in the Study and Writing of History, vol.* 3. Indianapolis, IN: Liberty Classics.
———. *Selected Writing,* vol. 3. Indianapolis, IN: Liberty Classics, "Human Sacrifice," 1985.
Aston, Margaret. *England's Iconoclasts: Laws Against Images,* vol. 1. Oxford: Clarendon Press, 1988.
Barish, Jonas. *The AntiTheatrical Prejudice.* Berkeley, CA: University of California Press, 1981.
Braudel, Femand. *The Mediterranean,* vol. 2. New York, N.Y.: Harper and Row, 1973.
Burckhardt, Jacob. *The Civilization of the Renaissance in Italy.* Phaideon Publishers, 1965.
Calvin, John. *Commentary on the Psalms,* Library of Christian Classics, vol. 23, Preface. London: SCM Press; Philadelphia: Westminster Press, 1958.
Chamberlin, *The Sack of Rome* . Dorset Press, 1985.
Dawson, Christopher. *The Christian View of History,* cf. God. Oxford University Press, 1977.
Durant, Will. *The Story of Civilization,* vol. 6. New York, N.Y.: Simon and Shuster, 1957.
Eisenstein, E. I. *The Advent of Printing and* the *Protestant Revolt,* cf. *Renaissance and Reformation History.* Minnesota Burgess Printing Co., 1974.
Erickson, C. *Bloody Mary.* Doubleday, 1978.
Firth, C. H. ed. *The Clark Papers,* vol. 1. The Camden Society, 1891.
Fraser, Antonia. *Cromwell, The Lord Protector.* New York, N. Y.: Alfred A. Knopf, 1973.

Friedman, Jerome. "Michael Servetus: Exegete of Divine History," *Church History,* vol. 42. 1974.

———. "Servetus and the Psalms: The Exegesis of Heresy," *Histoire de l'Exegese au XVI Siecle.* Geneva: Droz, 1978.

———. "Michael Servetus: The Case for a Jewish Christianity," *Sixteenth Century Journal,* vol. 4, no. 1. April, 1973.

Froude, James Anthony. *Short Studies of Great Subjects.* London, England: Longman, Green and Co., 1888.

Gardiner, Samuel Rawson. *The First Two Stuarts and the Puritan Revolution 1602–1660.* New York, N.Y.: Thomas Y. Crowell, 1970.

Green, John Richard. *A Short History of the English People,* vol. 1. New York, N.Y.: Colonial Press, 1899.

Hill, Christopher. *God's Englishman.* Harper & Row, 1970.

Johnson, Paul. *A History of the English People.* New York, N.Y.: Harper and Row, 1985.

Klaits, Dr. Joseph. *Servants of Satan: The Age of the Witch Hunts.* Bloomington, IN: Indiana University Press, 1985.

Levy, Leonard. *Origins of the Fifth Amendment* . Oxford University Press, 1971.

Luke, Mary M. *Gloriana: The Years of Elizabeth I.* New York, N.Y.: Coward, McCann & Geoghegan, 1973.

Mattingly, Garrett. *The Armada.* Boston, Mass: Houghton Mifflin, 1959.

McCrie, Thomas. *The Life of John Knox.* Edinburgh, Scotland: Nelson and Sons, 1905.

Miller, Perry. *Orthodoxy in Massachusetts 1630–1650: A Genetic Study.* Harvard University Press, 1933.

Morgan, Edmund S. *Inventing the People: The Rise of Popular Sovereignty in England and America.* New York, N.Y.: W. W. Norton & Company, 1988.

Parker, T. H. L. *John Calvin: A Biography.* London, England: Dent and Sons, 1975.

Prestwich, ed. *International Calvinism, 1541–1715.* Oxford: Clarendon Press, 1986 (paper).

Schaff, Philip. *History of the Christian Church,* vol. VII, The German Reformation, Part I. New York, NY: Charles Scribner's Sons, 1910.

Scott, Otto. *James I.* Vallecito, CA: Ross House Books, 1988.

Social England, 6 vols. New York, N.Y.: G. P. Putmans, 1897.

Thornton, E. M. *The Freudian Fallacy: An Alternative View of Freudian Theory.* New York, N.Y.: Doubleday, 1984.

Transactions of the Congregational Historical Society, XII. "Was Cromwell an Iconoclast?"

Trevelyan, George Macaulay. *England Under the Stuarts.* London, England: Methuen and Co., 1924.

Tyacke, Nicholas. *Anti-Calvinists: The Rise of English Arminianism c. 1590–1640.* Oxford: Clarendon Press, 1987.

Warfield, Benjamin B. *Calvin and Augustine.* Philadelphia, PA: Presbyterian and Reformed Publishing Company, 1980.

Wedgewood, C. V. *A Coffin for King Charles.* New York, N.Y.: Time, Inc. (paper), 1966.

Index

Syphilis   9

T

Taxes   16, 84, 91, 126, 200, 218, 239, 244, 246
   Cavaliers and   253
   illegal   164
   Mohammedan usage and   3
   ship tax   171
   tonnage and poundage   162, 185
Televangelists   270
Tetzel, John   7, 8
Textiles   156
"The Broken Heart" (Ford)   169
The Church of England's Old Antithesis to New Arminianism (Prynne)   169
The Education of Henry Adams (Adams, Henry)   iii
The Hunting of the Foxes from Newmarket and Triploe Heath by Five Small Beagles (pamphlet)   230
"The Merry Monarch". *See* Charles II (king of England)
The Moderate (newspaper)   226
The Perpetuitie of a Regenerate Man's Estate (Prynne)   169
The Siege of Rhodes (English opera)   248
The Unbishoping of Timothy and Titus (Prynne)   172
Theater   169, 195, 219, 247, 255
Theocracy   166
Thirty Year's War   17, 51, 148, 174, 194
   ended in 1648   231
Thirty-Nine Articles (Church of England)   98, 161
Thoroughness (system)   167, 170, 175, 178, 183
Thorton, E. M.   45
Thurloe, John   255, 260
   plots to murder the Protector and   258
Tillet, Louis du   48
Tilly   161
"Tis a Pity She's a Whore." (Ford)   169

Tithes   78, 240, 242, 243, 245
Tomlinson, Colonel   227
Tortures   36, 86, 102, 117, 122, 125, 185, 269
Trade war   246
Transubstantiation   32, 92
Treaty of
   Crepy   49
   Nantes   134
   Uxbridge   200
Trevelyan, George Macaulay   205, 214
Trie, Guillaume de   65
Trinity, The   64, 224
Tudor, Margaret   75
Turks   36, 49, 110, 128
   Europe menaced by   10
   Pasha, General Mustapha and   110
   pirates   178
   struggle between Christianity and Islam   109
   war against Hungary and   26
Twelve Years' Truce   142
Tyacke, Nicholas   129, 155
Tyndale, William   50

U

Udine, Giovanni da   25
Ulstermen   231
Unitarianism   62, 72
Unitarians   206, 255
United Provinces   135, 141, 142
Universal suffrage   16
Usher, Bishop   265

V

Valentine, Benjamin   163
Valois, Marguerite of (Catherine de Médicis' daughter)   35, 112
Van Oldbarnevelt, Johann   142, 143
Vane, Sir Henry   182
Vatican   4, 10, 18, 22, 26, 29, 33, 35, 39, 41, 46, 50, 54, 55, 56, 82, 84, 86, 87, 90, 93, 98, 101, 119, 120, 123, 125, 128, 140, 231, 248